Creativity 101
James C. Kaufman, PhD

Genius 101
Dean Keith Simonton, PhD

IQ Testing 101
Alan S. Kaufman, PhD

Leadership 101
Michael D. Mumford, PhD

Psycholinguistics 101
H. Wind Cowles, PhD

Intelligence 101
Jonathan Plucker, PhD

Anxiety 101
Moshe Zeidner, PhD
Gerald Matthews, PhD

James C. Kaufman, PhD, Series Editor

Director, Learning Research Center
California State University

Dean Keith Simonton, PhD, is distinguished professor and vice chair of the department of psychology at the University of California, Davis. He is the author of ten books and over 300 journal articles and book chapters on creativity, genius, leadership, aesthetics, and the history of psychology. His 1999 book, *Origins of Genius: Darwinian Perspectives on Creativity,* won the William James Book Award from the American Psychological Association. Simonton has also won awards from Divisions 1, 8, 9, and 10 of the APA as well as the UC Davis Prize for Teaching and Scholarly Achievement. He is a past president of the International Association for Empirical Aesthetics and the Society for the Psychology of Aesthetics, Creativity, and the Arts. His work has received coverage in prominent media outlets, such as CNN, the Discovery Channel, National Public Radio, *Newsweek, Time, The New Yorker, Fortune,* and *Business Week.*

Genius 101

Dean Keith Simonton, PhD

SPRINGER PUBLISHING COMPANY

Springer Publishing Company, LLC
11 West 42nd Street
New York, NY 10036
www.springerpub.com

Acquisitions Editor: Philip Laughlin
Production Editor: Rosanne Lugtu
Cover Design: David Levy
Composition: Apex CoVantage

08 09 10 11 / 5 4 3 2 1

Library of Congress Cataloging-in-Publication Data

Simonton, Dean Keith.
  Genius 101 / Dean Keith Simonton.
      p. cm. — (The psych 101)
  Includes bibliographical references and index.
  ISBN 978-0-8261-0627-8 (alk. paper)
  1. Genius.   I. Title.   II. Title: Genius one oh one.   III. Title:
Genius one hundred one.   IV. Title: Genius one hundred and one.
  BF412.S55   2009
  153.9'8—dc22   2008046852

Printed in Canada by Transcontinental.

TO BREE

Contents

Preface

When I was in kindergarten, my dad and mom purchased an edition of the *World Book Encyclopedia*. As it was specifically designed for school-age children and adolescents, my parents thought that it would constitute a good educational investment for me and my three younger sisters. The volumes were especially critical in a working-class home that had very few books of any kind. To me the encyclopedia was a wonder. Although I could not yet read, I loved to thumb through the pages, attracted by the plentiful supply of photographs, paintings, and drawings. At the time, it was my favorite picture book. What especially provoked my curiosity were the many photos and paintings of exotic people—dressed in odd costumes and sporting strange hairdos and facial hair. The volumes also included no pictures of anybody I knew, and certainly none of my parents, grandparents, or other relatives. Not even my kindergarten teacher! So I became very curious about what these folks had done for their portraits to be so honored. Of course, once I was able to read the entries associated with these faces, I gradually learned their secret. They had all done something important. In one way or another, they had left a lasting imprint on history through one or more notable achievements. I would now say that many if not most could be considered as *geniuses* in their chosen fields.

All that happened over half a century ago. By a circuitous series of serendipitous events that I have already narrated elsewhere (Simonton, 1990a, 2002c), I eventually found myself conducting scientific research on genius and the related topics of creativity, leadership, talent, and aesthetics. Over the past one-third of a century, I have published hundreds of articles and chapters, plus several books. Many of these contributions have been successful in shedding light on the phenomenon of genius. But almost all my publications were highly technical as well. For the most part, their primary audience was other scientists who were also studying phenomena associated with genius. Since my colleagues are most impressed with mathematical equations, statistical tables, and complex graphs, I naturally complied with their desires.

It is for this reason that I welcomed the chance to contribute this volume to the Springer Psychology 101 series. According to the invitation, the writing style was to be "scholarly light." The volumes should be scientifically accurate without being academically ponderous—providing a lively introduction rather than a plodding monograph. Such an opportunity was especially inviting given the stage I had reached in my career. Having published so much myself, and having read so much terrific work by my numerous colleagues, it seemed that the time was ripe for writing an accessible volume that would convey the essentials of what we know. So I have sat down to write chapters that give you the gist on genius. Better yet, you'll view the general picture without a single mathematical equation, statistical table, or complex graph. Don't believe me? Go ahead, thumb through the book's pages from cover to cover. Nothing but words, words, words, all arranged in intelligible English sentences (and sometimes even sentence fragments, as in the present instance!). A special bonus: absolutely no footnotes either! Just appropriate citations to the researchers who have contributed so much to our knowledge of genius, with the citations dutifully listed in the book's reference section—the only feature reminiscent of a scientific publication. The citations and references provide the "scholarly" in "scholarly light."

In previous books, I have acknowledged the many persons who have helped me reach the point where I could be asked to write a book like this. I need not repeat their names here. However, I am grateful to the series editor, James Kaufman, for offering me this opportunity, and to the acquisitions editor, Phil Laughlin, for a positive response to my prospectus and for his comments on the first draft. While I'm expressing public gratitude, I might also thank Phil for successfully nominating my 1999 *Origins of Genius*—when he was an acquisitions editor at Oxford University Press—for the William James Book Award.

I am also grateful to my wife, Karen Horobin, for providing me with an environment supportive of my writing activities. As a fellow university professor who works just as hard as I do, Kazie respects my career goals as much as I do hers. So we do our utmost not to interrupt each other's work. Yet when it's time for play, we really play!

I would like to add a word about the dedication. Back in 1990, I published *Psychology, Science, and History: An Introduction to Historiometry*. The book was dedicated to my toddler daughter, Sabrina Dee Simonton. Unfortunately, as the most technical and specialized of all my books, it was eventually remaindered—the only one of my books ever to suffer that horrid fate. I resigned myself to buying some excess copies to give to students and colleagues who expressed a special interest in the esoteric and difficult methods it so thoroughly describes. (Anybody else out there want a copy? Must I really save them for my grandchildren?)

In the meantime, my daughter has grown into a talented woman who had just completed her first year of college at the time that I began writing this book. As she grew bigger, her name got smaller. So she now deserves a new book dedication. Given all the 101-type courses she took in her first two years, this dedication seems singularly appropriate. My only regret is that I did not complete the book in time for her to have it assigned in one of her classes!

Who First
Studied Genius?

eniuses have been around for a very long time. In fact, perhaps the oldest identifiable genius is the Egyptian Imhotep, the architect who built the Step Pyramid at Saqqara sometime before 2600 B.C.E. Within a few generations, his architectural design evolved into the Great Pyramid of Giza, the only one of the Seven Wonders of the Ancient World that survives to the present day. Moreover, it is difficult to imagine the history of world civilization without the contributions of specific geniuses. Within the confines of the West, for example, just think of Greece without Aristotle and Alexander the Great, Italy without Dante and Michelangelo, Spain without Cervantes and Goya, France without Descartes and Napoleon, Germany without Goethe and Beethoven, the Netherlands without Rembrandt and Vermeer, England without Shakespeare and Newton, the United States without

Jefferson and Whitman, and Russia without Tolstoy and Lenin. Each culture would suffer a major loss, not just in prestige or influence but in recognizable identity besides. An English literature without Shakespeare's plays and poems would be like a London without the Tower of London, Westminster Abbey, St. Paul's Cathedral, or Big Ben.

Rather than conceive of the impact of geniuses in terms of national heritage, we can contemplate their significance with respect to particular domains of human achievement. Where would philosophy be without Plato, mathematics without Euclid, astronomy without Copernicus, physics without Einstein, chemistry without Lavoisier, biology without Darwin, medicine without Pasteur, art without Picasso, technology without Edison, or film without Bergman? Rather different, no?

Given the prominence of geniuses throughout the world's history, it should not surprise us that they have often become the subjects of biographers. Examples include Diogenes Laertius's *The Lives of the Eminent Philosophers*, written in the early 200s C.E., and Giorgio Vasari's *Lives of the Artists*, published in about 1550. These biographies obviously focus on creative geniuses. Yet other biographers have concentrated on exemplars of genius in other domains, such as politics and war. Plutarch's *Lives of the Noble Grecians and Romans*, written around 100 C.E., is a case in point. And almost two centuries earlier there appeared the biographies included in Sima Qian's (Ssŭma Ch'ien) *Records of the Grand Historian*, the classic history of early Chinese civilization.

These biographical contributions are all substantial. They often provide the only information we have about the geniuses they describe. But these biographies are humanistic—literary and historical—rather than scientific. They certainly are not examples of psychological science. Genuine scientific inquiries into the psychology of genius came much later. Indeed, such investigations did not appear until the 19th century. The investigators engaged in these inquiries adopted two main approaches: *psychometrics* and *historiometrics* (Simonton, 1999c).

PSYCHOMETRICS

Probably everyone who is reading this book has taken a psychological test—and most likely many such tests. Maybe you took a vocational interest test in junior high or a scholastic achievement test in high school. Perhaps you have visited Web sites that allow you to understand what makes you tick by assessing your personality or motives. You may even have taken an IQ test on the Internet or in the office of some school psychologist. Although these quantitative instruments vary greatly in what they measure and how they measure it, they have certain features in common. They consist of a series of questions focusing on one or more psychological variables. These variables may involve abilities, aptitudes, interests, values, dispositions, well, you name it. In some tests, the questions may follow a true/false format, others are multiple choice, and still others provide ratings along some scale, like a 7-point Likert scale that goes from "strongly agree" to "strongly disagree." Psychometrics is the subdiscipline of psychology devoted to the creation and application of such tests (Rudy, 2007). The word literally means "mind measurement."

The British scientist Francis Galton was a pioneer in this field. For instance, he devised various tests that assessed how people vary in reaction times, visual and auditory acuity, and color perception as well as height, weight, arm span, and strength. These *anthropometric* (or human measurement) assessments were thought to gauge important individual differences in abilities (Galton, 1883). Galton also invented the questionnaire and quickly applied the new method to the study of eminent scientists and artists. For example, one questionnaire asked great scientists— including Galton's cousin Charles Darwin—about their attitudes toward school and education (Galton, 1874).

Not only was Galton the first psychometrician to study genius, but he himself was a genius. Most psychologists today have to struggle to recruit research participants. Either they have to pay participants in hard cash or else they have to offer them extra

3

credit in an introductory psychology course. Probably many of my readers have served as subjects in laboratory experiments in this way—as I did when I became a psychology major. In contrast, Galton was able to convince participants to *pay him* for subjecting them to anthropometric instruments. At the 1884–1885 International Health Exhibition, 9,337 visitors paid him 3 pence each for the privilege!

Unfortunately, Galton's early psychometric measures were either inaccurate or irrelevant. In the former category was his assessment of mental imagery. The potential utility of the measure was undermined by its highly qualitative rather than quantitative nature. In the latter category was his measure of the highest pitch that a person can hear. Although this trait can be assessed with much more accuracy than mental imagery, it is, unlike mental imagery, not pertinent to anything particularly interesting—and certainly not to anything germane to genius.

Hence, psychometric research did not make much headway until instruments emerged that provided fairly accurate assessments of highly relevant variables. In this area the real pioneer was Lewis M. Terman, a professor at Stanford University. Terman's starting point was an early version of an intelligence measure developed in France by Alfred Binet and Theodore Simon (1905). In 1916, Terman revised and extended this test to produce the Stanford-Binet Intelligence Scale. A few years later he began a long-term study of 1,528 children who received very high IQ scores (mostly 140 and above) on the Stanford-Binet test. The results of this longitudinal inquiry were published in a series of volumes, the first appearing in 1925. The title of this series was *Genetic Studies of Genius* (Terman, 1925–1959). Terman studied his young geniuses from every possible aspect, including their family background, scholastic performance, physical health, personality traits, interests and values, and later their achievements in adulthood.

Although Terman conducted the first classic psychometric study of genius, he was by no means the only psychologist to employ this specific approach. Perhaps most notable among other contributors was Leta Hollingworth. She began her career making significant contributions to the psychology of women, but her interests eventually turned to young budding geniuses. In 1922, she began a 3-year study of 50 children with IQs that surpassed 155, publishing her findings in the 1926 work, *Gifted Children*. In 1916, she had actually begun investigating children with even higher IQs, starting with a child with an IQ of 187! Her conclusions, based on a dozen extremely bright kids, were published posthumously in a book entitled *Children Above IQ 180* (1942). Hollingworth's two works have become minor classics in the field. In any case, by the middle of the 20th century, psychometric studies of genius had become well established.

HISTORIOMETRICS

Psychometric research represents the most common way that psychologists investigate genius. Yet it's not the only method available. The principal alternative is a technique known as historiometrics. In this method, biographical and historical information is first quantified and then subjected to statistical analysis (Simonton, 2007d). The first bona fide historiometric study was published in 1835 by Adolphe Quételet, the Belgian mathematician and physicist who established that individual differences in physical traits were distributed according to the normal or bell-shaped curve. In his historiometric investigation, Quételet examined how creative productivity in eminent English and French dramatists—such as Shakespeare and Molière—changed across the life span. Unfortunately, because his inquiry was hidden deep within a much larger work on a more general subject, this contribution had very little immediate influence on the study of genius.

Quite the contrary can be said regarding the next major example of historiometric research. In 1865, Galton published a magazine article titled "Hereditary Talent and Character," which he subsequently expanded into the 1869 *Hereditary Genius: An Inquiry Into Its Laws and Consequences*. Because this book reports research that was conducted prior to Galton's psychometric investigations, it can be considered the first major scientific study of genius. It has also become a classic in the history of psychology. Because it deals with the question of whether genius is born or made, I will devote part of chapter 4 to discussing its contents. At that time I will also discuss the fascinating historiometric study by Alphonse de Candolle (1873), which offered a different take on the origins of genius. Right now I would like to mention some other early figures in the development of this distinct methodology.

Among the first psychologists to follow up Galton's research was James McKeen Cattell, an American psychologist. Cattell had even studied under Galton shortly after receiving his PhD. Much of Cattell's work is psychometric, and even more specifically anthropometric. He was the very one who introduced the term *mental test* (Cattell, 1890). Yet he also published several historiometric studies. Perhaps the most remarkable investigation was Cattell's first, a 1903 study in which he ranked the 1,000 most eminent geniuses of Western civilization. At the top of his list were Napoleon, a military genius, and Shakespeare, a literary genius. Just a year later came *A Study of British Genius* by Havelock Ellis, a British psychologist far better known for his revolutionary research on human sexuality. In his 1904 book, Ellis investigated over a thousand geniuses, looking at such variables as precocity, birth order, social class, education, pathology, marriage, and life span.

I hasten to point out that none of the above researchers—Quételet, Galton, Cattell, or Ellis—expressly referred to their research as historiometric. That was because the term hadn't been coined yet! In truth, the word was concocted by a geneticist, not a psychologist. His name was Frederick Woods. In 1909, he published "A New Name for a New Science," an article in which he says the method is used when "the facts of history of a personal nature [are] subjected to statistical analysis by some more or less objective method" (p. 703). In 1911, Woods published another article, in which he defended the approach as an *exact science.* In addition, he argued that the method was well suited to studying the "psychology of genius" (p. 568). Besides conceiving the term,

Woods also conducted historiometric research of his own. In 1906, he had studied the inheritance of intellectual and moral genius in royal families, and in 1913 he examined the influence of political genius on the welfare of the nations ruled. Yet in the long run, his primary contribution may be a single word: historiometrics.

The first psychologist to make it explicit that she was conducting historiometric research was Catharine Cox (1926). Cox was a graduate student of Lewis Terman at Stanford. Looking for a topic for her doctoral dissertation, she decided to do for historiometrics what her mentor had done for psychometrics. Terman had already begun his ambitious longitudinal study of high-IQ children. Terman's goal was to follow his subjects—affectionately called "Termites"—from childhood through adolescence to adulthood with the aim of showing that intellectual giftedness becomes adulthood genius. Yet this plan had to face an awkward fact: The average age of Terman's children at the beginning of the study was about 11 years. So Terman had a very, very long wait before he could find out how the story would turn out. In fact, Terman died before the final volume was published (Terman & Oden, 1959).

That's where Cox's dissertation came in. Terman (1917) had also explored a method of calculating IQ scores using historiometric methods. In particular, he examined biographical information on one of his heroes, Francis Galton. Terman took advantage of the fact that the Stanford–Binet IQ was then defined as a ratio of mental age (MA) to chronological age (CA) multiplied by 100 (i.e., $IQ = 100 * MA/CA$). Consequently, Terman could estimate IQ scores on the basis of Galton's precocious intellectual development. For instance, by the end of his first year of life, Galton knew his capital letters and 6 months later knew both the upper- and lowercase alphabets; he could read at age 2 1/2 and could read any English book before he was 5 years old (and what, may I ask, were you doing at the same ages?). In general, Galton was achieving things that most children do not achieve until they are almost twice his age. Galton's IQ must have approached 200—a very brilliant guy to be sure.

7

So what Cox did was to estimate IQ scores not just for one genius but for 301. She then examined the correlation between these IQ scores and the eminence that each individual had achieved, using the rankings done by Cattell (1903). She concluded that the greatest adult geniuses had been high-IQ children and adolescents. If there had been IQ tests hundreds of years ago, they would've been singled out as Termites! Cox's dissertation was accordingly published as the second volume in Terman's *Genetic Studies of Genius,* just one year after the first volume (Cox, 1926). If I had to identify the most monumental historiometric study of genius ever published, Cox's would be it. It may also count as one of the most ambitious doctoral dissertations ever published. In print, the study took up 842 pages filled with biographical data and intriguing statistics! Where else can you find the IQs of such diverse notables as Simón Bolívar, Benjamin Franklin, Carolus Linnaeus, Baruch Spinoza, George Sand (Aurore Dupin), Diego Velázquez, and Johann Sebastian Bach?

I'd like to close this section by honoring one last early proponent of historiometric methods: Edward L. Thorndike. This American psychologist was much better known for his classic experiments on animal learning—especially his puzzle boxes from which cats were obliged to escape. Yet later in his career he acquired psychometric interests, and in 1927 he published a book on the measurement of intelligence. This was just a year after the appearance of Hollingworth's *Gifted Children,* and in fact Hollingworth had earned her PhD under Thorndike in 1916, the year in which Terman produced the Stanford–Binet Intelligence Scale. A decade after his book on intelligence, Thorndike expanded his tool kit to include historiometrics. Specifically, he published a follow-up study of Woods' (1906) assessment of intelligence and morality in royalty (Thorndike, 1936). Finally, at the very end of his life he conducted a historiometric study that was published posthumously by his son (Thorndike, 1950). In this investigation, he calculated intellectual and personality scores for 92 geniuses. The study was his swan song. Despite all of his experimental and psychometric work, his final contribution to psychology was historiometric.

Thorndike illustrates a very useful point. Even though psychometric and historiometric methods are very different, psychologists may use both techniques if they choose. After all, several of the leaders in the study of genius felt comfortable with both approaches. Galton, Cattell, Terman, and Thorndike certainly did. Furthermore, the two methods, however divergent in technique, often lead to compatible results—a convergence that will become more apparent in later chapters. But before moving on, I would just like to acknowledge a third methodology in the psychological study of genius.

WHAT ABOUT PSYCHOBIOGRAPHY?

At this point some psychologists will stand up and shout: Wait! Aren't you overlooking something? Psychology must have more than just two ways to study genius! Well, yes, to say there are just two ways to study genius is both true and false. In the first place, other methods are used, but extremely rarely. A case par excellence is the laboratory experiment, the very method favored by the overwhelming majority of research psychologists. Laboratory experiments have many advantages—especially in the area of causal inference—but they also have major disadvantages. One drawback is the difficulty of getting world-renowned geniuses to subject themselves to such intrusions. People of the caliber of an Albert Einstein seldom sign up to participate. Perhaps some day the theoretical physicist Stephen Hawking might volunteer to spend a few days in an MRI machine, but that seems very unlikely. Such people don't need the extra credit.

Nonetheless, there is another method that is frequently applied to geniuses of every variety. That's psychobiography. A classic example is Sigmund Freud's (1910/1964) psychoanalytical study

9

of Leonardo da Vinci. Later, the noted psychoanalyst Erik Erikson published two notable psychobiographies, one on Martin Luther (Erikson, 1958), the founder of the Protestant movement, and the other on Mahatma Gandhi (Erikson, 1969), the most important practitioner of civil disobedience. Moreover, it is difficult to think of a single major genius who has not become the subject of at least one psychobiographical investigation. Examples include Socrates, Emily Dickinson, Fyodor Dostoevsky, Friedrich Nietzsche, Richard Wagner, Mary Baker Eddy, Adolf Hitler, and Abraham Lincoln. Indeed, one could almost define a genius as someone famous (or notorious) enough to attract the attention of a psychobiographer!

So why isn't psychobiography listed along with psychometric and historiometric research? The answer is simple: Psychobiography uses very different methods to answer very different questions (Simonton, 1999c). Unlike psychometrics and historiometrics, psychobiography constitutes a single-case qualitative approach. The whole study is devoted to a psychological interpretation of the life and work of a single genius. Most often the focus is on a peculiar event or idiosyncratic trait. For example, many psychobiographers have tried to fathom why Vincent Van Gogh cut off part of his left ear (Runyan, 1981). No doubt this is a captivating question. Yet the answer—if one is ever possible—would only tell us something about Van Gogh as an individual. It would not give any insights into the nature of genius as a universal phenomenon. Not every genius, artistic or otherwise, engages in self-mutilation. And not all self-mutilators are geniuses. Our goal throughout this book is to discuss the psychology of genius in general rather than the psychology of specific geniuses. For that reason, psychobiographers offer us little guidance. Our goal can only be reached by conducting investigations that subject multiple cases to quantitative analyses. Psychometric and historiometric inquiries provide the optimal methods for achieving our end.

What Is Genius?

ow would you answer the question posed by the title of this chapter? Too much to ask on the first day of class in Genius 101? Well, then, how would you address the more specific questions posed below?

If you had to identify at least one genius living in your own time, who would you name? Bill Gates? Nelson Mandela? Stephen Hawking? J. K. Rowling? Stephen Spielberg? Oprah Winfrey? Paul McCartney? Meryl Streep? Garry Kasparov? Mick Jagger? Kobe Bryant? Anyone? How would you defend your decision? What criteria are you using? Would your parents, best friend, or lover agree with you?

Say that you just met someone new at a party. She's about your age and looks pretty much like anybody else in your peer group. But during the conversation you find out that she is a member of an exclusive high-IQ society that only admits applicants who score 172 or higher on a standardized test. Would you call her a genius? Would you feel intimidated by her intellectual ability? Would you dismiss her as some nerd who probably has absolutely no street smarts? Would you turn away and decide to mix a little more with lesser intellects?

It's the first day of class in an upper-division psychology course. You sit next to somebody who looks awfully young. You think he's just visiting—perhaps he's the younger sib of one of your classmates. But afterward you learn that he's a college sophomore just 10 years old, that he's majoring in physics, and that so far he has never received a grade below an A, with A+ in the majority of his courses. In addition, he's first-chair violin in the university orchestra, plays highly competitive chess, and is fluent in English, Russian, Latin, and Greek and conversant with Arabic, Chinese, and Sanskrit. Would you call him a genius?

Had enough questions? Did you find them hard or easy? Do you think you might improve your answers if you read a little more about genius? Then read on. First we'll look at various ways of defining genius. Next we'll examine the diverse forms that genius may take. And then I'm going to do something downright mean to you. I'm going to ask you some more questions! Where do we draw the line between genius and other phenomena that are similar but should be kept separate? These inquiries will lead, I hope, to a more comprehensive definition of genius.

DEFINITIONS

Concepts can vary greatly in precision and application. Some concepts are extremely vague, like *weight*, whereas other concepts are exceedingly precise, like *kilogram*. Some concepts can be applied to a wide range of phenomena, such as *chance*, whereas others can only be applied to well-defined situations, such as *conditional probability*. The term *genius* is peculiar. It can be precisely defined or loosely defined. It can be applied to a diversity of phenomena or confined to just one or two. It all depends on how you use the term. The tremendous range in usage reflects the fact that genius is both a humanistic concept with a long history and a scientific concept with a much shorter history.

Humanistic Conceptions

The word genius goes way, way back to the time of the ancient Romans. Roman mythology included the idea of a guardian spirit or tutelary deity. This spiritual entity was assigned to a particular person or place. In the case of a person, it was like a "guardian angel" that looked after your welfare. Perhaps you've seen the classic 1946 film *It's a Wonderful Life*, in which such a benign being intervenes on behalf of the main character, who has just attempted suicide. The angel ("Clarence," played by Henry Travers) manages to convince the protagonist ("George Bailey," played by James Stewart) that life is truly worth living. That's a typically loose Hollywood rendition of the Roman genius.

Over time, this concept underwent a number of transformations, in which its meaning became secular rather than religious. In particular, it began to designate something unique or special about a given person. For example, we can say that a friend has a genius for taking multiple-choice tests. This meaning is seen in other European languages as well. In Spanish, for instance, when we speak of *una persona de mal genio,* we are not saying that the person is an evil genius but rather that he or she has a bad temper or disagreeable disposition. Although an individual's genius is no longer a spirit, it remains something that everybody has. It's what makes you distinct from anybody else. It may even be some unusual talent that sets you apart from others.

So far, so good. You have genius, I have genius, everyone has genius. Can't get much more egalitarian than that! But having genius is not the same as being a genius. The latter status is far more exalted. Only a small percentage of people in the world at any one time attain this high position. When I asked you at the beginning of the chapter to name a still-living genius, you probably didn't list everybody you knew, including yourself and your parents. Instead, you were more likely to conjure up a big name, someone famous and rare. Perhaps you even thought that true geniuses don't exist anymore, and named no one. Maybe the last genius in world history died with Churchill, Gandhi, Einstein, Sartre, Tagore, Stravinsky, Picasso, Hitchcock, or Martha Graham.

This elitist concept of genius is a later invention (P. Murray, 1989). The incipient forms of this usage appear in the Renaissance, but the idea really took off in late-18th-century Europe—during the time of the movement known as Romanticism. Genius came to be seen as an extraordinary, innate capacity. Most people were born without genius, and there was nothing one could do to make oneself into a genius. To illustrate this, the German philosopher Immanuel Kant said, in his 1790 *Critique of Judgement*, that "Genius is the talent (natural endowment)... for producing that for which no definite rule can be given" (Kant, 1790/1952, p. 525). As a consequence, "*originality* must be its primary quality" (p. 526). But because "there may also be original nonsense, its products must at the same time be models, i.e., be *exemplary*" (p. 526). In other words, although you can't become a genius through imitation, but only via innate talent, your genius inspires others to imitate you! The genius invents the exemplary rules that others will follow.

According to Cox (1926), Kant had a genius-level IQ, perhaps somewhere between 135 and 145, possibly even higher. So maybe Kant knew what he was talking about!

Scientific Measurement

Kant's ideas on genius are not without merit. We will come across echoes of his views in other parts of this book. Nonetheless, psychologists who study genius prefer a more clear-cut definition, and especially a definition that lends itself to quantification. Instead of dividing the world into geniuses and nongeniuses, it would be better to assess the magnitude of genius that each genius displays. Clearly not all geniuses are the same. To demonstrate this point, contemplate Kant's claim that the primary quality of genius is originality. Certainly some products of genius will be far more original than others. Almost anyone who receives a Nobel Prize in science or literature has had to create something original. Yet not all Nobel laureates are alike. In physics, for example, the breakthroughs of Albert Einstein, Niels Bohr, and Louis de Broglie surpassed the more somewhat conventional contributions of Charles Edouard Guillaume, Albert A. Michelson, and Manne Siegbahn. A bit lower still on the implicit originality scale are those who have never earned a trip to Stockholm to receive so high an honor.

In chapter 1, I noted that there are two main methods that psychologists apply to the study of genius. Not surprisingly, then, there are two principal ways to assess degrees of genius. You guessed it! One is historiometric, and the other psychometric.

Historiometric Genius. According to Kant, geniuses must not just be original but must also be exemplary. They should create products or ideas that inspire others to follow in their footsteps, in what Kant called imitation. Expressed differently, geniuses exert influence over others. They have an impact on both contemporaries and posterity. Their contributions survive the test of time. Yet how can this definition of genius be applied? One possibility is to sit down in a comfortable armchair, read stacks of biographies and histories, and then rate the big names of history according to their ultimate influence. In essence, this is what Hart (2000) did in *The 100: A Ranking of the Most Influential Persons in History.* In Hart's judgment, the top 10, in order, are Mohammed, the Islamic prophet, Isaac Newton, Jesus of Nazareth, Buddha, Kong Fuzi (Confucius), St. Paul the Apostle, Cai Lun (Ts'ai Lun), Johann Gutenberg, and Christopher Columbus. Most readers probably won't know the identity of the person ranked seventh, but he invented something that you use every day and that you're probably using at this very moment (unless you're reading this book in an electronic version). Yes, Cai Lun, a Chinese eunuch, is credited with inventing paper in 105 C.E. And without paper, how successful do you think Gutenberg's printing press would have been in the long run?

Needless to say, this approach leaves much to be desired. Because the influence of the big names is being assessed by a single person, there is ample latitude for the insertion of subjective bias. Someone else might judge impact in a different manner. For example, Hart tends to place religious leaders above political leaders, leaders above creators, and scientific creators above artistic creators. Thus, the highest-ranked artistic creator is William Shakespeare (aka, Edward de Vere, according to Hart), who comes in 31st, right between the economist Adam Smith and the chemist John Dalton. Leonardo da Vinci doesn't even make it into the top 100! Instead, tagging along at the end of this elite group are Justinian I, a Byzantine emperor, and Mahavira, the founder of Jainism.

Hence, what we need is a historiometric measure of genius that uses multiple sources, so that everybody's idiosyncratic opinions will cancel each other out. One such measure was mentioned briefly in chapter 1: Cattell's (1903) ranking of 1,000 eminent creators and leaders. This ranking was based on the amount of space granted to each individual in five biographical dictionaries and encyclopedias. Three of these reference works were in English, two in French, and one in German. I already mentioned the two who are at the top of the list—Napoleon and Shakespeare—but what about at the bottom? What are the names of those who came in 999th and 1,000th? The answer: Barthélemy Prosper Enfantin and François-Noël Babeuf, respectively. Who? Ever heard of either one before? Does it refresh your memory if I tell you that the first was a French social reformer of the 19th century and the second a French political activist of the latter part of the 18th century? Probably not! But I'm sure you all would agree that neither is as eminent as the two who came in first and second. So by this space measure, Napoleon and Shakespeare exhibit more genius than Enfantin and Babeuf.

Space measures based on standard reference works are very common in the historiometric research on genius. Besides being fairly easy to calculate, they are highly reliable: that is, indicators from different sources agree strongly on how much space they assign to different historical figures (C. Murray, 2003; Simonton, 1991c). It's unimaginable that some encyclopedia or biographical dictionary might allot more pages, columns, lines, or words to Babeuf than to Napoleon! Nevertheless, there is no such thing as a perfect measurement technique in the psychological sciences. Space measures are no exception. Sometimes a genius will be granted more space for reasons having nothing to do with his or her actual impact. For instance, Cattell's (1903) ranking has a tendency to place geniuses slightly higher if they happened to die at a very young age (Simonton, 1976a). Historical figures apparently get extra points for having their lives end in tragedy. This tragedy effect is especially conspicuous in the case of creative geniuses. When we hear of the youthful deaths of Pascal, Mozart, Byron, or Raphael, we may lament, "Oh, woe is me! What they might've done had they lived longer!" Their unrealized potential becomes projected achievement.

Fortunately, space measures can be supplemented or even replaced by various alternatives. Another possibility is to survey experts, asking them to nominate or rate a slate of candidates. Cattell was among the first to use this technique, applying it to the evaluation of scientists and psychologists. Almost every major form of exceptional achievement has been evaluated in this manner, from that of presidents of the United States to that of composers of classical music (Farnsworth, 1969; Simonton, 1986b). Even so, historiometric research can resort to still other methods besides space measures and expert surveys. Studies of scientific genius frequently use the number of times an individual's publications are cited in the professional literature (e.g., Simonton, 1992b, 2000c). The more citations a scientist receives, the higher is his or her presumed impact on the field. And studies of classical composers can use the number of times that a person's work is recorded or performed (Simonton, 1980c, 1980d, 1991b). Each of these methods has its own pros and cons.

Given the vast array of measurement strategies, you might wonder if they yield the same results. If each has advantages and disadvantages, might these differences undermine the degree of correspondence? The answer is surprising: The concordance is extremely large, as large as found in the best psychometric instruments (Simonton, 1990b). As a case in point, consider classical composers. Space measures, expert surveys, and performance frequency almost invariably place the same three composers at the top, namely, Beethoven, Mozart, and J. S. Bach. Other composers are consistently placed toward the bottom. To be sure, one source may place Beethoven first, another Mozart, and still another Bach. Yet these disagreements are to be expected. Each measure is weighting various criteria in slightly different ways. Notwithstanding the discrepancies, you will never find a historiometric measure that will replace Beethoven with Reicha or Mozart with Türk or Bach with Gebel—just to mention three of their exact contemporaries who never attained the highest levels of genius.

Quick quiz: Whose music have you heard most often? Beethoven's or Reicha's? Mozart's or Türk's? Bach's or Gebel's? Even if you only listen to rock, jazz, country, hip-hop, or pop, you are all likely to give the same answers.

Psychometric Genius. Historiometric measures have one major liability: They work best when you study dead people. Almost all of the geniuses investigated by Galton (1869), Cattell (1903), Cox (1926), and Thorndike (1950) were deceased. Admittedly, you could apply the same techniques to living contemporaries, but you would be taking a risk. Until the moment of death, you never know whether their supreme contribution still lies before them. Perhaps they are going to leave this world with a bang rather than a whimper. Copernicus published his revolutionary masterpiece in 1543, in the last year of his life. The first printed copy of *On the Revolutions of the Celestial Spheres* may have been presented to him on the very day he died. According to legend, it was placed in his hand as he lay on his deathbed in a stroke-induced coma. He briefly woke up, glanced at his magnum opus, and passed away peacefully. Whether this story is true or not, the historiometric assessment of genius certainly cannot rest in peace until the genius does.

That's where psychometric measurement comes in. Rather than wait until people have completed their careers, why can't we test them in advance? If genius depends on certain psychological characteristics, why not measure those characteristics? From that measurement we can decide whether we have a genius on our hands. Yet what personal attributes should we assess? Galton provided an answer back in 1869. He said that genius was contingent on what he called *natural ability*. The higher the natural ability, the greater is the magnitude of genius. But how do we gauge natural ability? If we were inclined toward Kantianism, we might say that we would only have to measure a person's capacity for originality. Galton had a very different idea. For him, natural ability meant "those qualities of intellect and disposition, which urge and qualify a man to perform acts that lead to reputation," where the reputation is that "of a leader of opinion, of an originator, of a man to whom the world deliberately acknowledges itself largely indebted" (p. 37). Moreover, Galton did "not mean capacity without zeal, nor zeal without capacity, nor even a combination of both of them, without an adequate power of doing a great deal of very laborious work" (p. 37). This combination he called "the concrete triple event, of ability combined with zeal and with capacity for hard labour" (p. 38). The upshot is "a nature which, when left to itself, will, urged by an inherent stimulus, climb the path that leads to eminence" (p. 38).

Sad to tell, Galton never really figured out how to measure any of these characteristics. His anthropometric instruments were decidedly inadequate. Furthermore, once psychologists got around to assessing these supposed qualities of genius, they concentrated their efforts on what they thought to be the most critical—the intellectual. I've already identified the man responsible: Lewis M. Terman. He defined genius as a high score on the Stanford–Binet Intelligence Scale. The specific criterion he introduced was IQ 140. This distinctive cutoff even became an official definition of genius. As one dictionary put it, a genius is "a person who has an exceptionally high intelligence quotient, typically above 140" (*American Heritage Electronic Dictionary,* 1992). It goes without saying that the more your IQ exceeds this figure, the more you can boast about your "geniusness."

Nonetheless, we should recognize a severe problem with this psychometric definition: The Stanford–Binet IQ is only applicable to children. It's not just that the items making up the test would be too easy for adults. It's also the case that the original definition of IQ only makes sense with respect to children. As noted in chapter 1, IQ was at first defined as the ratio of mental age to chronological age multiplied by a hundred. Consequently, if a child who was 6 years old was able to perform at a 12-year-old level, she would receive an IQ score of 200—the estimated IQ of Galton. In the specific case of the Termites, who were around 11 at the time of testing, they would have needed a mental age of 15.4 to get an IQ of 140 ($= 100 \times 15.4/11$). That seems sensible enough. But consider what happens when we apply this definition to an adult. Say someone is 40 with an IQ of 200. Does that imply that this person has the intelligence of an 80-year-old? Does that make any sense? Although a person who is 12 years old should be expected to have more intellectual ability than one who is 6 years old, it's not so obvious that the same expectation applies to adults. On the contrary, this once commonsense definition now seems totally absurd.

What was required was a shift in the conception of psychometric intelligence. That new conception was actually suggested by Galton in 1869. He argued that natural ability was normally distributed, just as Quételet (1835/1968) had indicated was the case for physical traits such as weight and height. Geniuses were located at the upper tail of the bell-shaped curve. In contrast, people of average intelligence were located in the middle of the distribution, the place where the peak appears. The question then becomes a simple matter of determining where to draw the line between geniuses and everybody else. What's the minimum IQ necessary for someone to be called a psychometric genius, even a low-grade one?

It must be obvious that any answer to this question must be arbitrary. One reason why it's arbitrary is that not all IQ tests are the same. Accordingly, a particular IQ score on one test may not be equivalent to the same score on another IQ test. To keep things simple, let's just overlook these niceties and present approximate thresholds (cf. Storfer, 1990). If we use Terman's cutoff of IQ 140, the person with IQ 140 easily scores in the upper 1% of the distribution. That is, out of 100 people, that person would be the brightest. But we could be more lenient, like the Mensa society. It only requires that members be in the upper 2% of the population, which translates to an IQ of around 130. Or we could also be more stringent. Only one person in a million would earn a score as high as 172. The odds of meeting someone with an IQ this high at a party would be extremely low. To have a reasonable chance to meet just one, you would have to be surrounded by a million partygoers. That's some big party!

So where would you place the boundary? Perhaps Terman's (1925) criterion of IQ 140 is as good as any. This figure is still 40 points higher than the average IQ and fully 20 points higher than the average IQ of a college graduate in the United States (Cronbach, 1960). People with IQ 140 are really smart people. An IQ in the 130–139 range would then qualify a person as a "borderline genius" or "quasi-genius." In reality, about five dozen of the 1,528 putative geniuses in Terman's longitudinal study had IQs in the 135–139 range, but he still allowed them to become Termites. Should we then revise the genius application to read "only those with IQs of 135 or better need apply"?

Some of you may now be saying to yourself, "Wait! How do we really know that a high IQ is equivalent to genius? Do we even know that IQ tests are measuring the right kind of intelligence? And what about the zeal and persistence that Galton talked about? How do we know that high-IQ people can produce the original and exemplary products that Kant mentioned?" Well, at this point, we don't. Yet the psychometric definition of genius has insinuated its way into the dictionary. So it has to be true. Right? We'll see.

MANIFESTATIONS

Whatever the actual association between historiometric and psychometric genius, we have a strong inclination to associate the two concepts. This connection was demonstrated in a recent survey of college students at both U.S. and Canadian universities (Paulhus, Wehr, Harms, & Strasser, 2002). The students were asked to "think of an ideal example of an intelligent person. Not a friend or family member, but someone who is well known— alive or not" (p. 1052). How would you respond to this question? The survey respondents came up with such names as Albert Einstein, Isaac Newton, Thomas Edison, Wolfgang Mozart, William Shakespeare, and Leonardo da Vinci. Every one of these figures would also be considered examples of historiometric genius. In addition, rough IQ estimates are available for three of those cited: Newton at 130–170, Mozart at 150–155, and da Vinci at 135–150 (Cox, 1926). In these three instances, historiometric and psychometric genius would seem to converge. No doubt that convergence would hold for Einstein, Edison, and Shakespeare as well.

The exemplars of intelligence have another feature in common: They are all known as exceptional creators. This commonality obliges us to examine the most prominent manifestation of genius. Later we will see, however, that it is not the only one.

Outstanding Creativity

What is creativity? What does it mean to say that someone is creative? The favored definition is that creativity satisfies two separate requirements (Simonton, 2000b). First, to be creative is to be *original.* If hundreds of others have already come up with the same idea, it can hardly be considered creative. Yet originality is a necessary but not sufficient criterion. As Kant pointed out earlier, total nonsense can be highly original—as the antics of absolute psychotics amply illustrate. From this undeniable reality arises the second quality: To be creative is to be *useful*. The original idea must work. If I decide to make an airplane out of cinderblocks, I will earn many points for originality but no points whatsoever for usefulness, and so my overall score on creativity is zero.

It is helpful to view creativity as the product of these two features. More specifically, we can say that $C = O \times U$, where C is creativity, O originality, and U usefulness. If either O or U is zero, then C is zero. Otherwise, creativity can result from various combinations of originality and usefulness. Sometimes a creative idea will be higher in originality than in usefulness, and other times it will be higher in usefulness than in originality. In the former category might be a work of art conceived in a revolutionary style that not everybody "gets." In the latter category might be a new home appliance that in large part provides the functions of already existing appliances but provides them in one single unit.

When studying creativity, psychologists often make a critical distinction between two kinds of creativity (Simonton, 2000b). On the one hand there is "little-c" creativity. This involves the creativity of everyday life. Life is full of problems that we have to solve. And we will often arrive at novel solutions that actually work, that get the job done. For example, perhaps you are cooking dinner for a special someone when you suddenly realize, just minutes before he or she arrives, that the pantry is missing an essential ingredient. So you scramble around the spice rack and discover a unique combination of herbs that will do the trick. The resulting recipe is original to you, and it yielded a satisfying dish, yet it may not impress anyone as a conspicuous innovation in haute cuisine. You were just fixing some sloppy Joes, after all. As they say, it's not rocket science.

On the other hand there is "Big-C" Creativity. In this case the originality is much more striking and the usefulness much more pervasive. Perhaps no one has ever come up with that idea before, and the idea revolutionizes a whole domain of creative achievement. To use Kant's notion, the resulting product may seem *exemplary* to the extent that it inspires imitators or at least recruits admirers or disciples. Shakespeare's *Hamlet* has not only enthralled theatergoers for centuries but has also stimulated many other creators to conceive operas, ballets, films, paintings, novels, and even other plays, such as Tom Stoppard's 1966 *Rosencrantz and Guildenstern Are Dead*. This means that the product $O \times U$ for *Hamlet* is several orders of magnitude higher than that of a makeshift recipe for sloppy Joes. Creativity of such a high order is called the work of genius. Big-C Creativity is what creative geniuses do for a living.

This last conclusion raises an interesting issue: In what domains of achievement can we expect to find creative genius? Does Big-C Creativity appear in all achievement domains, or in just a subset? I ask this question because there is a strong tendency to limit creative genius to the fine arts. For instance, when college students had to name exemplars of creativity rather than intelligence, Einstein, Newton, and even Edison disappeared from the lists (Paulhus et al., 2002). Only Mozart, Shakespeare, and da Vinci remained, to be joined by other artistic creators like Beethoven, Michelangelo, Picasso, Salvador Dali, Stephen Spielberg, and Walt Disney, and even such outstanding performers as Michael Jackson, Robin Williams, and Madonna. Very low on the list—even lower than Madonna!—can be found Sigmund Freud and Alexander Graham Bell, the only two geniuses on the list who have any claim to being scientists.

Of course, these are the opinions of college undergraduates. We might reject these identifications as the expressions of ignorance. What do *they* know? Not so fast. Even well-informed intellectuals display the same propensity to see the arts as more creative than the sciences. In fact, that viewpoint goes all the back to Immanuel Kant (1790/1952). The philosopher made it quite unambiguous that in his view, genius could only appear in the arts, not in the sciences. "Fine art is the art of genius" (p. 525). He even explicitly argued that Newton's *Principia Mathematica*, though an "immortal work," could have been produced by any-one with sufficient learning, whereas only a genius like Homer could have written the *Iliad* and the *Odyssey*. Poets, dramatists, painters, sculptors, architects, and composers could be geniuses, but not mathematicians, astronomers, physicists, chemists, and biologists. The expression "scientific genius" would be an oxymoron.

Kant's position falls in line with the position of those philos-ophers and scientists who believe that science doesn't *need* cre-ativity because there is something styled the scientific method, which obviates the need to be creative. For Francis Bacon it was an inductive method, for René Descartes a deductive method, and for Newton a hypothetico–deductive method. Despite this variety, science still had a method. Imitate the method, and you're a scientist. But no matter how successful you are, you're not a genius. If Newton doesn't count as one, how can the fate of Copernicus, Galileo, or even Einstein be any different?

Although Kant and the rest overstate their case, their posi-tion does contain a grain of truth. On the average, artistic genius requires more originality than scientific genius. The latter oper-ates under more constraints—imposed by fact and logic—than does the former. An artist can always take advantage of poetic license to stretch the truth; a scientist never can. This difference means that the personal traits of a scientific genius tend to fall somewhere between those of an artistic genius and someone en-gaged in small-c creativity. In a sense, the scientific genius is a practitioner of medium-c creativity.

Exceptional Leadership

When the U.S. and Canadian students had to name exemplars of intelligence, they occasionally identified leaders rather than creators (Paulhus et al., 2002). The nominees included Martin Luther King, Malcolm X, Bill Clinton, Jimmy Carter, Mikhail Gor-bachev, Pierre Trudeau, Diane Feinstein, Bill Gates, Lee Iacocca, and even Donald Trump! This suggests that genius can also appear in domains requiring leadership rather than creativity. This extension of the concept is consistent with Galton's (1869) *Hereditary Genius*. Besides discussing scientists, poets, novelists, painters, and composers, Galton also discussed politicians, commanders, and religious and judicial leaders. Additionally, this enlargement of the concept falls in line with Hart's (2000) rating of the 100 most influential persons in history. As observed earlier, leaders outrank creators, and religious leaders tend to outrank political leaders.

In the main, genius in the leadership domain of achievement appears to fall into the following four groups: (a) military genius, as in Genghis Khan, Alexander the Great, Napoleon Bonaparte, Attila the Hun, Cyrus the Great, Julius Caesar, Frederick the Great, Gustavus Adolphus, George Washington, Simón Bolívar, Francisco Pizarro, Hernando Cortés, Chief Joseph, and Shaka; (b) political genius, as in Ashoka the Great, Qin Shi Huang (Ch'in Shih-huang), Lenin, Mao Zedong (Mao Tse-tung), Augustus Caesar, Constantine the Great, Oliver Cromwell, Adolf Hitler, Joseph Stalin, Queen Isabella I, Queen Elizabeth I, Peter the Great, and Catherine the Great; (c) entrepreneurial genius, as in Bill Gates, John D. Rockefeller, Cornelius Vanderbilt, Andrew Carnegie, John Jacob Astor, and Henry Ford; and (d) religious genius, as in Mohammed, Jesus, Buddha, Moses, Zoroaster, Mahavira, Mani, Martin Luther, John Calvin, and Pope Urban II.

Admittedly, the last category of genius is mighty controversial. The attribution depends on your religious affiliation or theology. If you're Muslim, Mohammed was the Prophet of Allah, not a mere genius. Likewise, if you're a Christian, Jesus was the Son of God, and the term genius becomes demeaning if not heretical. Kant did not consider the possibility that the original ideas that serve as exemplary models for others to imitate might come through divine revelation or inspiration. Happily, there is no need to grapple further with this most delicate quandary. Very few psychologists, if any, have published research on so-called religious genius. So we can easily put the problem aside for a more enlightened future generation to ponder.

Prodigious Performance

When we talk about genius in domains of leadership, we are in a more precarious situation than when we speak of genius in domains of creativity. Leaving aside the question of religious genius, exceptional leadership doesn't always require the same level of natural ability as does outstanding creativity. This difference is even apparent in the IQ scores that Cox (1926) estimated for her 301 geniuses (Simonton, 1976a). The leaders in her sample had an average IQ about 10 points lower than the average IQ for the creators. This IQ gap would even be wider if we removed from her sample the political revolutionaries, a group with IQs about 20 points higher than her generals and admirals. Cox's results are compatible with the student survey that found far fewer leaders listed as exemplars of intelligence than creators (Paulhus et al., 2002).

Even so, it is possible to dip lower into even more doubtful cases. Frequently the term genius is applied to exemplars of prodigious performance of almost any kind. Anyone who has worked his or her way to the very top of the distribution with respect to performance in a given domain is said to be a genius. Thus, it seems okay to speak of chess genius when discussing Garry Kasparov or Bobby Fisher. Virtuosic facility with a musical instrument can similarly be referred to as indicating genius. We see this when the lofty label of genius is applied to virtuosos like Glenn Gould or Itzhak Perlman. The former was a piano genius and the latter is a violin genius. On the same principle, this elite designation can work for the rock guitarist Jimi Hendrix, the sitar player Ravi Shankar, or the jazz vocalist Ella Fitzgerald.

Even more dubious are occasions where the word is bandied about in sports. Was Michael Jordan a basketball genius or Joe Montana a genius in football? To some observers, such largesse in bestowing the term may appear absurd. Yet Galton himself (1869) was guilty of the practice. Along with his eminent creators and leaders, he included oarsmen and wrestlers! And if physical athletes can be geniuses, what about mental athletes? Consider Shakuntala Devi, the phenomenal human calculator (Jensen,

1990). She can multiply two numbers like 7,686,369,774,870 and 2,465,099,745,779 in just 28 seconds—in her head! Or calculate the eighth root of the number 20,047,612,231,936 in just 10 seconds! How many of us can even calculate the square root of a much smaller number in just 10 seconds? Should Shakuntala Devi be called a calculating genius?

In all of the above applications, we are talking about grown-ups who perform at prodigious levels. But what about the child prodigy? Take Mozart, for instance. According to Cox (1926), Mozart began composing around age 5, and by the age of 7 he had published his first works, namely, four sonatas for violin and keyboard. By the age of 15, he had composed 18 symphonies, two operettas, and an opera, plus numerous concerti, chamber works, and church compositions. He was even appointed grand ducal concert master at age 13. In addition to all these precocious accomplishments, he became an outstanding keyboard virtuoso and launched himself on successful concert tours while a mere boy. When he was 14, he attended a performance in the Sistine Chapel of Allegri's *Miserere*—a most intricate piece written for two choirs of four and five parts—and then proceeded to write the entire work down from memory. The transcript required only minor corrections! And, naturally, he demonstrated perfect pitch, at age 7. These feats are certainly prodigious. If Mozart had died before entering adulthood, could we still call him a genius?

From a scientific perspective, the answer would be both yes and no. That's because we only have two assessment criteria. By the criterion of psychometric genius, we could argue that Mozart would count as a genius even if he had died even younger than he did. Cox's (1926) IQ estimate, based on Mozart's patently precocious development, would have earned him a place among the Termites. Still, the judgment comes out differently when we use the criterion of historiometric genius. Mozart may have been highly prolific, but his early works were far from original. Indeed, the early Mozart was proficient but imitative. And as Kant reminds us, imitation is not genius. Mozart didn't discover his unique voice until he was in his late teens, and he didn't start producing indisputable masterpieces until he was in his mid-20s (Hayes, 1989). So if had died around 20, say, he would at best have earned a brief footnote in music history as the promising but short-lived son of Leopold Mozart, a noted music teacher, violinist, and minor composer.

DEMARCATION

At the end of the previous section, I argued that we only have two rightful standards for calling someone a genius. One is psychometric and the other historiometric. Of these two touchstones, the first is the easier and the more unequivocal in application. Just have the person take an intelligence test, as Terman (1925) did. If that's not possible, because the person is inconveniently deceased or otherwise indisposed, then try to estimate the individual's intelligence using available biographical data (e.g., Cox, 1926; Simonton, 1986c, 2006c; Thorndike, 1936, 1950; Woods, 1906). Historiometric genius, by comparison, is much more difficult and uncertain as a standard. To help you gain an appreciation of the problem, I would like you to contemplate six cases, deciding whether they should count as genius or not. What are the criteria you will use in making the decision?

Evil Genius

Some of you may have taken offense, even gotten an adrenaline rush, when Hitler was listed earlier as an example of political genius. Those of you who know your history may also have taken exception to the listing of Genghis Khan. I could probably have provoked the ire of even more readers if I had included Osama bin Laden. Once I participated in an A&E television program called *The Mystery of Genius*. My own remarks were confined to creative and military genius, but when I watched the show for the first time on TV, I was shocked to discover that it also included notorious spies! Why not talk about criminal genius, while we're at it? Why not Al Capone or some infamous Mafia godfather? In more general terms, should evil genius still count as genius?

I don't have a definite answer, but I would like you to assess a research finding from a study of 342 European monarchs (Simonton, 1984e). Although the sample included kings, queens, and sultans like Louis XIV of France, Frederick the Great of Prussia, Christina of Sweden, Catherine the Great of Russia, and Suleiman the Magnificent of the Ottoman Empire, not all of the political leaders in the sample attained fame and fortune, and some were outright failures—including Catherine's incompetent and impotent husband, Peter III. Tellingly, a leader's historiometric eminence was found to be a U-shaped function of his or her rated morality. In other words, the greatest monarchs were either good or evil, famous or infamous. More mediocre rulers were less extreme in their moral behavior. So if you can't go down in history as a saint, at least you can leave your mark as a sinner. How many of you have watched or read Shakespeare's play *Richard III?* You get the idea.

Accidental Genius

We'd like to think that a genius attains distinction by some effort, even lots of effort. Remember what Galton (1869) said about the capacity for doing really hard work. Yet perhaps someone could be lucky enough to be at the right place at the right time. Consider the well-known case of Alexander Fleming. In 1928, he noticed quite by chance that a culture of *Staphylococcus* had been contaminated by a blue–green mold. Around the mold was a halo, indicating that it was emitting a chemical that inhibited the bacteria's growth. Fleming identified the mold as *Penicillium notatum* and eventually isolated the active substance he called penicillin. In time, penicillin became a miracle drug, saving millions of lives. In 1944, Fleming was knighted, and a year later he shared the Nobel Prize in Medicine with Howard Florey and Ernst Boris Chain.

Events like this are very common, so common that they have a name: *serendipity* (Cannon, 1940; Roberts, 1989). Some famous examples include discoveries about the interference of light (Grimaldi in 1663), the geometric laws of crystallography (Haüy in 1781), animal electricity (Galvani in 1791), laughing gas anesthesia (Davy in 1798), electromagnetism (Oersted in 1820), ozone (Schönbein in 1839), photography (Daguerre in 1839), synthetic coal-tar dyes (Perkin in 1856), the D-line in the solar spectrum (Kirchhoff in 1859), dynamite (Nobel in 1866), the phonograph (Edison in 1877), vaccination (Pasteur in 1878), saccharin (Fahlberg in 1879), X-rays (Röntgen in 1895), radioactivity (Becquerel in 1896), induced sensitization (anaphylaxis; Richet in 1902), classical conditioning (Pavlov in 1902), vitamin K (Dam in 1929), sulfa drugs (Domagk in 1932), Teflon (Plunkett in 1938), and Velcro (de Maestral in 1948). Yet should we dismiss any claims to genius because the discoveries were serendipitous? If you were lucky enough to be in Fleming's laboratory on that fateful day in 1928, and beat him to the petri dish, would you have earned yourself a knighthood and a Nobel?

Before you lament your misfortune, you should know that serendipity seldom falls into the lap of couch potatoes. Most recipients of chance discoveries worked very hard before the big event and continued to work very hard after the big event. Thus, Fleming had made important contributions to bacteriology, immunology, and chemotherapy prior to 1928. For instance, he had discovered the enzyme lysozyme 6 years earlier. After 1928, Fleming endeavored to get chemists to help him isolate the antibiotic agent in the mold, and he engaged in clinical trials to test its effectiveness. Although penicillin did not become a viable medication until after the work of Florey and Chain, it was Fleming who set the whole process in motion and acted as an impetus to the drug's development. Still think he was just an accidental genius?

Neglected Genius

This problem has plagued the concept of historiometric genius ever since its inception. In the Austrian Empire, Gregor Mendel discovers the laws of genetics in 1865, dies in 1884 with his breakthrough virtually ignored, and is posthumously resurrected in 1900 when three different scientists independently rediscover his results. Two years after Mendel's death, a woman dies in the United States. Having published fewer than a dozen poems during her brief lifetime, she leaves behind more than 1,500 unpublished poems that are both original and exemplary. Only after the posthumous publication of these compositions does Emily Dickinson become known as one of the country's greatest poets (and, much later, become one of my personal favorites). Finally, let's go to Mexico, where Frida Kahlo dies at an even younger age than Dickinson (47 rather than 55). The wife of the great Mexican muralist Diego Rivera, and one-time lover of the Russian revolutionary Leon Trotsky, she leaves behind nearly 150 paintings, more than a third of which are self-portraits. After her death, these paintings gain ever more admirers until the movie star Salma Hayek can play the title role in a 2002 film titled simply *Frida*.

Don't we just *love* these stories? I think they have a special appeal to everyone suffering from what may be called the Walter-Mitty complex (after James Thurber's fictional character). Some of us may live in a secret world in which we come up with revolutionary scientific discoveries, write poetic masterpieces, or paint unqualified masterworks. Sadly, nobody knows it. Even so, from these examples we can hope, however vainly, for posthumous vindication if not acclamation. Even if it would be nice if we didn't have to die first, we can still draw some comfort from the idea that geniuses are often neglected in their own time.

If you are one of these dreamers, all I can say is, "Dream on!" Neglected geniuses are the exception rather than the rule. Any rule has an exception, but it wouldn't be a rule if it didn't hold up most of the time. In English orthography, we have the handy spelling guide "*i* before *e,* except after *c,* or if sounded as *a* as in *neighbor* and *weigh.*" This works for *relieve* and *receive,* but not for *weird.* The cases of Mendel, Dickinson, and Kahlo are plain weird. Their exceptionality has been demonstrated in several empirical studies. For instance, the relative eminence of Renaissance Italian artists has remained rather stable over several centuries (Ginsburgh & Weyers, 2006). Occasionally some also-ran will make a brief appearance, only to lapse again into obscurity. And the luminaries like Leonardo da Vinci, Michelangelo, and Raphael will sometimes shuffle about in competition for first place. Yet the generation-to-generation fluctuations do not produce any big surprises. The same transhistorical stability holds for other domains, such as literature, science, and even psychology (Over, 1982; Rosengren, 1985; Simonton, 1984f). This consistency across time even applies to individual creative products. The reception of an opera at the time of its debut predicts its popularity centuries later (Simonton, 1998b), and a comparable stability applies to the perceived merit of Shakespeare's 154 sonnets (Simonton, 1989b). Fame is not as fickle as people so often suppose.

To sum up, once a genius has survived the test of time, he or she doesn't have to be retested. A few geniuses, like Mendel, Dickinson, and Kahlo, may not pass the test until it's too late for them to bask in the glory, but once they pass, they pass, and their standing with posterity becomes reasonably secure. The reputations of Mendel, Dickinson, and Kahlo will still have ups and downs, but it's highly unlikely that any of them will face the oblivion that seemed to be their destiny when they died. Once you make it into the pantheon, you've made it—even if you find yourself demoted to the basement from time to time.

Inverse Genius

Perhaps inverse genius is not the best term. It's just hard to come up with another. I'm thinking here of something so bad, it's good. Like a movie so terrible that it becomes classic camp. The films of Ed Wood might fit the bill. He's gone down in history as the world's worst director ever. His 1959 *Plan 9 From Outer Space* is sometimes called the worst film ever made. Yet in 1994, he became the subject of the biopic *Ed Wood* with Johnny Depp in the title role! And several of his films, not excluding *Plan 9 From Outer Space*, are available for viewing from Netflix, the Internet DVD supplier! Certainly there are much better filmmakers who are still waiting for their films to get the attention that has been bestowed on Wood's monstrosities!

Or ponder the poet named William McGonagall. Never heard of him? He is to Shakespeare what Hitler is to Churchill; McGonagall is the worst poet in the English language. His poetry is so bad that gleeful fans are still reading it today. The Web site dedicated to his memory at http://www.mcgonagall-online.org.uk/ features many of his highly mortal lines from his all too numerous horrid poems. The poem "Glasgow" contains this gem: "So let the beautiful city of Glasgow flourish / And may the inhabitants always find food their bodies to nourish." The case of McGonagall reminds me of the annual Bulwer-Lytton Fiction Contest sponsored by the English Department at San José State University, California, just a short drive from where I work at the University of California, Davis. Contestants must "compose the opening sentence to the worst of all possible novels." The prize's namesake, Bulwer-Lytton, began one novel with this line: "It was a dark and stormy night." Sound familiar? It was sometimes quoted by Charles Shulz in his Peanuts comic strip. It's the line sometimes typed out by Snoopy as he sits atop his doghouse, trying to hammer out his take on the Great American Novel. Anyhow, you can win $250 if you come up with an opening bad enough to be good. The "Lyttony of Grand Prize Winners" includes the name of Gary Dahl, who in 1975 became a millionaire by convincing lots of people to purchase "Pet Rocks." In 2000, he had the Bulwer-Lytton prize to add to his résumé.

So what's your opinion? Do you believe that Ed Wood, William McGonagall, and Gary Dahl can all be considered geniuses? If not, why not?

Sham Genius

I'm an aficionado of classical music, and *numero uno* on my list of favorite composers is Beethoven. Maybe fanatic is a more apt word than aficionado. Anyway, I once lamented to a friend how I regretted that the master only composed a little more than 100 substantial works—far fewer than Bach, Handel, Haydn, or Mozart, my other favorites. Indeed, Beethoven's major compositions are fewer than the number of symphonies composed by Haydn—104 symphonies by Haydn versus Beethoven's measly 9 symphonies. The relative scarcity meant that you could listen to Ludwig's music for fewer hours before you had to repeat. It's not that Beethoven's music isn't worth rehearing. Not at all! It's just that I would love to be able to listen to more operas besides the one, more piano concerti besides the five, more symphonies besides the 9, more string quartets besides the 16, more piano sonatas besides the 32—more, more, and more.

So my friend asked a very reasonable question: Why doesn't somebody else just compose more works that sound just like Beethoven? Tentatively, I answered that composers with genius enough to create new works by Beethoven would have so much genius that they would create compositions of their own. In retrospect, that was a very Kantian answer. Genius and imitation are antithetical. But are they really?

Take a time machine to Holland right after World War II. The Dutch authorities are rounding up those who collaborated with the Nazis during the German occupation of their country. Among those arrested was Han van Meegeren, a minor artist and sometime art dealer. His offense was selling a prized Vermeer painting to Hermann Göring, a would-be connoisseur and Hitler confidant. Jan Vermeer is the painter portrayed by Colin Firth in the 2003 film *Girl With a Pearl Earring*. As that movie suggested, Vermeer was a slow worker, so not too many paintings survive—only about a tenth of those that Rembrandt left behind. So Vermeers are rare national treasures, making the crime that van Meegeren committed all the more grave. He certainly was not going to get much sympathy in the Dutch courts.

Yet van Meegeren came up with an astonishing defense: He himself had created the painting, not Vermeer! Not only that, but van Meegeren claimed to have painted six "Vermeers" as well as two paintings attributed to Pieter de Hoogh, another Dutch master. Who could possibly believe that tall tale? To prove his case, he asked to be provided with canvas and paint. He then proceeded to craft an entirely new Vermeer, right before everyone's eyes! He didn't finish the painting, however, because he discovered that he was now going to be prosecuted for art forgery rather than collaboration with the enemy. After various tests, the other forgeries were confirmed, and van Meegeren was condemned to serve a 1-year prison sentence. Curiously, he even became something of a national hero. He had fooled the disreputable Göring into believing he was buying masterpieces instead of forgeries. Dutch ingenuity triumphed over German tyranny.

If these paintings had actually been created by Vermeer, they would have been considered masterworks. And the paintings were not mere copies of Vermeer's work, but rather original creations—albeit in imitation of someone else's artistic style. Perhaps that's the key. A la Kant, van Meegeren was imitating a genius, not being a genius. He was slavishly following another's exemplary work. What's your judgment? Authentic or sham genius?

With the advent of computers, this question has taken on a new twist. Several computer programs have been written that purport to make scientific discoveries or create works of art. For example, David Cope has written a program called EMI (Experiments in Musical Intelligence), which fashions music that sounds like it was created by famous composers (Cope, 1996). The program has generated a new rag "by" Scott Joplin, a new mazurka "by" Chopin, a new invention "by" J. S. Bach, and even a new piano sonata "by" Beethoven. So I can listen to more music by my favorite composer! You can, too, because excerpts can be heard at Amazon.com or on MP3s downloaded from Cope's Web site (http://arts.ucsc.edu/faculty/cope/mp3page.htm). Yet the music is by definition imitative. The compositions might even be called computer-generated forgeries. As such, they can be viewed as another form of sham genius. So what I said to my friend still stands.

Computer Genius

While we're on the topic of apparently brilliant computers, how many of you have ever played chess with your computer? How many of you have found yourself soundly beaten by a dumb machine? Perhaps years of learning the game have been undone by some program that fits on your laptop! It's not surprising that computer chess programs can defeat your amateur skills. These programs have been around for a very long time (Levy & Newborn, 1982). At first, they didn't do so well vis-à-vis human beings. The programs were inadequate because they tried to play chess the way human beings play chess. These were termed knowledge-based programs because they actually knew what they were doing.

Only when computers became really, really fast were they able to bypass the need to know how to play chess. In place of chess strategy and tactics, computer programs could adopt a brute-force approach, calculating the long-term repercussions of any particular move on the chessboard. The programs became clairvoyants who could see well into the future. Being able to anticipate the consequences of every single move is certainly going to give you the edge over a measly human brain. Our wetware is just too slow and clumsy in comparison to their hardware.

At first, the new chess programs weren't very ambitious. They were content to beat the average recreational player. With time, however, the programmers became increasingly bold, taking on chess grand masters. In 1989, the program DEEP THOUGHT challenged Garry Kasparov. Despite having the capacity to evaluate 700,000 positions per second, it lost the matches. Yet it wasn't an easy victory for the champion. Finally, in 1996, an upgraded brute-force program called DEEP BLUE managed to defeat Garry Kasparov, the human chess champion of the world (Hsu, 2002).

Although, in later matches, Kasparov has sometimes managed to outwit the machine, it is now evident to everyone that the days of human chess supremacy are now over. Earlier in this chapter we seemed willing to acknowledge the legitimacy of chess genius. Should DEEP BLUE, then, be counted as an exemplar along with Kasparov?

How about if I ask a different but analogous question? Imagine a marathon competition in which the world's top runner is matched up against the world's fastest and most agile Grand Prix sports car. Who do you think would win? Would this triumph provide us with any insight into what it takes to be a great track athlete? Should the car be allowed to enter the Olympics and compete with human beings for a gold medal? Would you be more impressed if a two-legged robot like *Star Wars'* C3-PO replaced the sports car in the race and won? Wouldn't the marathon competition then be on more equal terms?

Speaking more generally, can a computer genius really be a human genius? Even if computers manage to outdo a human being, should they still get the same credit if they cheat?

INTEGRATION

I believe it's possible to come up with a conception of genius that overcomes the demarcation problems just discussed. Moreover, I think the conception can make some headway toward integrating both psychometric and historiometric definitions. The conception also brings in the seminal ideas of both Galton and Kant.

We begin by emphasizing that geniuses are *generators*. They generate identifiable products. These products can assume many forms, depending on the domain in which the genius is manifested. Examples include ideas, ideologies, theories, inventions, discoveries, novels, plays, poems, paintings, musical compositions, designs, solutions, policies, programs, strategies, tactics, decisions, interventions, reforms, initiatives, and laws. The generative feature is so critical to the definition of genius that it provides a means to assess the magnitude of genius. For the most part, the greatest geniuses have the most progeny (Albert, 1975). They are not one-idea people or one-shot successes. Hence, the more prolific the individual, the more secure is his or her claim to genius.

Note that this productivity stipulation helps solve the problem of the accidental genius. A serendipitous event led Edison to the invention of the phonograph. Yet if he had only relied on serendipity, he couldn't possibly have generated over a thousand inventions—so many that he still claims the record for patents issued by the U.S. Patent Office! Lady luck may strike once or twice, but not multiple times over the course of a career.

I hasten to add that this generative quality is a necessary but not sufficient feature of genius. The products generated must also exhibit originality, just as Kant noted. Original products meet three specifications:

1. At the most minimal level, originality means that the product must not have already been produced. If you reinvent the wheel, you will be very disappointed when you try to file a patent application. In fact, that is the main business of patent offices. They must determine whether a new invention is really new. If its claims overlap those of already awarded patents, the application is rejected.

2. Beyond that, originality also means that the product is not imitative. Recall that Kant thought imitation was opposed to genius. Genius originates products that *others* imitate. It is for this reason that we deny any genius behind van Meegeren's Vermeer paintings or EMI's Beethoven piano pieces. The products are imitative and thus unoriginal. When I listen to one of EMI's compositions, it sounds like Beethoven, all right, but like the master imitating himself! The work seems more similar to any of his sonatas than the sonatas seem to each other! The product is more akin to a caricature than a creation. This point underlines another aspect of the originality requirement: Geniuses should not imitate other geniuses, but

also they should not imitate themselves! When they decide just to do more of the same thing—whether out of external incentives or out of internal laziness—they're in trouble. At that instant their originality has evaporated.

3. At the same time, a special originality should appear in the entire corpus of products generated by a genuine genius. This third aspect of originality concerns the representation of something distinctive or unique about that genius. In artistic genius, this uniqueness may reveal itself in a personal style and perhaps personal thematic material. Thus, the poems and plays of William Shakespeare can easily be distinguished from the works of his contemporaries—so obvious is the difference that a computer can discern it (Elliott & Valenza, 2004). Computers can even identify the composer of a piece of classical music just from the first four notes (Paisley, 1964). Even scientific geniuses have a discernible way of doing science. The theoretical physicist Ludwig Boltzmann once observed that "a mathematician will recognize Cauchy, Gauss, Jacobi, or Helmholtz, after reading a few pages, just as musicians recognize, from the first few bars, Mozart, Beethoven, or Schubert" (qtd. in Koestler, 1964, p. 265). When Newton anonymously submitted a solution to a mathematical puzzle that had been posed as a challenge to the international community, the recipient immediately discerned "the claw of the lion." Notice that this final aspect of originality gets back to the ancient Roman concept. Our genius is what individualizes each one of us. It's what makes us special.

Still, original products alone do not a genius make. If they did suffice, then McGonagall would be a literary genius right up there with Shakespeare! When we discussed creative genius, we mentioned the joint necessity of originality and usefulness. Kant referred to the need for the originality to be sensible rather than nonsensical. The product had to be taken as a model or exemplar of works in a particular domain of fine arts. McGonagall's poetry fails to pass this test. Definitely not exemplary! Unlike

Kant, however, we've already agreed that the phenomenon of genius need not be confined to the fine arts. On the contrary, genius can appear in virtually any domain of human achievement. In the case of outstanding creativity, it can emerge in the diverse disciplines of science and philosophy, in the varied genres of literature and music, and in the visual arts, which can include domains as diverse as painting, drawing, sculpture, architecture, calligraphy, and even cinema. When genius assumes the guise of exceptional leadership, it can also appear in several manifestations, although the military, political, and entrepreneurial varieties are perhaps the least contentious. We have even allowed that some types of prodigious performance might be seen as examples of genius.

But where should we draw the line? I believe that the boundary should be decided according to two criteria.

First, genius should only appear in a *broadly valued domain* of human achievement. This criterion gets back to Galton's (1869) linkage of genius with the reputation of a person "to whom the world deliberately acknowledges itself largely indebted" (p. 37). It is doubtful that this standard would allow some of the more vicious forms of evil genius to be included. Organized crime does not count as a domain of achievement that's highly valued in society at large (however much it is admired within a delimited subculture). By comparison, military leaders like Genghis Khan and Attila the Hun would probably be encompassed by the term genius. Hitler's status is more of an enigma. Nevertheless, his candidacy may fail according to the next criterion.

Second, the achievement must involve the *acquisition of domain-specific expertise* that puts severe demands on anyone wanting to enter the domain. These demands will likely require that any aspirant possess "ability combined with zeal and with capacity for hard labour" (Galton, 1869, p. 38). Of the three components in Galton's "triple event," the enthusiasm (or zeal) precondition needs little elaboration. It is exceedingly unlikely that anyone will acquire world-class expertise in a given domain without having a considerable fascination with the area. Great artists must absolutely love art, notable scientists must have an intense passion for science, top-notch generals must get excited about the strategies and tactics of war, and chess champions must exhibit a total obsession with the game. Besides providing the basis for acquiring the requisite expertise, such zeal helps sustain active involvement in the domain throughout the life span. Practicing an expertise without zest for the domain is the shortest route to career burnout. The other two parts of the triplet require more explanation.

With respect to ability, it should be evident that most domains of achievement presume that a person will have sufficient intelligence to master the obligatory knowledge and skills. Take almost any scientific domain. First you must have enough smarts to get your BA or BS in some science major. As touched upon earlier, this indicates an IQ of around 120. Then nowadays you must, almost invariably, get a higher degree in your chosen scientific discipline. This presumes an IQ at least 10 points higher, already putting you on the threshold of psychometric genius (Cronbach, 1960). For some areas, such as physics, the intellectual prerequisite may be higher still—say, an IQ of around 140. A glance through the undergraduate and graduate curriculum at any top-flight research university proves beyond doubt that there's no such thing as "physics for dummies." A physics watered down sufficiently to be intelligible to someone of average intelligence would not be physics. It would be tantamount to teaching that Einstein won the Nobel Prize for saying that "everything is relative." One study of 64 eminent scientists found that their IQ scores tended to range between around 120 to 200, with averages between 135 and 170 (Simonton, 2002b; cf. Roe, 1953). The ranges depended on the discipline (physics, biology, or social science) and the specific IQ measure (mathematical, verbal, or spatial). Most of the scientists studied could be considered geniuses or at least borderline geniuses.

And what about the "capacity for hard labour," the third part of Galton's triplet? One of the recurrent myths of genius is that it involves a talent so immense that it precludes the necessity of actually knowing what you're doing. Instead of mastering a domain, you use your talent. This myth is implicit in Kant's belief that genius cannot be taught, that you must have it from the moment of conception. I'm afraid the truth is far more pedestrian. Research on high achievers has proven that no one can escape a long period of apprenticeship, starting as a mere ignorant and incompetent novice (Ericsson, Charness, Feltovich, & Hoffman, 2006).

Earlier I observed that Mozart had been composing for about 20 years before he began producing undoubted masterpieces. Actually, Mozart's development as a genius was a bit slow. In most domains that support superlative achievement, young talents are governed by the *10-year rule* (Ericsson, 1996; Hayes, 1989). This rule specifies that it takes a full decade of extensive and intensive study and practice before you're ready to make major contributions to a given domain. This degree of effort is not for the faint of heart. You have to be persistent, methodical, meticulous, and dedicated to acquire the knowledge and skill that underlie extraordinary achievement in most domains.

Take special care to note that the above provisos, taken together, automatically disqualify certain achievement domains as potential homes to genius. For many domains, the highest accomplishments emerging in the domain will lack some essential ingredient. In most sports, for example, originality is not at a premium. The job of Tiger Woods is to get as many birdies or eagles as possible in every round of golf. The task for Barry Bonds is to get as many RBIs as possible in every game, or at least to get himself on base for a potential score later in the inning. In fact, pace Galton, I do not believe that most champion oarsmen and wrestlers get by on the score of originality. I'm not saying that geniuses cannot appear in any sport. Perhaps Kobe Bryant's ability to overcome almost any defense reveals a spontaneous originality of the highest order. And probably some team coaches meet the originality criterion. In U.S. professional football, possible qualifiers include Bill Walsh of the San Francisco 49ers, who is credited as the inventor of the West Coast Offense, and Bill

Belichick of the New England Patriots, who built a dynasty in the era of salary caps and free agency.

Other achievement domains may be deficient in terms of some other criterion. My pet example is the set of categories by which you can get yourself into the *Guinness Book of Records*. A few years ago, a student on my campus asked if I was willing to serve as an official witness to his attempt to break one of these records. Which one? The number of paperclips strung together in a 24-hour period! Do you think it requires much intelligence to learn how to hook paperclips together? Do you believe that it takes a decade of practice before you're ready to challenge the world record? Do you even think it demands an intense zeal for paperclip stringing? No, no, and no, respectively! So there's no such thing as paperclip-stringing-together genius. Now I'll answer your questions. No, I declined to serve as a witness. And no, he didn't succeed—the string got tangled up, making it impossible to determine its length.

And think over the triumph of DEEP BLUE over Garry Kasparov in this context. Can a brute-force program even be said to possess any legitimate chess expertise? Isn't it more like a weight lifter who, when asked to play a game of chess, offers to arm wrestle instead?

Three last test cases are left to the student as an exercise. First assignment: the people listed in the second paragraph of this chapter. Second: that super-IQ woman you met at the party. Third and last assignment: that child prodigy you sat next to in your psychology class. Yes? No?

APPLICATION

So now let's apply what we've learned in this chapter: How can you know if you're a genius? Just ask yourself three questions. Did you have the intelligence, enthusiasm, and endurance to acquire the needed expertise in a broadly valued domain of achievement? Did you actually do so, devoting the approximately 10-year period required? Did you take advantage of this domain-specific expertise to make one or more contributions that are considered by those in your field to be both strikingly original and highly exemplary? If the answer is always yes, then congratulations! You're now a *certified* genius!

Naturally, if you are a younger reader, your answers will sometimes be no, but unfairly so. It's still too early to respond to such questions. Not to worry! We can rephrase them in the future tense so that they become predictors rather than identifiers. Will you have the intelligence, enthusiasm, and endurance to acquire the needed expertise in a broadly valued domain of achievement? Will you actually do so, devoting the approximately 10-year period required? Will you take advantage of this domain-specific expertise to make one or more contributions that are considered by those in your field to be both strikingly original and highly exemplary? If the answer is always yes, then congratulations! You're now a *potential* genius!

Is Genius Generic?

At the close of chapter 2, I offered an integrative conception of genius. Not content just to combine ideas from Kant and Galton, I even tried to unify the historiometric and psychometric definitions. Supposedly, you can't qualify by the former definition without having some claim to the latter. More specifically, you can't become a historiometric genius without making contributions that are both original and exemplary; you can't make those contributions without first acquiring the necessary expertise; you can't obtain the necessary knowledge and skill without first possessing sufficient intelligence—intelligence at the level of a genius or perhaps a borderline genius. Given enough brains, you can master any domain for which you have ample fervor and fortitude. Supposedly, then, any psychometric genius can become a historiometric genius.

This stance can be said to date back to Samuel Johnson, the scholar who compiled the first dictionary of the English language. In 1781, he said that "the true Genius is a mind of large general powers, accidentally determined to some particular direction" (p. 5). I must admit that the adverb "accidentally" doesn't seem to fit what we discussed in chapter 2. But it could be made to do so if the word means that a chance set of causes are responsible for determining a person's interests and values. One combination of genes and early experiences might induce a fascination with and appreciation for, say, science. Another fortuitous mix of genetic and experiential factors may instill in a young talent a preoccupation with politics. These accidents of birth and life then channel the general intelligence toward the acquisition of what it takes to achieve eminence in a particular domain. So one happenstance yields Newton, while another produces Napoleon.

Notice that Johnson's (1781) idea seems to suggest that genius is generic rather than domain specific. This position seems compatible with Galton's (1869) view that genius is dependent on a high level of natural ability. Yet on closer examination, Galton's point of view appears more domain specific. After all, when Galton established family pedigrees for eminent creators, leaders, and athletes, those pedigrees tended to be restricted to particular domains. The Darwin family produced lots of scientists, but no artists or leaders. The Brontë sisters (Charlotte, Emily, and Anne) were all novelists, but their brother (Patrick) was a far less successful poet and painter, who would no doubt not be known today were it not for his three sibs. This specificity suggests that natural ability should be expressed in the plural: natural abili*ties*. Each person might have a capacity for acquiring expertise in a somewhat circumscribed domain. A person who masters physics in record time might find that poetry will always remain beyond all comprehension. Natural ability comes to mean something more akin to a special *talent*.

Of course, if we conclude that natural ability must be tailored to a singular area of expertise, this implies that expertise is particular to each domain. Being creative in physics has nothing to do with being creative in poetry. Outstanding creativity has nothing to do with exceptional leadership, and neither has any connection to prodigious performance. If domain expertise is really so specialized, then we have to marvel all the more at those geniuses who have managed to achieve in more than one domain; the universal geniuses or polymaths are then the wonders of the world. Johann Wolfgang von Goethe was a German poet, novelist, playwright, and natural scientist who created original and exemplary products in all four domains—including such unqualified masterpieces as the dramatic poem *Faust* and the epistolary novel *Sorrows of Young Werther*—all the while making a good living in a succession of political positions. Cox (1926) estimated Goethe's IQ as lying between 185 and 200. Does this mean that he was a "mind of large general powers" accidentally directed toward multiple domains of achievement? Or was he fortunate enough to be born with several separate talents?

The existence of universal geniuses also wreaks havoc with the 10-year rule introduced in chapter 2. If it requires a full decade to attain sufficient domain mastery to make original and exemplary contributions, then how can one become a genius in more than one domain? Two domains would require 20 years, three domains 30 years, and so on. Soon you'll run out of life span and not have enough years to make bona fide contributions. Naturally, one could make a case that expertise in some domains overlaps, so it may take fewer than the normally prescribed years. For Goethe to learn how to write poems, plays, and novels may have only required, say, 20 years instead of 30. Yet given that he was already producing major poems, plays, and novels by his early 20s, even 20 years seems like too long a time requirement.

Besides, what about the other polymaths who achieved excellence in truly disparate domains? Just think about the achievements of the following geniuses: Aristotle (Greek, 384–322 B.C.E.): metaphysics, logic, biology, psychology, political science, ethics, and aesthetics; Al-Kindi (Arab, 801–873 C.E.): astronomy, geography, mathematics, meteorology, music, philosophy, medicine, physics, and political science; Abhinavagupta (Indian, fl. ca. 975–1025): philosophy, aesthetics, criticism, poetry, drama, music, theology, logic, and dance; Shen Kuo (Chinese, 1031–1095): mathematics, astronomy, geology, meteorology, zoology, botany, pharmacology, ethnography, poetry, technology, engineering, politics, government, administration, and war; Omar Khayyám (Persian, 1048–1131): poetry, astronomy, mathematics, and philosophy; Hildegard of Bingen (German, 1098–1179): music composition, drama, natural history, philosophy, medicine, poetry, and religion; Blaise Pascal (French, 1623–1662): mathematics, physics, literary prose, philosophy, and religion; Mikhail Lomonosov (Russian, 1711–1765): physics, chemistry, poetry, geology, linguistics, and education; Thomas Jefferson (American, 1743–1826): political leadership, political philosophy, horticulture, architecture, archaeology, paleontology, technology, and education; and Thomas Young (British, 1773–1829): optics, physics, physiology, mathematics, medicine, Egyptology, linguistics, and music. Psychology even has its own polymath: Herbert Simon (American, 1916–2001), who attained eminence not just in cognitive psychology but also in computer science, public administration, economics, management, statistics, and philosophy of science. Is it really possible to collapse accomplishments so diverse into a mere handful of inclusive domains whose expertise acquisition can fit within a mere decade?

Hence, the question that drives this chapter has two parts. The first concentrates on the nature of intelligence and the second on the nature of domain expertise.

GENERAL INTELLIGENCE OR MULTIPLE INTELLIGENCES?

In chapter 2, I mentioned that college students named Albert Einstein, Isaac Newton, Thomas Edison, Wolfgang Mozart, William Shakespeare, and Leonardo da Vinci as ideal examples of what it means to be intelligent (Paulhus et al., 2002). But are these half dozen geniuses all intelligent in the same manner? Do you truly think that they have some intellectual facility that makes them all illustrate the same characteristic? Does it help or hinder your answer to these questions when I tell you that Oprah Winfrey was also listed among the exemplars of intelligence? Whatever the first six have in common intellectually, does she share it with them? In short, when you say that someone is highly intelligent, what do you mean? Do you think that all intelligent people are intelligent in the same way? Or do you believe that the intelligence of Oprah is very different from the intelligence of, say, Einstein or Mozart? And what do psychologists say about this issue?

To answer the last question, I want to examine three alternative positions on the nature of cognitive ability. The first holds that intelligence is a single coherent construct, a unified dimension that underlies performance on all mental tasks. The second maintains that there are many varied kinds of intellectual ability, so varied that they represent independent intelligences. And the third position argues for a sort of integration of the previous two, in the sense that diverse intelligences can be arranged in a hierarchy with general intelligence at the top.

Unified Intellect

When Terman (1925) began his longitudinal study of 1,528 geniuses, he clearly conceived intelligence as a cohesive entity. The level of intelligence was specified as a single IQ score on the Stanford–Binet Intelligence Scale. Those who scored 140 or higher were then designated as geniuses. By following these kids through to adulthood, Terman hoped to show that they would end up as authentic achievers in a wide range of domains. In line with Samuel Johnson's (1781) assertion, these children would have their "large general powers" directed toward diverse achievements according to a variety of circumstances. One might become the next Newton, another the next Mozart, and yet another the next Cervantes.

Terman's concept was not without merit. Indeed, the concept of a general intelligence had already received substantial support in the work of Charles Spearman (1904). Spearman showed that the grades schoolchildren received on seemingly unrelated subjects were highly correlated. Moreover, statistical analyses indicated that these grades as well as performance on other intellectual tasks could be explained in terms of a general factor, a factor that eventually became known as Spearman's g (see Spearman, 1927). Each measure of human cognitive performance contained two components, the g factor that was shared by all tests or assessments, and a special factor s that was unique to each measure. Although measures would vary in how much they *loaded* on Spearman's g, any gauge of intellectual ability would have a substantial loading on the general intelligence factor.

Research on the g factor has developed considerably since the time of Spearman. Suitable intelligence indicators have proliferated, and the available statistical methods, such as factor analysis, have become increasingly sophisticated. As a consequence, psychologists may know more about general intelligence than they know about most individual-difference variables (see Jensen, 1999). Furthermore, general intelligence has been shown to correlate with a range of positive outcomes. In particular, assessments of general intelligence are correlated with (a) successful adaptation to the demands of daily living (Gottfredson, 1997) and (b) job performance in a diversity of occupations (Ones, Viswesvaran, & Dilchert, 2005). In addition, general cognitive ability correlates positively with achievement in domains that are directly linked with genius. For instance, if we are willing to welcome leadership among these domains, then it is pertinent to note that general intelligence is associated with the performance of leaders in a variety of situations (Simonton, 1995). Thus, a meta-analysis of 151 independent samples obtained a correlation of .27 (Judge, Colbert, & Ilies, 2004). (Quick review session: The correlation coefficient r ranges between −1.00 and 1.00, with 0 indicating no relation between two variables.) But do such statistical associations prove that genius is generic? Are those leaders who gain extremely high scores on an intelligence test more likely to be political, military, or entrepreneurial geniuses than their less brilliant colleagues? Let us think about the pros and cons.

Pro g → Genius. The evidence in favor of this connection is both psychometric and historiometric. On the psychometric side is Terman's longitudinal study. In 1959, a few years after Terman's death, the fifth volume of *Genetic Studies of Genius* was finally published under the title *The Gifted Child at Mid-Life* (Terman & Oden, 1959). The Termites were now in their mid-40s, and thus it was possible to see how the story turned out. Terman made the following observation about the achievements of the men in the sample:

> Nearly 2000 scientific and technical papers and articles and some 60 books and monographs in the sciences, literature, arts, and humanities have been published. Patents granted amount to at least 230. Other writings include 33 novels, about 375 short stories, novelettes, and plays; 60 or more essays, critiques, and sketches; and 265 miscellaneous articles on a variety of subjects. The figures on publications do not include the hundreds of publications by journalists that classify as news stories, editorials, or newspaper columns, nor do they include the hundreds, if not thousands, of radio, television, or motion picture scripts. (p. 147)

A sine qua non of genius status according to the historiometric definition is the generation of products. And by that requirement, Terman's kids may have made the grade.

This positive conclusion appears to be reinforced by the historiometric research reported in the second volume of *Genetic Studies of Genius,* namely, Cox's (1926) *Early Mental Traits of Three Hundred Geniuses.* Cox calculated the actual correlation between her geniuses' estimated IQ and their ranked eminence according to Cattell's (1903) space measures. The result was $r = .25$, about the same size as the correlation between general intelligence and leader performance mentioned earlier. Subsequent historiometric studies have reported even larger correlations. Hence, the intelligence scores that Thorndike (1950) estimated for 92 creators and leaders was shown to correlate at .35 with another eminence measure (Simonton, 1991d; see also Walberg, Rasher, & Hase, 1978; Walberg, Rasher, & Parkerson, 1980).

Within the specific domain of political leadership, the relative eminence of 342 European monarchs studied by Woods (1913) correlated at .32 with their assessed general intelligence (Simonton, 1983). The three most intellectually brilliant monarchs—Frederick the Great of Prussia, William the Silent of the Netherlands, and Gustavus Adolphus of Sweden—are also among the most illustrious in modern history. Similar correlations, ranging between .31 and .35, are found between IQ estimates extrapolated from Cox (1926) and the greatness ratings of U.S. presidents (Simonton, 2006c). The brightest president ever, Thomas Jefferson, is considered among the best, whereas Warren Harding, the least bright (to be nice), is placed among the worst (see also Simonton, 1986c).

To sum up, historiometric studies suggest that historiometric genius correlates at between .25 and .35 with estimates of psychometric genius. So far so good. But...

Con ℊ → Genius. Things are not what they seem. Why don't we scrutinize Terman's proud boast about his Termites (Terman & Oden, 1959). Wow, "nearly 2000 scientific and technical papers"—sounds very impressive! But we must remember that this statistic applies only to the men in his longitudinal study, and then only to the men who became scientists. How does this output work out on a per capita basis? It's hard to say, but we are told that 70 of these men ended up with entries in *American Men of Science.* So let's be liberal and assume that all 2,000 papers were produced by just the eminent 70. That means that Terman's male scientists had each generated about 29 publications by the time they reached their mid-40s. In contrast, U.S. scientists who become Nobel laureates in a scientific discipline tend to have about twice that many publications by the same age (Zuckerman, 1977). In point of fact, not one of the Termites, male or female, attained so high an honor. Even worse, one of the boys who was tested back in the 1920s but wasn't bright enough to be included in the sample did manage to earn the Nobel Prize in Physics. This laureate was William Shockley, the coinventor of the transistor (Eysenck, 1995). Shockley didn't have enough general intelligence to become a psychometric genius but did have enough to lay some claim to being a historiometric genius.

Nor does the picture get much brighter when we turn our gaze to the Termites who did not go into the sciences. The fact of the matter is that not one could be considered to have made the grade as a historiometric genius. Aggravating matters all the more, the Termites' domains of achievement are predominantly of an academic nature, such as humanistic scholarship. Even if they are not academic, their achievements are predominantly verbal. Exceptional accomplishments in the visual arts and music are very rare. Suddenly their intelligence does not seem so general after all.

The historiometric results also turn out to be less clear-cut on further scrutiny. Cox's (1926) inquiry is a case in point. Her elite sample certainly includes a much broader assortment of achievement domains than those found among the Termites: politicians, commanders, revolutionaries, religious leaders, philosophers, scientists, poets, dramatists, novelists, essayists, historians, painters, sculptors, and composers. This would imply that general intelligence has a broad impact. Yet here's the catch: These unquestioned geniuses were not assessed on general intelligence. They did not all take the Stanford–Binet test when they were 11 years old, nor could they have. So what did Cox do? She and her collaborators estimated IQs using biographical data on childhood and adolescent accomplishments. And a large proportion of these accomplishments were confined to specific domains. Recall the precocious feats of Mozart? They were all in music. Likewise, Pascal's IQ estimate of 180 is predicated largely on his mathematical precocity. At age 12, he rediscovered Euclidian geometry totally on his own (working his way up to the 32nd proposition), at 16, he completed a treatise on conic sections that astounded no less a mathematician than Descartes, and at 19, he devised the first calculating machine that could do addition and subtraction. For the most part, Cox's IQ scores were based on domain-specific indicators of intellectual development. Hence, advocates of the *g* factor can find no comfort here. Similar specificity problems may plague the other historiometric studies.

And one more damning fact should be taken into consideration: People who score at the genius level on general intelligence tests seldom produce original and exemplary work worthy of their stratospheric IQs. Marilyn vos Savant was once listed in the *Guinness Book of World Records* as having the highest recorded IQ (McFarlan, 1989). She took the Stanford–Binet at the chronological age of 10 and attained the ceiling mental age for the test (22 years, 10 months), giving her a score of 228 $[=100*(22+10/12)/10]$. Although she has scored somewhat lower on adult tests, she must still be counted as one of the brightest human beings on this planet. So how many of you have heard of her? If I had asked you to name an exemplar of intelligence, would her name have come to mind? Would you have identified her before identifying Oprah Winfrey? For some of you, the answer may be affirmative, namely, those of you who read her weekly column "Ask Marilyn" in *Parade* magazine. Here she gives smart answers to the (sometimes dumb) questions of her readers. No Nobel Prize, no cure for cancer, not even a better mousetrap. By comparison, her presumably less IQ-smart husband, Robert Jarvik, invented the Jarvik-7 artificial heart!

Is it possible that her intelligence is *too* general to be specifically useful? Is it tantamount to someone in excellent physical condition who cannot possibly compete in an amateur triathlon, make a basket from the freethrow line, catch a short pass in football, or even get a hit off a softball lobbed gently over the plate?

Diverse Intellects

Some psychologists become almost apoplectic when the topic of the *g* factor comes up. I won't name names, but I've heard otherwise sensible academics get into yelling matches over the issue.

There seem to be two kinds of psychologists—those who believe in general intelligence and those who don't. The latter are perhaps the more interesting. Those who agree to reject the idea of a unified intellect cannot agree on how many kinds of intelligence there actually are. It's as if they've opened up a real can of worms. There's either one intelligence or there's any integer number between 2 and ∞.

To offer one example, at somewhat less than infinity, J. P. Guilford (1967) proposed a structure of intellect model that stipulates 120 different abilities. More accurately, it's a three-dimensional model consisting of all the possible combinations of operations (cognition, memory, divergent thinking, convergent thinking, and evaluation), products (units, classes, relations, systems, transformations, and implications), and contents (figural, symbolic, semantic, and behavioral). As another homework assignment, you can contemplate a few of the possibilities. To give an example, if someone's performance was superlative in evaluative operations, transformational products, and semantic contents, what kind of genius would he or she be? Not easy? Perhaps we should work out the answer in class.

Fortunately, not all psychologists are so rambunctious with permutations. Robert J. Sternberg (1996) has been kind enough to limit his intelligences to just three. The first is *analytical* intelligence, which comes very close to what is tested by most standard IQ tests. The second is *creative* intelligence, which taps the kinds of abilities most often associated with creativity tests (see Simonton, 2003a). The third is *practical* intelligence, which concentrates on the application of knowledge to real-life situations. According to this triarchic theory, you can be high on one, medium on another, and lower on another. Different people will have distinct profiles on the three intelligences. If a person has the right profile for his or her occupation or profession, then she or he can be said to be high in *successful* intelligence.

A final example comes between these extremes. This is Howard Gardner's (1983) theory of *multiple intelligences*. There were initially seven, namely, linguistic, logical-mathematical, spatial, bodily-kinesthetic, musical, intrapersonal, and interpersonal. Moreover, each of these seven was later coupled with an exemplary genius: the poet T. S. Eliot, the theoretical physicist Einstein, the artist Picasso, the choreographer Martha Graham, the composer Stravinsky, the psychoanalyst Sigmund Freud, and the political leader Gandhi, respectively (Gardner, 1993). As if seven were not enough, still later, Gardner (1998) deliberated about three additional intelligences: naturalist, spiritual, and existential. It remains to be seen whether the number of Gardner's intelligences eventually surpasses 120. I heard someone joke once that the ability to come up with new intelligences should itself count as an 11th intelligence! Gardner could then boast the multiple-intelligence-generating intelligence par excellence.

Unfortunately, none of these multidimensional conceptions of intelligence has yet been subjected to the same degree of empirical scrutiny as has general intelligence. Neither Guilford nor Gardner has developed instruments to measure all (or even any) of their hypothesized abilities. Although Sternberg has devised such measures, they have yet to undergo the same kind of validation as seen in the Stanford–Binet and other standard tests. It would be especially interesting to repeat Terman's (1925–1959) longitudinal study with three types of high-intelligence children. Would those high in analytical intelligence come out pretty much the same as the Termites? Would those exceptional in creative intelligence end up becoming notable artists, composers, and filmmakers? And would those extraordinary in practical intelligence become high-achieving politicians, commanders, and entrepreneurs?

Hierarchical Intellect

Many psychologists now favor a compromise position between single and multiple intelligences. Various intelligences are configured into a hierarchical arrangement with the more narrowly defined intelligences at the bottom and general intelligence at the top. Probably the best-known proponent of this view is

John B. Carroll (1993). After reanalyzing cognitive ability test scores from hundreds of data sets, he claimed that the abilities operated at three levels or strata. At the lowest but most varied level (Stratum I) are the highly specialized tests of particular abilities. At the middle, more abstract level (Stratum II) are more inclusive forms of cognitive ability that are far fewer in number (such as general memory and learning, auditory perception, visual perception, and processing speed). Finally, at the apex (Stratum III) is the g factor, in line with Spearman's (1904, 1927) seminal work. The first stratum spanned 69 tests, the second stratum 8 factors, and the third stratum a single factor. The upshot is a unity-in-diversity model of intelligence.

Complicated? Not at all! To appreciate the simplicity, just compare this hierarchical configuration of intelligences with other hierarchical arrangements. For example, in the classification of life forms we must deal with a hierarchy consisting of several levels, such as kingdoms (e.g., Animalia), phyla (e.g., Chordata), classes (e.g., Mammalia), orders (e.g., Primata), families (e.g., Hominidae), genera (e.g., *Homo*), and species (e.g., *sapiens*)—not even counting all of the super-, sub-, and infra-taxonomic groups! Likewise, a minimum military hierarchy might follow the following sequence: general, colonel, major, captain, sergeant, corporal, and private (and most chains of command have many more ranks than this). By comparison, the hierarchical model of intelligence contains only three levels, with a single kingdom or general at the top—good old Spearman's g—and with numerous but narrow cognitive capacities constituting the species or private soldiers at the bottom.

My personal position favors the hierarchical model of intellect. Dozens of very specialized abilities can be grouped together into middle-level factors that represent more inclusive capacities. Yet the latter are ultimately subordinated to an all-encompassing general factor, Spearman's g. This model does not preclude the possibility that one individual's general intelligence might have a different mix of low-level abilities from the mix seen in other individuals. It just means that on the average, across lots of diverse people, various cognitive capacities tend to positively correlate with each other. Because the separate skills are coordinated by the superordinate faculty, it becomes easier for someone with especially high g to acquire competence in more than one domain of achievement. Although we tend to think of polymaths as very rare, their less intimidating cousins—those who have attained distinction in "only" two or three areas—are actually fairly common.

The last-mentioned conclusion was demonstrated in a historiometric study of 2,102 creative geniuses (Cassandro, 1998). The creators were assessed on their versatility, defined as having achieved eminence in more than one domain or subdomain. Although 61% were not versatile by this definition, 15% were eminent in more than one subdomain within a domain (e.g., poetry and drama within literature), and fully 24% were eminent in more than one domain (e.g., literature and science). Hence, more than one-third exhibited creative versatility of some kind. Shakespeare is an example of a genius in the first category of versatility, Goethe a genius in the second category.

Cox's (1926) sample of 301 creators and leaders also contains many undeniable cases of intra- and interdomain versatility (R. K. White, 1931). Even more telling than the frequencies are the correlations: The versatility of these geniuses is positively correlated with both IQ and eminence, two variables that, as already noted, are also correlated with each other (Simonton, 1976a). Expressed differently, the intellectually most brilliant of Cox's geniuses not only attain higher eminence but also attain eminence in more domains. This implies that Cox's IQ measures were not so domain specific after all. They may have been based mostly on one primary domain, but that specialized assessment served as a proxy for a more general intelligence.

I wish we could say the same thing about the Stanford–Binet Intelligence Scale that Terman used to select his sample. The test excluded too many achievement domains to capture a genuinely broad intellect. That is one reason why the most successful of the Termites tended to achieve eminence in a much more constrained set of domains. Terman measured analytical intelligence and found 1,528 youngsters who were most likely to attain success in some highly academic area. This narrowness may have denied him what he wanted more than anything else—a bona fide historiometric genius. As an academic myself, I know that we professors seldom attain the same degree of distinction as T. S. Eliot, Einstein, Picasso, Martha Graham, Stravinsky, Sigmund Freud, or Gandhi, none of whom were bona fide academics. We cannot even claim Einstein as one of us. Although he held regular professorships in the middle part of his career, he did everything possible to avoid the main responsibilities of academic life, like teaching and professional service. Except for his research, he was no better as a professor than he was as a student.

I will not say anything more than this. Frankly, I'm chicken. I worry about what will happen after this book is published. At the next conference I go to, some anti-*g* psychologist may start yelling at me! I'd rather not get into a competition to see who can scream the loudest. So please don't tell anybody else what I just wrote. It's our little secret.

DOMAIN-SPECIFIC EXPERTISE OR GENERAL PROBLEM-SOLVING TECHNIQUES?

Whether intelligence is unified or multiple, all budding geniuses must go through some sort of apprenticeship period in which they acquire the expertise that will enable them to make original and exemplary contributions to their chosen domain of achievement. Even an Einstein cannot circumvent this necessity. At 16, Albert pondered a question to which few physicists—and certainly few teenagers—would even have given a moment's thought. What would a light wave look like if you could travel alongside it at the speed of light? Einstein needed a full decade before he could answer the question, and reach a surprising answer, too. It's impossible to catch up with a light beam, so you could never observe a static wave. Paradoxically, no matter how fast you traveled, the wave would always be traveling ahead of you at the speed of light! The velocity of light is always constant. That answer was embedded as a core assumption in Einstein's special theory of relativity.

But what was the expertise that Einstein mastered in the intervening years, between the question and the answer? Did he acquire a lot more knowledge and skills in the domain of physics? Or did he acquire some broadly applicable methods for finding solutions to problems? To address this issue, I will first turn to what psychologists have said about problem-solving research in cognitive psychology (see, e.g., Klahr, 2000; Newell & Simon, 1972). After that I will propose a resolution that attempts an integration of two divergent positions.

Algorithms Versus Heuristics

You're at a restaurant and the bill arrives. You've now got to add the tip. Dinner and wine cost $74.15 and you want to tip your server 15%. Not having a calculator handy, what do you do? Presumably you move the decimal point over to the left, and do some rounding to get $7.40. You then add half of this amount, namely, $3.70 (or, for some readers, $3.50 + $0.20), yielding $11.10 as the total tip. You then add this amount to the cost of dinner and wine, to produce the final sum on the credit card receipt, arriving at $85.25. What did you just do? You solved a problem. And how did you do it? By applying a finite series of arithmetic operations that converted what you knew ($74.15) to what you needed to know ($85.25). This step-by-step procedure works for any input. Solution guaranteed, every time.

Methodical routines such as the above are called *algorithms,* a word that derives from the surname of Muhammad ibn Musa al-Khwarizmi, a 9th-century Muslim mathematician and astronomer. Al-Khwarizmi had published a work on what is now known as algebra (derived from the title of his book), in which he set down the rules for solving linear and quadratic equations. In fact, textbooks in mathematics and the mathematical sciences are replete with such algorithmic methods for solving problems. A typical section of the text might start with a specific problem, demonstrate a solution, generalize that procedure so that it can apply to every problem of a similar type, and then end with some exercises or "problem sets" (the answers to the even-numbered problems being given in the back of the book). So if you have taken introductory calculus, you will experience no difficulty solving a problem like this: if $y = 2x^2 - 3x + 2$, $dy/dx = ?$. It's even easier than calculating the tip after dinner!

I am sure that for a portion of the decade that led up to his special theory of relativity, Einstein devoted himself to building up an inventory of algorithms in mathematics and physics. Judging from his 1905 journal article, he had to learn how to solve algebraic problems as well as problems involving Newtonian mechanics and Maxwell's equations for electromagnetic phenomena. But I am equally confident that such algorithms could not have been all that he learned. This is because algorithms have somewhat limited applicability. In the first place, algorithms tend to be highly domain specific. You use one algorithm to solve a problem in mechanics, another to solve a problem in electromagnetism. Besides that, algorithms are designed to solve problems that are well defined and for which the rules for solution have already been established. They are not especially well designed for solving problems that lead to original and exemplary solutions. To be specific, in no single one of his textbooks would Einstein have encountered an algorithm that would provide a direct solution to the problem he conjured up when he was 16 years old. He couldn't just plug in a number—I'm now traveling at 299,792,458 meters per second alongside a beam of light—and obtain an equation describing the form of the light wave.

This means that Einstein probably relied on another approach to problem solving, namely, the application of *heuristics.* A heuristic is a crude rule of thumb or all-purpose course of action that facilitates the discovery of a solution but without any assurance that a solution will in fact be found. Also unlike algorithms, heuristics tend to be much less domain specific, many applying to any and all possible problems. Among these domain-free heuristics are (a) hill climbing, where you always select the path that gets you closer to the goal; (b) means-ends analysis, where you break down the problem into more easily solved smaller problems; (c) working backward, where you assume that you have the solution and then weave your way back to the problem; (d) analogy, where you compare a phenomenon you understand well with a phenomenon you don't understand very well; and (e) trial and error, where you try out all possibilities to see which one works (either haphazardly or systematically).

One especially useful set of heuristics involves converting one problem to another problem. For instance, an abstract or general problem might be transformed into a concrete problem or special case. Or a mathematical problem might be converted into a problem that can easily be visualized. Indeed, one of Einstein's favorite problem-solving strategies was the *Gedanken* or "thought" experiment. Rather than make deductions by means of abstract mathematics, he would imagine a hypothetical situation and then work out the implications. It was by this means that he arrived at his special theory of relativity, as well as his general theory of relativity a decade later. Yet Einstein's *Gedanken* experiments didn't always arrive at the right answer, as he learned when he tried to use them to overthrow the Copenhagen interpretation of quantum mechanics. A *Gedanken* experiment is not an algorithm.

Observe that heuristic problem solving, unlike algorithmic problem solving, is more congruent with Kant's assertion that geniuses produce "that for which no definite rule can be given" (Kant, 1790/1952, p. 525). Algorithms are rules; heuristics are not. However, the application of heuristics often leads to the discovery of new algorithms that can be used to solve problems similar to the ones already solved. The discovered algorithms thus become exemplary and thereby subject to imitation by subsequent creators. When Einstein came up with the special and general theories of relativity, he in effect provided the scientific community with a new set of computational rules for solving problems in physics. In lieu of the algorithms of Newtonian mechanics, physicists would use the algorithms of relativity theory. While in some instances the two sets of algorithms would give the same answer (e.g., the path of a baseball as it travels from pitcher to catcher), in other instances the two sets of answers would diverge (e.g., the precession of the perihelion of Mercury). Whenever they differ, the relativistic calculations are preferred.

Algorithmic Versus Heuristic Computer Programs. To further our understanding of the difference between algorithms and heuristics, and to appreciate their relevance to an understanding of the nature of genius, let's take a glance at two kinds of computer programs that engage in problem solving of a rather high order:

1. *Expert systems* are computer programs that aspire to reproduce human expertise in a given domain of expert knowledge (Duda & Shortliffe, 1983). A classic example is MYCIN, a program designed to diagnose infectious diseases of the blood and even to recommend appropriate antibiotics (Buchanan & Shortliffe, 1984). Such systems typically consist of a large number of if–then statements. An example would be as follows: If the organism found in the blood has the following properties (e.g., stains gram positive, has coccus shape, forms chains) then it can be identified as such-and-such (e.g., *Streptococcus*). Interestingly, MYCIN performed better than most physicians but did not do as well as specialists in the diagnosis of bacterial infections. In any case, most expert systems operate according to algorithms rather than heuristics. Furthermore, these systems are deliberately imitative of human experts. Experts known as knowledge engineers tease out the expertise of experts in a given domain and then relay that information to the computer programmers. So the domain experts, not the engineers or programmers, establish the rules that the systems

blindly imitate. Because of this restriction, these systems do not make new discoveries in the domain. So expert systems cannot be cited as examples of computer-simulated genius.

2. *Discovery programs,* in contrast, purport to make actual discoveries (Langley, Simon, Bradshaw, & Zythow, 1987; Shrager & Langley, 1990). Moreover, they claim to do so by applying heuristics rather than algorithms. Even more strikingly, these programs can reproduce the discoveries made by scientific geniuses using the same data that those geniuses used to make the original discoveries. For example, the program called BACON—named to honor Francis Bacon's inductive method—rediscovered Kepler's third law of planetary motion after it was given the raw data on planet orbital periods and maximal planet–sun distances. BACON achieved this feat by applying a highly constrained trial-and-error heuristic to the given data. If Kepler is commonly considered a genius—he ranked 75th on Hart's (2000) list of the 100 most influential people of history and 90th on Cattell's (1903) list of the 1,000 most renowned people in Western history—then can we say that BACON, unlike MYCIN, is a genius?

Sorry to say, the answer may still be no. The objection is simply put: The discovery programs should really be called *rediscovery* programs. That's all they do: rediscover what has already been discovered, using the same data that led to the earlier discoveries, or similar data. The heuristics that are embedded in the programs have a definite post hoc appearance. The programs are written after the fact to reproduce discoveries already made, using heuristics that the discoverer seems to have used. Isn't that cheating? It took a tremendous amount of effort before poor Kepler was able to hit on the third law, yet the computer programmers cast a backward peek and manage in a jiffy to replicate what he did. It just doesn't seem fair. Fair or not, it also seems imitative, perhaps as imitative as MYCIN. The only difference is that BACON impersonates scientists making discoveries while MYCIN mimics physicians making diagnoses.

Strong Versus Weak Methods. Sometimes algorithms are referred to as *strong* problem-solving methods, heuristics as *weak* methods (cf. Klahr, 2000). It's not difficult to see why. Not only do heuristics fail to guarantee a solution, but for any given problem it is not always clear which of several available heuristics will work best. That's why I have argued that all heuristic methods are best subsumed under a single meta-heuristic that I call the trial-and-error application of heuristics (Simonton, 2004c). When confronted with a highly original problem whose solution is most likely to generate an exemplary product, the problem solver must often go back and forth between various heuristics until the issue is resolved. This flexibility is necessary, in part, because no heuristic is infallible. Each has its assets and deficits. For example, the hill-climbing heuristic works just fine until you run into a "local maximum" that is remote from the "global maximum"—something that you might not realize for weeks if not years. Similarly, reducing an abstract general problem to a concrete special case is vulnerable to the choice of that case. It may or not be representative of the larger problem, so that the specific solution leads you in the wrong direction. And so forth. Hence emerges the need for a trial-and-error meta-heuristic.

To illustrate the complexities attending real-life problem solving, the great scientist Hermann von Helmholtz (1898) once confessed that

> I only succeeded in solving such problems after many devious ways, by the gradually increasing generalisation of favourable examples, and by a series of fortunate guesses. I had to compare myself with an Alpine climber, who, not knowing the way, ascends slowly and with toil, and is often compelled to retrace his steps because his progress is stopped; sometimes by reasoning, and sometimes by accident, he hits upon traces of a fresh path, which again leads him a little further; and finally, when he has reached the goal, he finds to his annoyance a royal road on which he might have ridden up if he had been clever enough to find the right starting-point at the outset. In my memoirs I have, of course, not given the reader an account of my

wanderings, but I have described the beaten path on which he can now reach the summit without trouble. (p. 282)

The last sentence makes an important point: We seldom appreciate the sheer chaos of heuristic problem solving, because the final scientific publication only gives the direct path finally discovered, not the circuitous route by which the scientist got to the destination. It is the final path that's then written into the discovery programs discussed formerly. This allows the programs to make rediscoveries but probably prevents them from making new discoveries. The shortcut to the top of Mount Kilimanjaro will not get you to the top of Mount Everest, and vice versa.

Integration: Darwinian Genius

In 1859, Charles Darwin provided a scientific explanation for the evolution of life. Although the explanation is most often referred to as the theory of natural selection, it can be more accurately referred to as a theory of variation–selection. That's because selection depends on variation. No variation, no selection. Even more to the point, the variation side of Darwin's theory is in many respects more provocative than the selection side. On the one hand, it may seem obvious, even tautological, to affirm, in line with selection theory, that those trait variants that bestow more fitness are most likely to survive in the gene pool. Little debate here. On the other hand, Darwin's core assertion about the variation process was contentious in his own time, and it continues to be so today: The variations display no volition or intelligence. Yes, according to Darwin, the variations are generated without secure foresight into which variants are most likely to survive and reproduce. The variations are not preadapted for success, and many will be out-and-out maladaptive. Darwin viewed variation as ignorant of future outcomes and therefore inherently wasteful. Only a small proportion of all competing variants will prevail.

In a sense, Darwin's theory can be taken as an implicit theory of creativity—the creativity associated with the *Origin of Species,* as the title has it. It is a theory of how new forms emerge from old. Indeed, the theory even features a direct relation with the definition of creativity chosen in chapter 2. To be creative, a product must be original and useful. New species emerge when original variants prove more useful than old variants. Given this analytical linkage, it should not surprise us that Darwin's theory soon influenced thinking about human creativity. The creative process in *Homo sapiens* could be perceived as working via processes analogous to those credited with the evolution of that very species from shared ancestors among the anthropoid apes. The first genius to make this connection was the psychologist and philosopher William James (1880). Just a little more than 20 years after the first edition of *Origin* appeared, James published an article titled "Great Men, Great Thoughts, and the Environment," in which he outlined a Darwinian theory of creativity. James maintained that "social evolution is a resultant of the interaction of two wholly distinct factors: the individual, deriving his peculiar gifts from the play of psychological and infra-social forces, but bearing all the power of initiative and origination in his hands; and, second, the social environment, with its power of adopting or rejecting both him and his gifts" (p. 448). James also depicted the mental processes by which the individual generates originality:

> Instead of thoughts of concrete things patiently following one another in a beaten track of habitual suggestion, we have the most abrupt cross-cuts and transitions from one idea to another, the most rarefied abstractions and discriminations, the most unheard of combination of elements, the subtlest associations of analogy; in a word, we seem suddenly introduced into a seething cauldron of ideas, where everything is fizzling and bobbling about in a state of bewildering activity, where partnerships can be joined or loosened in an instant, treadmill routine is unknown, and the unexpected seems only law. (p. 456)

In other words, the process is haphazard rather than deliberate, chaotic rather than ordered, combinatorial rather than logical.

The process is certainly not algorithmic. It doesn't even seem that heuristic, at least not in any systematic fashion. The process appears much too blind, which brings me to...

The BVSR Model. About a century after Darwin's *Origin,* and exactly 80 years after James's essay, the psychologist Donald Campbell (1960) argued that creativity and discovery take place by means of an expressly Darwinian process. He named this process *blind variation and selective retention,* which is sometimes shortened to the acronym BVSR (Cziko, 1998). The selective-retention part of the process is governed by a set of criteria that must be satisfied for an ideational variation to be retained for further use. For instance, of all the potential solutions to a given problem, that one that meets the specified conditions will be preserved. As in the case of Darwin's original theory, this second step is the least interesting and least controversial aspect of the BVSR model. More provocative is the first step of the process—that which generates blind variations. Campbell insisted that true creativity and discovery require a certain amount of groping in the dark. The originator has to engage in some procedure in which the outcome of any given trial is uncertain. Any given ideational variant may or may not fulfill the twofold requirement of originality and usefulness that is the hallmark of creativity and discovery.

If you read over again the remarks of Helmholtz (1898) quoted above, you'll see that they describe a blind-variation process. Every occasion on which Helmholtz was "compelled to retrace his steps" indicates a prior moment when he chose the wrong path, not knowing that his progress would be stopped. The "fortunate guesses" imply the existence of unfortunate guesses. And Helmholtz acknowledges that "accident," which is inherently blind, has about a big a role as "reasoning," which presumably shows more foresight. In brief, Helmholtz's introspective report provides conclusive evidence that his own problem solving was guided by a BVSR process.

Campbell (1960) offered some suggestions about what kinds of mental processes would generate the blind variations.

Although such ideational variants can come from many sources—BVSR is *not* a single-process model—among the most interesting are those involving combinatorial thought. In support of his suggestions, Campbell quoted the French mathematician Henri Poincaré (1921), who observed how "Ideas rose in crowds; I felt them collide until pairs interlocked, so to speak, making a stable combination" (p. 387). Campbell also mentioned the work of another French mathematician, Jacques Hadamard (1945), who argued for a combinatorial model of mathematical invention based on a survey of eminent achievers in mathematical sciences. Remember Einstein's report that "combinatory play seems to be the essential feature in productive thought" (qtd. in Hadamard, 1945, p. 142). Remember, too, how James (1880) said that creativity demanded the "most unheard of combination of elements" (p. 456). These combinatorial processes roughly parallel the genetic recombinations that introduce most of the variants on which natural selection operates in biological evolution.

Campbell (1960) allotted some space to discussing how his model might contribute to our understanding of genius. To give just one example, he observed that "thinkers can differ in the number and range of variations in thought trials produced. The more numerous and the more varied such trials, the greater the chance of success" (p. 391). Despite these observations, he never elaborated his BVSR model into a full-fledged Darwinian theory of creative genius. That elaboration did not take place until many years later. The model would eventually become enlarged into an ambitious theory.

The BVSR Theory. Caveat emptor: Every time you buy a textbook you do so at your own risk! The danger is especially high when the text's author is an active researcher in the field. You know that sooner or later the author is going to assign a page or two (or three) to describing his or her own pet research findings. Well, that moment has now arrived, and I find it impossible to pass up the opportunity. For the past 20 years, I have been expanding Campbell's (1960) bare-bones model into a precise and comprehensive theory. It all began with my 1988 book, *Scientific Genius*, and continued through my 1999 *Origins of Genius*, which has the telltale subtitle *Darwinian Perspectives on Creativity*. Despite many criticisms and complaints—do you really expect me to give references to my critics?—to the present day I have persisted in testing the predictions and evaluating the explanations of the theory (e.g., Simonton, 2005b, 2007b). As a card-carrying, royalty-earning author, I'm inclined to say simply, "Buy my book!" Yet because you may have purchased the book you already hold in your hand, that command may be too much to obey. So let me give you a thumbnail sketch of the theory, for free.

I said that the BVSR theory is far more precise and comprehensive than Campbell's (1960) old BVSR model. The precision comes from the mathematical models that have been derived from the theory (Simonton, 2004c). One of the models concentrates on the prediction of creative productivity (Simonton, 1997a). For example, the model predicts how the output rate changes across the life span and even predicts the ages at which creators make their first major contribution, their best contribution, and their last major contribution. So far these predictions have been confirmed for samples of 2,026 distinguished scientists (Simonton, 1991a), 69 famous American psychologists (Simonton, 1992b), 120 great and not-so-great classical composers (Simonton, 1991b), and even 78 composers who created award-winning scores and songs for motion pictures (Simonton, 2007a). Another mathematical model makes precise predictions with respect to a phenomenon that we'll discuss at length in chapter 6. This is the phenomenon in which two or more scientists or inventors make the same contribution independently of each other (Simonton, 2004c). Sadly, the only route to appreciating the precision is to do the math, something not particularly desirable in an introductory book. So I'll leave this aspect of the BVSR theory to your imagination.

Consequently, rather than detail the precise nature of the theory, I'll say more about the comprehensive nature of the theory. Instead of examining the theory's precision, we can discuss the range of phenomena that it can successfully explain. Explanation is not as powerful as prediction, but in the current state of psychological science, the former is most often the best we can do. Anyhow, among other things, this Darwinian theory has been used to explicate (a) the distinctive mental processes that contribute to genius-grade, Big-C Creativity; (b) the personality characteristics associated with creative genius, including the incidence of the mad genius; (c) the family backgrounds and educational experiences that contribute to the creative development of future geniuses; and (d) the political, economic, and cultural environments that are most conducive to the emergence of genius in the major domains of creative achievement (Simonton, 1999a, 1999b). Because it is absolutely impossible to treat all of these explanatory features, I will just focus on (a), leaving (b)–(d) for curious readers with spare change in their pockets.

A key concept in BVSR theory is that the blindness of the variations is a quantitative rather than a qualitative attribute. It's not that variations are either blind or sighted, but rather that variations vary in the relative prominence of blindness and sightedness. In different terms, the thought processes generating ideational variations can be placed along a continuum, with totally blind processes at one extreme and totally sighted processes at the other extreme, but with most processes falling somewhere between the endpoints. To appreciate the sheer range of this bipolar dimension, let's go back to the distinction between algorithms and heuristics. Essentially, algorithmic processes are the epitome of sightedness. The vast majority of algorithms are so mundane as to be almost trivial—like the routine used to calculate a restaurant tip in your head.

Even so, algorithms do not always rest at the farthest spot on the bipolar dimension. Some algorithms let in a dose of blindness—most often in the form of "trial values" or "initial parameter estimates." Take long division. (Put your calculators away, please.) Now calculate the IQ of someone whose mental age is 15.5 but whose chronological age is 7.8. Did you do it right off the bat, or did you try one or two trial values while you cranked out the solution? Obviously, if you happened to be Shakuntala Devi, the calculating prodigy we mentioned in chapter 2, you would have just laughed hysterically. Those of you whose arithmetic is much more rusty would have engaged in one or two episodes of trial and error before you finally arrived at an answer. That is, you would have picked some digit to multiply by the divisor and discovered that it was either too small or too large, requiring that you try another digit, one integer higher or lower. After a modicum of such blindness, you would eventually have settled on IQ = ___ (you can get out your calculator now).

The blindness of algorithms can become even more prominent than this. Sometimes the problems become sufficiently difficult that some ambiguity emerges about which algorithm to use. Those of you who have studied integral calculus know what I mean. There are several methods for integrating a given function—by substitution, by parts, by successive reduction, and so on—but it's not always obvious which method will work for a particular function. So in lieu of a trial value, you have a trial algorithm. You try integration by one method, you get mathematical gobbledygook that you couldn't reduce to simpler terms even if your life depended on it, and so you try another method. All in vain, you later discover, when your calculus teacher finally tells you that the function cannot be integrated by any of the methods you have learned! Your instructor gave you a trick question!

Some algorithms may let in some trickles of blindness, but heuristics often open the floodgates. The trial-and-error heuristic is explicitly a blind-variation process. First try this, then that, and then the other thing until you finally succeed. By the same token, the trial-and-error meta-heuristic that I introduced earlier is also a blind-variation process. To be sure, some trial-and-error procedures are more sighted than others. Perhaps you have enough expertise to rule out a large proportion of the possible trials. Nevertheless, it would not even count as trial and error if no blindness whatsoever intruded on the process.

For the other heuristics, the blindness is more subtle but still ever present. The analogy heuristic? What analogy? Any given phenomenon can be compared with an indefinite number of other phenomena. Which one are you going to try first? If you hadn't been exposed to the idea in high school science class, would you have guessed that the structure of an atom is analogous to the solar system? Gutenberg's invention of the printing press was based on an analogy to the wine press. Is it obvious to you that the equipment used to make an alcoholic beverage would help someone who wanted to mass-produce Bibles for pilgrims?

Or look at the hill-climbing heuristic—the rule of thumb that says you always move in the direction that seems to get you closer to the goal (like always going up to reach a peak). We have already mentioned the problem of local maxima. How do you decide whether to risk coming down the slope in the hope of encountering the global maximum? You may already be at the global maximum! And how will you ever know if you don't descend the slope? Or what happens if your starting place is in the midst of a totally flat plain? In which direction do you go to initiate your "hill" climbing? Have you ever been confronted with a problem where you did not even know where to begin? You had no idea what was up, what down, what north, and what south?

Go ahead, I dare you. Closely scrutinize other heuristic problem-solving techniques—whether means–ends analysis or working backwards. Can you prove that these heuristics contain not one iota of blindness? Good luck!

It goes without saying that the pole representing the outermost extent of blindness is pure chance or randomness. This is the realm of 100% serendipitous discoveries, of unadulterated aleatory music and art. The splash and dribble paintings of Jackson Pollock come very close to this terminal point. And much computer creativity has a random-number generator at its source (Boden, 1991).

But why am I telling you all this? It's because different domains of creativity vary immensely as to where they stand on this blindness–sightedness dimension. Generally, artistic genius is much more blind and scientific genius is much more sighted.

Within the arts and sciences, additional distinctions intrude. Highly formal, academic, or classical artists tend to be more sighted than highly expressionistic, avant-garde, or romantic artists (cf. Ludwig, 1998). Scientists in the hard sciences like physics and chemistry tend to be less blind than scientists in the soft(er) sciences like psychology and sociology (Simonton, 2004d). And these contrasts in terms of where a domain falls on the blindness–sightedness dimension then influence the personality characteristics associated with creative genius in that domain, including the incidence of the mad genius; the family backgrounds and educational experiences that contribute to the creative development of future geniuses in that domain; and the political, economic, and cultural environments that are most conducive to the emergence of genius in that domain (Simonton, 1999b).

Don't take my word for it. Read my books and articles!

FINAL OBSERVATION

Some of you may have spotted a gradual shift in the center of attention. We began talking about general intelligence. In that conversation, we managed to call upon various forms of genius, not just creative genius. Somehow we ended up talking exclusively about creative genius. Maybe this shift in emphasis can be justified by the fact that Big-C Creativity is so often viewed as the supreme manifestation of this human singularity. And maybe not. Accordingly, I'd like just to end this chapter with a final remark about genius in general.

If we accept Kant's old conception of a genius as one having the capacity of generating products that are both original and exemplary, then I would reason that the BVSR process extends beyond the confines of creativity. The commander figuring out the best disposition of his troops on the night before a battle to be fought on unfamiliar turf, the head of state endeavoring to find a way around an unprecedented political or diplomatic impasse, the

CEO attempting to think up an innovative product or marketing strategy that will save the company from declaring bankruptcy—these are all situations that favor someone with the aptitude for engaging in some degree of blind variation. It is necessary to explore all possibilities, to work out the implications of all contingencies, and to offer serious consideration to near impossibilities. In this light, the BVSR model may define the generic thought process that unifies all valid categories of genius.

Or is this final observation a mere blind variation that awaits selective retention?

Is Genius Born or Made?

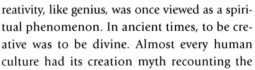reativity, like genius, was once viewed as a spiritual phenomenon. In ancient times, to be creative was to be divine. Almost every human culture had its creation myth recounting the miraculous accomplishments of some spiritual power. Such creative agents include the Creator of the Judeo–Christian–Islamic tradition, Odin of Norse mythology, Ormazd of Zoroastrianism, and Brahma of the Hindu trinity. Members of our down-to-earth species exhibited craft rather than creativity. Rather than artists, we were artisans—workers who had the skill to make certain artifacts. To be sure, over time, individual human beings were also seen as manifesting creativity. Yet even then, the ultimate source of that human creativity often remained spiritual.

This halfway point appears in the classical Greek myth of the Muses. As the story goes, Zeus, the supreme deity in the pantheon, fathered nine daughters with Mnemosyne (the personification of memory). Each of these daughters was put in charge of a separate domain of human creativity—heroic or epic poetry, lyric and love poetry, sacred poetry, tragedy, comedy, music, dance, astronomy, and history. Each immortal Muse provided a guiding spirit or source of inspiration for the mortal creator. In a sense, each Muse was the genius for all creators contributing to the same domain.

This myth has inspired some everyday expressions. For instance, I might say that I have lost my muse when I'm stymied by writer's block—and my muse has left me more than once when writing this book. In the 1999 film *The Muse*, Sharon Stone—who is much better remembered for her more profane role in the 1992 *Basic Instinct*—plays a "goddess" who aids a screenwriter who has lost his creative edge. The film illustrates the fact that human creativity was once conceived as the gift of the gods or spirits. Even during the Italian Renaissance, this spiritual ascription endured. For example, Giorgio Vasari (ca. 1550/1968) began his biography of the "divine" Michelangelo by declaring that "the great Ruler of Heaven" specifically placed the artist on the earth to serve as an exemplar of artistic genius (p. 347).

As Western civilization became more secular in emphasis, and especially during the Enlightenment, the concept of creative genius progressively lost its sacred accoutrements. Yet it was still often seen as innate. "Genius must be born, and never can be taught," affirmed the English dramatist John Dryden (1693/1885, p. 60). In chapter 2, we saw that this point of view was enshrined in Kant's very definition of genius. Genius was a talent, a natural endowment. It could not be learned. It was purely innate. "Now since learning is nothing but imitation, the greatest ability, or aptness as a pupil (capacity), is still, as such, not equivalent to genius," said Kant (1790/1952, p. 526).

Nonetheless, about the time that Kant was expressing this extreme position with regard to nature, an almost exact contemporary was presenting an opposing take on the origins of creative genius. This contemporary was Joshua Reynolds, the eminent British painter who helped found the Royal Academy of Arts in 1768, becoming its first president, and receiving a knighthood the following year. Sir Joshua (1769–1790/1966) explicitly warned his students at the Royal Academy:

> You must have no dependence on your own genius. If you have great talents, industry will improve them; if you have but moderate abilities, industry will supply their deficiency. Nothing is denied to well directed labour; nothing is to be obtained without it. Not to enter into metaphysical discussions on the nature or essence of genius, I will venture to assert, that assiduity unabated by difficulty, and a disposition eagerly directed to the object of its pursuit, will produce effects similar to those which some call the result of *natural powers*. (p. 37)

Reynolds seems to be affirming, contra Kant, that imitation *can* produce genius, whatever a person's natural abilities might be! You just have to work hard enough to nurture whatever minimal talents you possess. Imitate the exemplars and your own work can become exemplary.

Kant did not refer to Reynolds in his *Critique of Judgement*, but we can guess how he might have responded. Kant could counter that Reynolds is precisely the person he has in mind, the person who substitutes imitation for genius. This argument might seem ad hominem, but it's really not. Kant believed that true geniuses invent their own rules. This originality is definitely mandatory in the fine arts, including Reynolds's own domain of painting. Moreover, the rules originate not from training but from innate talent. From Kant's perspective, for Reynolds to argue the contrary could simply betray the sorry state of the British visual arts at the end of the 18th century. After all, Reynolds was widely considered the greatest English painter of his day, with Thomas Gainsborough as his only rival. Were they mere imitators rather than bona fide geniuses?

But, alas! These are all opinions and speculations! What do the data say? Is genius just a matter of nature, as Kant claimed? Or can it be nurtured, as Reynolds believed? Well, let's see. We'll look first at the nature position, then at the nurture position, and finally at the modern position. How does contemporary research weigh in on this debate?

nATURE POSITION: YOU'RE BORN!

Do you have to be a genius to study genius? Perhaps not. Those of us who do research in the field may be able to name colleagues who are clearly not geniuses (although one or two might count as inverse geniuses). Yet it's a historical fact that the first scientist to devote a whole book to the study of genius was himself a genius. His name was Francis Galton. In chapter 1, you were told that Terman (1917) estimated Galton's IQ to be close to 200, a genius-grade score by any psychometric definition. You also learned back then that he wrote the book *Hereditary Genius* in 1869. Finally, in chapter 2, you found out about how Galton defined genius in that book. Galton argued that geniuses are those who possess an exceptional amount of natural ability. That is, geniuses would score in the upper tail of the normal distribution in intelligence, enthusiasm, and perseverance. For most of you reading my book, those bits of information may be all that you know. Even so, can you draw a key inference from the title of Galton's 1869 masterpiece?

You guessed right! Galton put forward the position that genius was inherited. Or more accurately, he maintained that natural ability was hereditary. And if parents had genius-level natural ability, their offspring were more likely to be geniuses than were the offspring of parents with average natural ability. So if natural ability is inheritable, geniuses should come from identifiable lineages. To make his case, Galton introduced the *family pedigree* method. In this technique, you examine whether specified traits are passed down through family lines. Just as some lineages will have lots of members who are unusually tall, so other lineages will have many members who are exceptionally bright. Much of

Hereditary Genius is devoted to documenting the prominence of distinguished family lines.

To be specific, Galton examined several major forms of outstanding achievement. Indeed, as mentioned in chapter 2, he had a fairly broad conception of genius. Besides politicians, commanders, writers, scientists, poets, composers, painters, religious leaders, and lawyers, he added such oddities as oarsmen and wrestlers. Anyhow, in most of these domains of achievement, he compiled extensive lists of eminent personalities who had some degree of familial connection. With respect to scientists, for example, he pointed out that Charles Darwin, the originator of the theory of evolution by natural selection, was the grandson of Erasmus Darwin, an early evolutionist. Furthermore, Galton noted that Charles Darwin had several notable sons, and even mentioned that other unnamed family members attained some success. Was Galton alluding to himself? He was also descended from Erasmus Darwin and thus was Charles Darwin's cousin! Perhaps only Victorian modesty prevented Galton from engaging in more unambiguous self-aggrandizement!

Galton did more than amass long honor rolls of illustrious family members. He also did the math. Always excessively fond of counting and statistics, he determined that frequencies in the occurrence of genius varied according to degree of kinship. In the main, the closer the family relationship, the higher the number of cases of genius co-occurence. Parents, children, and siblings showed the highest frequency, grandparents, uncles/aunts, nephews/nieces, and grandchildren the next highest frequency. The lowest frequency occurred among great-grandparents, great-uncles/aunts, great-nephews/nieces, great-grandchildren, and first cousins. This pattern of statistical expectations fits Charles Darwin pretty well. He had four eminent sons (George, an astronomer, Francis, a botanist, Leonard, a eugenicist, and Horace, a civil engineer), a scientifically eminent grandfather (Erasmus, cited earlier) and grandson (Sir Charles Galton Darwin, a physicist), and one well-known cousin-scientist (Francis Galton, who should also be well known to you by now). Three of his sons were elected fellows of the Royal Society of London (FRS), an honor that can be compared with getting a Nobel Prize today. The same three also became knights commander of the Order of the British Empire (KBE), which allowed them to put "Sir" before their given name. And Charles's grandson and cousin also became fellows of the Royal Academy and knights. Although Charles's son Leonard did not receive the same amount of acclaim, he personally mentored the famed evolutionary biologist and statistician Ronald Fisher (creator of the F test and the null hypothesis). All in all, it is hard to imagine a family pedigree more renowned than Darwin's.

Other researchers have shown that it's still easy to identify family clusters of scientific genius (e.g., Bramwell, 1948; Brimhall, 1922, 1923a, 1923b). In fact, such familial connections are evident in the Nobel Prizes granted in the science categories. Since the introduction of these prestigious awards in 1901, six father-son pairs have been so honored. The most recent example is that of the Kornbergs: Roger D. Kornberg received the 2006 Nobel Prize in Physiology or Medicine, an honor previously bestowed upon his father, Arthur Kornberg, in 1959. Besides fathers and sons, this award has also been conferred on one mother–daughter pair, one brother–brother pair, and one uncle–nephew pair (Nobel Laureates Facts, n.d.). What is more, only in one out of the nine cases was the prize earned for the same accomplishment (viz., the father and son Braggs in 1915). To appreciate the import of these stats we have to remember that the Nobel has an extremely low base rate. The overwhelming majority of even the most famed scientists never get the chance to go to Stockholm to accept the Nobel gold. So the chances of two members of the same family doing so would seem infinitesimal.

Needless to say, the clustering of geniuses in families is not confined to scientific genius. Yet rather than give you my own examples, let me ask you to come up with your own examples as your first take-home exam. To make the exam easy, you have permission to confine your examples to luminaries in popular culture. Before you sit down to take the exam, it may be best to do a practice test. I'll name some names and then you come up with other close family members who also attained fame and fortune (albeit not every time in the same domain or to the same degree). Ready? Okay, here it goes: Mario Andretti, Drew Barrymore, Warren Beatty, Barry Bonds, Jeff Bridges, Jamie Lee Curtis, Michael Douglas, Carrie Fisher, Jane Fonda, Angelica Houston, Brett Hull, Michael Jackson, Peyton Manning, Wynton Marsalis, Groucho Marx, Lee Petty, Vanessa Redgrave, Julia Roberts, Martin Sheen, Kiefer Sutherland, Shawn Wayans, and CeCe Winans. Got the idea? Now it's your turn. It's due this coming Monday, so you have the whole weekend. And you've got permission to use *Wikipedia* if you want. Talk about easy tests!

NURTURE POSITION: YOU'RE MADE!

Did all of you turn in your take-home exam? Good! Wasn't it fun? Isn't it like playing Six Degrees of Kevin Bacon but using a different kind of relationship–blood connection instead of film connection? And how well did you do? Did you come up with many more family ties than I suggested in the practice exam? And how were the relationships distributed? Did the frequencies decline as the family relationships got more remote? Weren't parent–child or sibling linkages the most common? But now I want to ask you a totally different question: Does the family pedigree method prove, in actual fact, that genius is born and not made? Did Michael Jackson become the "King of Pop" because he inherited good genes? Or was his talent nurtured in his early years with the Jackson Five? Might these data also support the nurture rather than nature position?

Galton's own contemporaries were not all convinced by the lengthy inventories of familial connections in *Hereditary Genius* (1869). Just a few years later, the French-Swiss botanist Alphonse de Candolle (1873) published an extensive investigation proving

85

quite the opposite. Focusing on scientific genius, Candolle showed that such eminence is most likely to appear in a distinctive set of political, social, cultural, educational, and religious conditions. The environment in which a person grows up trumps the genes that he or she may have inherited. What was particularly ironic about Candolle's counterargument is that he, like Galton, came from a family of notable scientists. In *Hereditary Genius*, Galton actually named Alphonse and his father Augustin, who was one of the greatest botanists of all! Alphonse even had a son of his own, Anne, who attained some recognition as a botanist as well. If anyone would be inclined to endorse Galton's flattering position, it would seem likely to be Alphonse de Candolle. But he didn't endorse Galton's position, and he collected data to contradict Galton. If genius tends to run in family lines, it is because family members—above all, first-degree relatives—are apt to grow up in a similar time and place.

Galton took Candolle's argument to heart, and responded at once. His response depended on developing a totally new scientific method, the questionnaire. He wrote up a series of questions and then circulated his questionnaire among members of the Royal Society, including his cousin Charles Darwin. The questions included items about family background and educational experiences. Galton published his findings in *English Men of Science: Their Nature and Nurture* (1874). The subtitle is significant for two reasons. First, Galton established the terms *nature* and *nurture* in the scientific study of genius. These two words were juxtaposed in Shakespeare's *The Tempest*, when Prospero laments: "A devil, a born devil, on whose nature / Nurture can never stick" (act 4, scene 1, lines 188–189). Still, it was in Galton's subtitle that these two words became part of psychology's terminology (cf. Teigen, 1984). Second, the subtitle shows that Galton had backed off from advocating an uncompromisingly genetic determinism. Nurture could play a role alongside nature. For instance, Galton was the first to inquire about the impact of birth order, an unmistakably environmental variable. Your genes do not depend on your ordinal position in your family.

Unfortunately, rather than adopt Galton's fairly concilia-tory concession, recent researchers have often taken a one-sided stance on behalf of nurture. Genius is made, not born. The talent or natural endowment that Kant believed was the defining fea-ture of genius was declared to be pure myth or crazy superstition (Howe, 1999). Instead, it was argued that genius is the outcome of various environmental influences. Probably the most critical of these influences is something called *deliberate practice* (Erics-son, Krampe, & Tesch-Römer, 1993; Starkes, Deakin, Allard, Hodges, & Hayes, 1996). You cannot become a genius without intense effort. You must study, learn, do exercises and drills until you get it all down pat. Even worse, you have to spend a very long time engaged in this acquisition of domain-specific exper-tise. You can't do it in a single year, or even in 5 years. On the contrary, you need a full decade of devotion to expertise acqui-sition before you have what it takes to make your mark in the world. In chapters 2 and 3, we referred to this necessity as the 10-year rule. No decade of dedicated training, no genius!

This nurture viewpoint may remind you of what Sir Joshua said about genius. Without "directed labour" (a.k.a. deliberate practice), you can go nowhere, no matter how talented you are. And because practice makes perfect, abundant practice can com-pensate for any dearth of natural endowment. In a book review, I once referred to this over-the-top position as the "drudge theory" (Simonton, 2001, p. 176). Geniuses are just drudges. They grimly engage in tedious, dreary, deliberate practice, weekday and week-end, day and night, until they've put in their time. Only after they conclude their 10-year sentence in solitary confinement can they finally march out the prison door with scarlet letters emblazoned across their chest: "I am now a certified genius!"

Okay, okay. You can tell that I have some antipathy toward this fanatical position. But my views are not just a matter of per-sonal opinion. There are data suggesting that the position runs roughshod over the complexities of nurture and the power of na-ture (Simonton, 2000a). I mentioned in chapter 2 the problems that universal geniuses must create for this dogma. If the 10-year rule is valid, how can anyone ever achieve excellence in more than one domain? Here are two added problems.

To begin with, the 10-year rule is an average, not a fixed threshold value. As you learned in statistics courses, the mean also has a standard deviation. Some geniuses will take less than a decade and some more. This variation is substantial, like 10 ± 5 years or more (e.g., Simonton, 1991b). And this variation has consequences, paradoxical consequences: Those who take less than the average time in expertise acquisition are more likely to exhibit more genius! In a study of 120 classical composers, brief apprenticeship periods were associated with composers who became highly eminent, were highly prolific, and had a longer productive career (Simonton, 1991b). Those who took longer than 10 years tended to be less eminent, to be less productive, and to have abbreviated careers.

The second problem with the drudge theory seems no less paradoxical. One would expect that the relationship between the amount of expertise and the level of genius would be best described by a positive monotonic function. This means that it would invariably increase. To be sure, after a while the curve might level off as the developing genius finally mastered all the necessary domain-specific expertise (Ericsson, 1996). This is the law of diminishing returns on your investment. Once you get it perfect, additional practice cannot make it more perfect, but it will not become less perfect. Yet this doesn't happen. Evidence from multiple sources reveals that in some domains, excessive expertise can be counterproductive, inducing a downturn in performance (Simonton, 2000a). This might be called an overtraining effect. Ironically, one of the best methods to ameliorate this adverse effect is to engage in cross-training, that is, to expand expertise in another area (Simonton, 2000a). Thus, composers are more likely to maintain a high level of creativity if they constantly change genres rather than composing consistently in the same genre over and over again. This is like telling Tiger Woods that he will improve his golf game if he stops from time to time to play croquet or perchance cricket!

The advocates of expertise acquisition are so keen to disprove Galton's genetic determinism that they throw the baby out with the bathwater!

MODERN POSITION: YOU'RE BORN AND MADE!

I once conducted a historiometric study of what it takes to make it big in psychology (Simonton, 2000c). The sample consisted of 54 psychologists who had attained some degree of eminence in the field. Some were of the highest eminence—like Francis Galton, Sigmund Freud, Ivan Pavlov, Jean Piaget, and B. F. Skinner. Others were more obscure. How many of you have heard of G. E. Miller, J. R. Angell, or...or...what's-his-name? Why can't I recall that psychologist's name for the life of me? Is it because he or she failed to leave a lasting impression on the field? Were such people also-rans with minimal long-term impact? If so, what's the basis for the impact? I hypothesized that durable influence depends on the positions that each psychologist in my sample took on six controversial issues that divide the discipline. Should psychology's methods and theories be objective or subjective, quantitative or qualitative, elementaristic or holistic, personal or impersonal, static or dynamic, and exogenist or endogenist? The last pairing is the most interesting to us here because it encompasses the current debate. Nurture is exogenist (involves external causes, such as deliberate practice) whereas nature is endogenist (involves internal causes, such as genetic endowment).

And here's the shocker: The long-term impact of these 54 psychologists, as gauged by the citations they receive from modern psychologists, is a curvilinear U-shaped function of the position they took on these divisive questions. In other words, those who are most frequently discussed today are those who advocated immoderate positions on the issues. By comparison, psychologists who argued for compromises ended up compromising their own standing with posterity. Psychologists show more interest in those who advocate immoderate positions, even when moderate stances are more likely to be correct (cf. Simonton, 1976b). Galton became a big name because he put so much stress on genetic endowment, even becoming a proponent of eugenics. Behaviorists like B. F. Skinner or John B. Watson, in contrast, found their ticket to fame by emphasizing an equally absurd environmentalism. Think about it: Are the most famous individuals in psychology best known for being right or for being wrong? Do the citations they receive in the research literature reflect agreement or disagreement with their views? When was the last time you ever heard a psychologist speak of Freud or Piaget in a totally approving manner?

All this is fine and dandy. The above study may explain why so many researchers go out on a limb regarding the nature–nurture issue. Yet I'll still risk my own long-term impact on the field by assuming a more reasonable standpoint in the sections that follow. I first discuss the effect of environmental factors and then turn to the effect of genetics.

Environmental Effects

Although Candolle (1873) was the first scientist to investigate the impact of environmental variables on the emergence of genius, his variables did not operate at the individual level. Instead, they all functioned at the sociocultural level—in the political, economic, social, cultural, and religious context. Consequently, while Candolle's findings can explain why one nation has more great scientists than another at a given time, they cannot explain why some scientists in a given nation are greater than their contemporaries from the same nation. At the time of Isaac Newton, England was chock full of scientific notables, but not all became as famous as he. How many of you have heard of the chemist and physiologist John Marrow, who was born only a year after Newton? Why did Newton become one of the greatest scientists of all time, while Marrow did not? Presumably Newton displayed more genius, creating more products that were more original and exemplary. Yet where did that genius come from? To answer this question, we have to examine the environmental circumstances that differ across individuals born at the same time and in the same place.

This brings us back to Galton's 1874 survey results. His questionnaire was distributed among the most eminent scientists of his time. Almost all were born and raised in Great Britain. Hence, all emerged under the same general sociocultural conditions. As a result, Galton's questions concentrated on the developmental experiences in which his survey respondents could be expected to vary. Later researchers soon followed suit, although they often adopted different methods. Thus, Ellis relied on biographical information in his 1904 *Study of British Genius.* Moreover, while some investigators, like Galton and Ellis, studied historiometric genius, others turned their attention to the environmental experiences of psychometric genius. The first to do so was Terman (1925), in the first volume of his *Genetic Studies of Genius.* In the years since this pioneering research, a huge literature has accumulated on the environmental factors that affect the growth of genius (Simonton, 1987a, 1999b).

These factors can be grouped into two categories: (a) general effects that apply to practically every domain of achievement; and (b) specific effects that are tailored to particular domains.

Domain-General Environment. Charity begins at home, and so does genius. At least this holds for almost all domains of outstanding creativity, most domains of exceptional leadership, and even a large proportion of the domains featuring prodigious performance. Specifically, geniuses are more likely to come from homes that are intellectually and culturally stimulating (Bloom, 1985; Cox, 1926; Roe, 1953; Schaefer & Anastasi, 1968; Terman, 1925; Walberg et al., 1980). The stimulation may come from an abundance of books and magazines, family trips to museums of art and science, and perhaps even travel to foreign nations. One or both parents will often be professionals—doctors, lawyers, professors, teachers, engineers, or perhaps ministers, rabbis, or priests—who have attained higher levels of formal education than the average (Albert, 1994; Ellis, 1904; Galton, 1874; Raskin, 1936; Roe, 1953; Terman, 1925). Not only are the parents somewhat older (and hopefully wiser) than the average before they start their families (Bowerman, 1947; Ellis, 1904; Galton, 1874; Raskin, 1936), but they also usually put considerable emphasis on the value of learning, not just for occupational success but also for its own sake (e.g., Bloom, 1985; Roe, 1953). The parents also tend to take an enhanced interest in their children's special talents (Bloom, 1985; Feldman & Goldsmith, 1986; McCurdy, 1960; Walberg et al., 1980). Interestingly, although geniuses are less likely to come from poor or working-class homes, they are also unlikely to come from upper-class or wealthy homes (Cox, 1926; Ellis, 1904; Galton, 1874; Roe, 1953). Those at the lower end of the socioeconomic scale lack the opportunities to develop their talents. Those at the upper end of the scale may have the opportunities but lack the incentive to develop their talents. Rich kids can too easily rest on their parents' laurels. Monetary inheritance interferes with intellectual investment in the future.

Well, that's pretty much it! Now to the specialized influences.

Domain-Specific Environments. Toward the end of chapter 3, I presented the Darwinian theory of genius, with a focus on its application to creative genius. This theory posits the involvement of a blind-variation and selective-retention or BVSR process. At the time, I also observed that the diverse domains of creativity vary in terms of how far they depend on this process. Some domains rely more on strict algorithmic problem solving, whereas others depend more on loose and unpredictable heuristics like trial and error. I also alluded to the fact that the degree of a domain's dependence on Darwinian genius will be associated with "the family backgrounds and educational experiences that contribute to the creative development of future geniuses" in that domain. It's now time to provide some details, because the theory provides some very specific predictions (Simonton, 1999b, 2004c).

Let's start with the family background of genius. Domains, such as the exact sciences, that minimize the blind-variation process will tend to attract geniuses who come from more conventional, stable, homogeneous home environments, whereas those, such as the subjectively expressive arts, that maximize the blind-variation process will tend to favor geniuses who grew up in more unconventional, unstable, and heterogeneous home environments (Simonton, 2004c). Hence, artistic geniuses are less likely than scientific geniuses to come from ordinary, conforming, middle-class homes but are more likely to have parents who come from very different backgrounds (whether ethnic, religious, or geographical), and they are more likely to have endured traumatic experiences in childhood or adolescence, such as the death of a parent or economic hardship (e.g., Berry, 1981; Brown, 1968; Ellis, 1904; Moulin, 1955; Post, 1994; Raskin, 1936; Simonton, 1986a). For example, writers honored with the Nobel Prize in Literature are far more likely than laureates in the sciences to have "either lost at least one parent through death or desertion or experienced the father's bankruptcy or impoverishment" (Berry, 1981, p. 387; see also Kaufmann, 2000–2001). At the other extreme, scientists who received the Nobel Prize in Physics "seem to have remarkably uneventful lives" (Berry, 1981, p. 387).

Are you thinking about where you fit in here? Was your home environment conventional, stable, and homogeneous or unconventional, unstable, and heterogeneous? That may not be an easy question, so I will ask some others. How many of you are the firstborn in the family? How many of you were born last? Those of you who were born in the middle of the pack, now raise your hands! Much easier to answer, no? But why did I ask these questions?

According to theory and relevant data, those domains that emphasize blind variation are more likely to be populated by those born later in the family, whereas those domains that emphasize sighted variation are more likely to recruit firstborns. Galton (1874) himself was the first to show that eminent scientists are more likely to be born first. The same was found by Anne Roe (1953) in her study of 64 illustrious scientists (one of whom was her own husband), and by too many other studies to name (e.g., Chambers, 1964; Clark & Rice, 1982; Helmreich, Spence, Beane, Lucker, & Matthews, 1980; Helson & Crutchfield, 1970; Terry, 1989; but see Feist, 1993). In contrast, artistic creators are more likely to be born later in the family lineup (e.g., Bliss, 1970; also see Eisenman, 1964).

This birth-order disparity reflects the fact that, on average, firstborns are prone to experience a more conventional and confined upbringing than their younger siblings (Sulloway, 1996). Being their parents' favorites, they grow up trying to fulfill parental expectations. This is evident in the tendency for firstborns to predominate in high-prestige domains like science, medicine, law, and other professions (Schachter, 1963). The laterborns dramatically diverge, more probably entering higher-risk and sometimes lower-status domains of achievement, like creative writing and even dangerous sports (Bliss, 1970; Nisbett, 1968). In line with this divergence, although everyday scientists and status quo politicians are more likely to be firstborns, revolutionary scientists and revolutionary politicians are more likely to be laterborns (Stewart, 1977, 1991; Walberg et al., 1980; Zweigenhaft, 1975). Put simply, the youngest sibs in the family are born to rebel (Sulloway, 1996).

As a lover of classical music, I find it worthy of note that great composers are more likely to be born earlier rather than later in the family (Schubert, Wagner, & Schubert, 1977). This implies that classical music is more like science than like art, more status quo than revolutionary. Given the highly formal and abstract nature of most masterpieces in the repertoire, this may contain a grain of truth. A symphony, quartet, trio, or sonata may have no explicit content, unlike a painting, sculpture, poem, or novel. A classical composer is like someone who presents mathematical proofs in sound.

Be that as it may, the contrast between the blind- and sighted-variation domains extends beyond the home. It crops up again during education and training (Simonton, 1999b, 2004c). On the one hand, the domains that need sighted variation the most are replete with geniuses who got superior grades in school, attained higher levels of formal education, and received training that was close to the domain in which they achieved eminence. On the other hand, the domains that need blind variation the most are crammed with geniuses who got inferior grades in school, managed only lower levels of formal education before they dropped out, and often received training that was rather marginal to the domain in which they eventually gained fame. In Kantian terms, the former domains require more imitation than talent and the latter domains require more talent than imitation (see, e.g., Goertzel, Goertzel, & Goertzel, 1978; Simonton, 1986a). Indeed, this very pattern replicates when we inspect another environmental factor, namely, mentors and role models (Simonton, 2004c). Geniuses who require more sighted variation tend to have only one or two mentors and models, and no matter how many they have, the mentors and models are very similar or homogeneous. But those geniuses who need more blind variation tend not only to have more mentors and models but to have mentors and models who are more heterogeneous, even contradictory. Expressed differently, the more original the genius must be to reach the heights in a given domain, the more that genius requires a rich influx of clashing perspectives and conflicting techniques (see, e.g., Simonton, 1984a, 1992b, 1992c).

Genetic Effects

Behavioral genetics is the scientific discipline committed to understanding how genes affect behavior in animals. In psychology, the discipline is more narrowly dedicated to comprehending the genetic basis of individual differences, where those differences may entail both intellectual and personality traits. When we say that a child is a "chip off the old block" or "like father, like son," is it because the child inherited a certain trait from its progenitor? Even though the discipline of behavioral genetics was not formally defined in the 19th century, Galton can be considered the first behavioral geneticist. Not only did he pioneer the family pedigree method in *Hereditary Genius* (Galton, 1869), but he also initiated the use of twins to tease out genetic effects (Galton, 1883). As he said, twins supply the "means of comparing the effects of nurture and nature" (p. ix). In addition, Galton developed the concepts of correlation and regression, which play a major role in behavioral genetic methods. Naturally, behavioral genetics has progressed substantially since Galton's day. Its techniques have become far more sophisticated and subtle. Probably the most significant advance, however, is a simple one: the analysis of identical twins who have grown up in separate homes (Bouchard, Lykken, McGue, Segal, & Tellegen, 1990). The more technical term for this focal group is MZA (monozygotic twins reared apart). Because such twins have identical genetic constitutions but diverging environmental experiences, any similarities in their intelligence or personality can be strongly attributed to genetic endowment.

Whatever the details, behavioral geneticists like to use their data to calculate the *heritability* of traits on which people may differ (Falconer, 1989). Heritability is always a positive decimal fraction and is usually represented by the symbol h^2. What it tells us for a given trait is the proportion of variation in the population that can be attributed to genetic variation in the same population. If $h^2 = 0$, then the trait is not genetically inheritable, but if $h^2 = 1.00$, it is entirely inherited. Of course, most heritabilities are much smaller than 1.00 and will vary appreciably from one trait to another (Bouchard, 2004). On the one hand, the heritability of general intelligence is .80 or higher, meaning that no less than 80% of the population's variation in performance on intelligence tests can be ascribed to genetic variation. On the other hand, interests and values may only have heritabilities in the .30s. Between these extremes come the heritabilities for many personality traits. They fall somewhere in the .40s and .50s.

The question you now may be asking is as follows: What's the heritability of genius? In the case of psychometric genius, I've already given you the answer: $h^2 \geq .80$. If genius is defined by your score on an IQ test, and variation in IQ scores reflects the magnitude of genius, then 80% of genius comes from the genes. This assumes that you are dealing with the entire range of scores in the population. If the range is narrower—for example, involving just college students—then h^2 will be much smaller.

Yet if you're more interested in historiometric genius—the kind exhibited by outstanding creators, exceptional leaders, and perhaps prodigious performers—then the answer is more problematic. That's because extraordinary achievements require much more than intelligence. They also depend on a large number of abilities, motives, personality traits, interests, and values. Stated differently, historiometric genius is necessarily multidimensional, whereas psychometric genius is supposedly unidimensional (if you trust in Spearman's g).

Making matters even more complicated, genius is decidedly nongeneric when it comes to the specific inventory of relevant intellectual and personal traits. Although general intelligence is probably a component of all guises of genius, other characteristics will most likely differ depending on the domain of achievement. Leaders may be more extroverted and motivated by a need for power, whereas creators may be more introverted and driven by a need for achievement. Artistic creators may be more emotionally unstable and neurotic, whereas scientific creators may be more cool, calm, and collected, like Spock, the Vulcan character in *Star Trek*. In fact, empirical research shows that this is the case. Each domain of high achievement features a defining profile of characteristics, some cognitive and others dispositional (Cox, 1926; Feist, 1998; Roe, 1953; Simonton, 1999d, 2008b).

This interdomain variation is illustrated in the case of the contrast between artistic and scientific genius. A meta-analysis summarized the empirical findings of dozens of studies based on thousands of research participants (Feist, 1998). Even if the artists and scientists shared some traits—both were open to experience, introverted, hostile, driven, and ambitious—they diverged on many more. On the one side, the artists were more imaginative, impulsive, norm-doubting, nonconforming, independent, aloof, cold, anxious, and emotionally sensitive. On the other side, the scientists were more flexible, dominant, arrogant, self-confident, and autonomous. Admittedly, the samples from which these conclusions were drawn did not consist entirely of Big-C Creators. Most of the studies only included little-c creators. Even so, it is probable that the differences between Big-A Artists and Big-S Scientists are even more pronounced than those between little-a artists and little-s scientists. Genius brings divergence. In any case, all of the personality traits mentioned have substantial heritabilities, ranging somewhere between .30 and .70 (Simonton, 2008b).

The problem now becomes how to combine these traits and their heritabilities to obtain an overall estimate of the heritability of artistic genius, scientific genius, political genius, and the like. This happens not to be an easy task. One source of the difficulty is that multidimensional talents are of two distinct types: additive and multiplicative (Simonton, 2005d).

Additive Inheritance. This form is the simpler: The discrete contributions of the various genetic traits are merely added together to produce the general trait. For instance, scientific genius may be a composite of general intelligence, special visual–spatial ability, an interest in science, an orientation toward things rather than people, and low religiosity, plus the personality traits mentioned in the previous section: openness to experience, flexibility, introversion, drive, ambitiousness, hostility, dominance, arrogance, self-confidence, and autonomy (Feist, 2006; Simonton, 2004c, 2008b). Because every one of these traits has a corresponding h^2, it should be possible to obtain a global heritability coefficient. The math needed to make these calculations is pretty tricky. Furthermore, the calculations require some rather technical information (the correlations among the traits, the correlations between the traits and whatever criterion we're using to judge genius, such as eminence, the trait reliabilities, etc.).

Instead of presenting you with more details, let's just cut to the chase. One recent investigation provided rough lower-bound estimates of both scientific and artistic creativity (Simonton, 2008b). It calculated that the global heritability of scientific creativity might range between .10 and .20. Given that several vital traits were omitted, the eventual range would very likely be considerably larger, perhaps between .20 and .30. The overall heritability of artistic creativity could be even higher than scientific creativity. The estimates for scientific and artistic creativity can be compared to those of another study, which estimated heritability of leadership to be around .17 using similar methods (Ilies, Gerhardt, & Le, 2004). Because the estimate from this other study incorporated just six relevant traits (general intelligence and the Big Five personality factors), this figure, too, is an underestimate, though we don't know by how much. I would guess that the global heritability of most forms of significant achievement is somewhere around .30 or .40. That is, between 30 and 40% of the variation in achievement might be credited to genetic endowment. That gives Galtonian nature enough wiggle room to leave an impression on the emergence of genius.

Multiplicative Inheritance. I hate to upset the apple cart, but the genes may contribute to genius by a more complex process than assumed by the foregoing estimates. Rather than being additive, inheritance may be multiplicative (Lykken, 1982). Put another way, genius may require a discrete and coherent configuration of intellectual and personality traits. Multiplicative inheritance is far more difficult to understand than additive inheritance, which probably explains why behavioral geneticists haven't discussed the phenomenon until relatively recently (Lykken, 1982; Lykken, McGue, Tellegen, & Bouchard, 1992). Nevertheless, it has been given a special name, *emergenesis* (Lykken, 1982). And there is already some empirical evidence that both creativity and leadership are subject to emergenic inheritance (Lykken et al., 1992; Waller, Bouchard, Lykken, Tellegen, & Blacker, 1993).

Unhappily, this form of genetic endowment is so complicated that it's not yet possible to derive a formula for estimating global heritability. Nonetheless, the mathematics behind the multiplicative models does enable us to arrive at three crucial implications.

First, estimates of overall heritability based on additive inheritance will be biased downward if the process is deep down emergenic (Simonton, 1999d). At present there's no way of gauging the amount of bias, but it might be equal to a decimal point or more. The global heritability might be around .40 or .50.

Second, if inheritance is multiplicative or emergenic, then genius may not run in family lines (Lykken et al., 1992). If you have to inherit all of the traits making up the configuration, then missing one trait is about the same as missing them all. In a way, each component trait has veto power over the other traits. If one component ain't happy, nobody ain't happy. This may seem a strange idea, but ponder Galton's (1869) assertion that genius requires intelligence, enthusiasm, and perseverance. What would happen if a person possessed just two of these three? Say, if the person was enthusiastic and persistent but dumb? Sounds like a thumbnail sketch of William McGonagall, the poet we met in chapter 2. Or intelligent and enthusiastic but lazy? How many people of ability and ardor fail to accomplish anything because they fail to do their homework or to work out the details? Or intelligent and persistent but halfhearted? Doesn't this describe a pedant who writes monotonous monographs and who, as your professor, puts you to sleep in class?

In any event, emergenesis accounts for why genius parents do not always have genius kids—as was the case with Albert Einstein. It can also explain the appearance of genius kids who did not have genius parents. In the latter category are Newton, Beethoven, and Michelangelo, all of whom lack a distinguished pedigree according to Galton's (1869) own data. But what about the Darwin family and other, similar lineages? Might these be instances of environmental rather than genetic effects? Didn't the Darwins all pass from childhood through adolescence in a home setting most of us can only envy?

Third, and probably even more interesting, multiplicative inheritance generates a very different frequency distribution than does additive inheritance. Where the latter yields a normal, bell-shaped curve, like that discussed in chapter 2, the former produces a highly skewed curve with a very long upper tail. For example, if the inheritance of creativity is emergenic, then the vast majority of people will have little or no creativity while a very small percentage will be astronomically creative. I know it's hard to fathom what this means, so imagine two hypothetical cases (Simonton, 1988c). First, if intelligence were an emergenic trait, then the person with the highest IQ in a population of 10,000 would have a score of around 341, more than 100 points greater than Marilyn vos Savant's personal best on any test! Second, if height were an emergenic trait (but with the same mean and standard deviation), then the tallest man out of 10,000 men would be 10 feet 9 inches tall! That's more than 2 feet taller than the Ukrainian veterinarian, Leonid Stadnyk, the world's tallest man, who measures "only" 8 feet 5 inches—and he's the tallest out of a population counted in the billions. If our imaginary fellow had played NBA basketball, he could've made Wilt Chamberlain wilt. I'll warn you, the guy's on my fantasy team.

These examples might look like a reductio ad absurdum argument against multiplicative inheritance, but they aren't. It's a fact that many kinds of remarkable accomplishments are distributed precisely in this fashion (Walberg, Strykowski, Rovai, & Hung, 1984). Creative productivity is an example (Simonton, 1997a). A very small percentage of the creators in any domain accounts for most of the products. Typically, the top 10% who are the most prolific account for nearly half of all the products, whereas those in the bottom half of the distribution account for only about 15% of the products (Dennis, 1954a, 1954b, 1955). Mind boggling, isn't it? You can fire half of the scientists or artists in the world and lose only about a seventh of the output! It is for this reason that the productivity of creative geniuses seems so off the scale. Galton published over 200 works. Mozart composed over 600 works despite living only 35 years. These people sit at the upper tail of an inordinately skewed distribution.

By the way, the same type of distribution applies to the accumulation of wealth. There's something called the Pareto law or 80:20 rule that says 80% of the financial assets are owned by 20% of the people. In the United States, the richest 1% of the households has more money than all of those in the bottom 90%. If Bill Gates divided his money equally among all U.S. households, how much cash do you think your family would get? Do a little Web surfing to find out! Gates is an authentic entrepreneurial genius on the rightmost tail of the distribution! He's like being 10 feet 9 inches tall with an IQ of 341.

BORN TO BE MADE—AND YOU'LL MAKE IT BIG!

One of the wonders of behavioral genetics is that the discipline contributes to our appreciation of environmental factors. Surprisingly, the quantification of nature leads to a quantification of nurture. In addition to determining the impact of genetics, behavioral geneticists assess the impact of the environment, too. In twin studies, for instance, researchers can partition environmental influences into shared and nonshared effects (e.g., Bouchard, 1994). The shared environment is what everybody in the same family shares. Most siblings share the same parents, the same home, the same neighborhood, and so forth. The nonshared environment is what's not the same for children in the family. Birth order is a prime example, but other examples include friendships and peer relationships. One curious finding is that nonshared effects are usually substantially greater than shared effects (Bouchard, 1994; Plomin & Rende, 1990). The impact of the shared environment can be negligible. Being raised by the same parents and living in the same home can be largely irrelevant. Accordingly, identical twins reared apart will be more similar to each other than they will to their foster sibs. Their foster parents leave no imprint.

This surprising outcome would seem inconsistent with what I said earlier about domain-general environmental effects. After all, I then described an idyllic home environment rich in intellectual and cultural stimulation. Yet this apparent contradiction leads to another fascinating finding from behavioral genetics: Many so-called environmental effects are nothing more than genetic effects that operate incognito (Plomin & Bergeman, 1991; Scarr & McCartney, 1983). The environment is a consequence of genetic endowment. Allow me to give two illustrations.

First, let's go back to the intellectually rich home that the parents provide for their budding geniuses. Where did the parents get that environment? Did they buy their house with bookshelves prestocked with classics and coffee tables already covered in highbrow magazines? Or did they spontaneously create a home that met their own needs? Because the parents were very intelligent, they themselves needed intellectual stimulation, and so they decorated their rooms in a manner that fitted their tastes. They also passed down to their offspring the very same intelligence that induced them to craft their home's intellectual environment. Remember that general intelligence has one of the highest heritabilities of any human characteristic. Perhaps this direct genetic contribution exceeds the indirect environmental contribution made by a scholarly and cultured living room and study. The child could have been raised in a foster home with no books at all and still come out with the same brains. This is why the IQs of MZA twins are more similar to the IQs of their biological parents than to those of their foster parents, even though the latter are responsible for the twins' experiential world (Bouchard & McGue, 1981). Shared genes, not shared surroundings, are essential to intellectual growth.

Next, let's put a child who has inherited a high level of general intelligence in a foster home initially ill equipped to supply her intellectual needs. Is she just going to accept the fait accompli? Or will she begin shaping her own environment as soon as she is old enough to do so? What will she ask her parents to get her for birthday or holiday presents? Once she gets an allowance, what will she spend her money on? What will she do during her leisure time? Will she ask permission to go to the public library or start bugging her parents to take her to fascinating places? Is it possible that she might transform her bedroom into a cozy little study crammed with intellectually challenging books? Will she become known as a bookworm? And if all this happens, doesn't it seem plausible that her genetic intelligence created her environment rather than that her environment created her intelligence? This is why the IQs of MZA twins become more similar to each other as they get older (Bouchard, 2004). Imagine the paradox: As the environment is given increasingly more time to influence the twins' intellectual development, it has an ever decreasing impact relative to what the twins inherited at the moment of conception!

The above discussion has focused on domain-general environmental effects, but parallel arguments can be constructed for domain-specific effects. We learned earlier that both scientific and artistic creativity have roots in the genes. If creative artists have a strong propensity to be open to experience, imaginative, driven, ambitious, impulsive, norm-doubting, nonconforming, independent, hostile, aloof, cold, introverted, anxious, and emotionally sensitive, then their parents will share those of the just-mentioned traits that have high heritabilities. Like child, like parent. One would believe that some of these parental traits would then have some consequence for the child's home environment. Can you figure out which traits might generate homes that are noticeably unconventional, unstable, and heterogeneous? Is it possible that some of these traits might even increase the likelihood that one of the parents would have a shortened life expectancy, and thereby expose the child to traumatic parental loss? The possibilities are endless.

After contemplating such gene–environment ambiguities, I'm now prepared to take one final swipe at the drudge theory (honestly the last, I promise). For sure, you can't become a genius without first mastering domain-specific expertise. Unless we're willing to admit ear wiggling as a brand of genius, that's an inescapable prerequisite. With the proviso mentioned before about individual variation, we can also accept the 10-year rule as a crude approximation. This means not 10 years studying and practicing just an hour each week, nor even an hour a day, but rather 3–4 hours a day, every day (Ericsson et al., 1993; Starkes et al., 1996). Given that level of commitment, how are you going to pick your future domain of genius? Will you just flip a coin to decide between being an artistic genius or a chess genius? Will you let yourself be "accidentally determined to some particular direction," in Samuel Johnson's words? Or is your decision going to reflect to a high degree your interests, values, personality, and intrinsic abilities? If you discover that deliberate practice in a given domain is too challenging or too mind-numbing or too meaningless, will you continue to spin your wheels? Or will you search for something else that's more your cup of tea? Something that you find accessible, that excites you, that's worthwhile, even valuable?

Once when I was a teenager I got into my head that I wanted to be a rock guitarist. Jimi Hendrix was only 6 years older than I was, Eric Clapton just 3 years older, and Duane Allman just 2, so certainly the time was ripe! I would force myself to the utmost to practice at least an hour a day. A measly hour and I just couldn't do it. I would repeatedly glance over at the clock on my desk, hoping the time would move much faster. My mind would wander off to faraway places. Even as I struggled to play over and over again some recalcitrant passage until I got it down cold, these wayward thoughts would distract me, and I would start making mistakes—new ones that I hadn't made before. I was getting nowhere, very slowly.

I'm confident that my fruitless experience is not unique. Perhaps you felt that way about piano lessons, soccer practice, language exercises, or algebra problem sets. Galton (1869) included enthusiasm along with perseverance. Without adequate zeal how can you have sufficient "capacity for hard labour"? It's a story that repeats itself over and over in countless lives. You will only become a genius if your genetic makeup lightens up the labor so you'll never let up.

Is Genius Mad?

Did you see the 2001 movie *A Beautiful Mind?* This was the biopic starring Russell Crowe, who portrays John Nash, a brilliant mathematician who succumbs to paranoid schizophrenia on his way to a Nobel Prize in economics. How many films have you seen that depicted a mad scientist? They go way back. Some forget that the actor in the title role in the 1931 classic *Frankenstein* was not the legendary Boris Karloff but rather the far more obscure Colin Clive, whose character famously screamed "It's alive! It's alive!" when his outrageous creation came to life.

Nor is Hollywood's fascination with crazy geniuses confined to the scientific domain. From Kirk Douglas as Van Gogh in the 1956 *Lust for Life* to Ed Harris as Jackson Pollock in the 2000 *Pollock,* how many troubled artists have you encountered on the silver screen? If we turn to the stars in popular music, the numbers of movie titles proliferate all the more. Have you seen the 1991 picture *The Doors,* starring Val Kilmer as Jim Morrison? It's representative of the genre: the early struggle against obstacles, the rise to fame, the weird behaviors and inevitable addictions, the tragic early death.

Hollywood seems to have a preoccupation with insane brilliance. Indeed, in the same year that saw the movie *Frankenstein* there also appeared a film explicitly titled *The Mad Genius,* starring John Barrymore (Drew's grandfather) and directed by Michael Curtiz (who a decade later directed the classics *Yankee Doodle Dandy* and *Casablanca*). Accordingly, multiple generations of moviegoers have become quite familiar with the popular image of the eccentric scientist or the tormented artist.

I'd like to say that this is all Hollywood flitter and fluff. But it's not. The notion that genius might be linked to madness goes back to antiquity. The Greek philosopher Aristotle is reputed to have observed that "Those who have become eminent in philosophy, politics, poetry, and the arts have all had tendencies toward melancholia" (qtd. in Andreasen & Canter, 1974, p. 123), while the Roman philosopher Seneca held that "No great genius has ever existed without some touch of madness" (Seneca, n.d./1932, p. 285). The idea of the mad genius persisted all the way to modern times and was even promulgated in scientific circles. Not only was genius mad, but it was associated with criminality and genetic degeneration. One author identified the four potential outcomes of an inferior genetic endowment:

> *First,* and most prominent in the order of frequency is an early death. *Second,* he may help swell the criminal ranks. *Third,* he may become mentally deranged and ultimately find his way into a hospital for the insane. *Fourth,* and least frequently, he startles the world by an invention or discovery in science or by an original composition of great merit in art, music or literature. He is then styled a genius. (Babcock, 1895, p. 752)

This quotation appeared not in a popular magazine or flier distributed on a busy boulevard but in the *Journal of Nervous and Mental Disease.* Founded in 1874, this journal is the oldest scientific monthly in its field; the journal was already more than 20 years old when the above statement was published, and the journal is still published today. So we're not talking about the opinions of a mere quack.

Yet, notice the quandary we're put in by such opinions: If geniuses are mad, then how can they be geniuses? However often the expression "mad genius" is bandied about, we must acknowledge that it seems an oxymoron. To be sure, it's easy enough to see how insanity can generate originality. That seems to be a specialty of insanity, if not an intrinsic part of its definition! Still, it's much more difficult to see how insanity can produce something truly exemplary—something worthy of imitation or admiration by others. If the insane could generate ideas, actions, or products that are so admirable, then why don't we all go to mental institutions to pick out our role models and mentors? Indeed, why would we have any such asylums at all? It would make more sense to place every psychotic in a laboratory or art studio, each with an entourage of disciples or apprentices dedicated to mastering the eccentricities of their selected expert!

How do we resolve this paradox? I have a suggestion: Before we speculate about it, why don't we first look at the relevant empirical findings? Once we have the facts in hand, we'll have a stronger basis for understanding the connection.

WHAT DO THE DATA SAY?

The empirical research relevant to the mad-genius issue uses three major methods. Two of them are already familiar: the historiometric and the psychometric. To these two can be added a third, namely, the psychiatric. Because of the obvious link between psychiatry and insanity, this method might seem the one most directly related to the question. Whether this is true or not, I will make a psychiatry sandwich by discussing the psychiatric findings in between the historiometric and psychometric results. As we'll see, although each approach has its own unique strengths and weaknesses, they all seem to converge on the same overall conclusions.

Historiometric Results: Retrospective Assignments

The historical record is replete with putative exemplars of mad genius (Simonton, 1994). This was made strikingly clear by several researchers who have compiled extensive lists of great geniuses who have succumbed to one mental illness or another (e.g., Prentky, 1980; Rothenberg, 1990). Even if we confine the listings to creative geniuses, the inventory is rather large. The geniuses who experienced a serious disorder at some point in their lives include scientists Isaac Newton, Charles Darwin, Francis Galton, and Sigmund Freud; philosophers Jean-Jacques Rousseau, Friedrich Nietzsche, and Sören Kierkegaard; novelists Honoré de Balzac, Fyodor Dostoevsky, and Franz Kafka; playwrights Friedrich Schiller, Federico García Lorca, and Tennessee Williams; poets Emily Dickinson, Arthur Rimbaud, and Ezra Pound; painters Michelangelo, Amadeo Modigliani, and Mark Rothko; and composers Robert Schumann, George Gershwin, and Sergei Rachmaninoff. This is an international collection of big names in a diversity of achievement domains.

Too often these disorders are terminated in a most tragic and direct fashion—suicide. Among the individuals in this category are Alan Turing, George Eastman, Ernst Hemingway, Jack London, Horacio Quiroga, Heinrich von Kleist, Vladimir Mayakovsky, Vachel Lindsay, Sylvia Plath, Anne Sexton, Virginia Woolf, Vincent Van Gogh, and Peter Tchaikovsky, And those who tried unsuccessfully to engage in self-murder include the Comte de Saint-Simon, William James, Dorothy Parker, Guy de Maupassant, Maxim Gorky, and Hugo Wolf.

At other times, the mental illness adopts a more subtle but still pernicious guise—alcoholism. The list of alcoholic geniuses in literature alone reads like an honor roll of authors who have contributed masterpieces to that domain of achievement

(F. Post, 1996). A partial register would include the names of James Agee, W. H. Auden, Charles Baudelaire, Hilaire Belloc, Robert Benchley, James Boswell, Dion Boucicault, Robert Burns, Truman Capote, John Cheever, Samuel Taylor Coleridge, James Gould Cozzens, Hart Crane, Stephen Crane, e e cummings, Theodore Dreiser, William Faulkner, F. Scott Fitzgerald, Dashiell Hammett, Lillian Hellman, Ernest Hemingway, Victor Hugo, Samuel Johnson, James Joyce, Jack Kerouac, Charles Lamb, Ring Lardner, Sinclair Lewis, Jack London, Robert Lowell, Malcolm Lowry, John Phillips Marquand, Edna Saint Vincent Millay, Joaquin Miller, Christopher Darlington Morley, Alfred de Musset, John Henry O'Hara, Charles Olson, Eugene O'Neill, Dorothy Parker, Edgar Allan Poe, William Sydney Porter (O. Henry), Edwin Arlington Robinson, Theodore Roethke, Jean-Paul Sartre, John Steinbeck, Wallace Stevens, Algernon Charles Swinburne, Alfred Tennyson, William Makepeace Thackeray, Dylan Thomas, James Thurber, Mark Twain, Paul Verlaine, Evelyn Waugh, Tennessee Williams, and Thomas Wolfe.

In fact, it sometimes appears that alcoholism is one of the necessities of literary genius. As short-story writer O. Henry put it, "Combining a little orange juice with a little scotch, the author drinks the health of all magazine editors, sharpens his pencil and begins to write. When the oranges are empty and the flask is dry, a saleable piece of fiction is ready for mailing" (qtd. in Davis & Maurice, 1931, p. 361). No bottle, no book.

Psychopathology can be found in other forms of genius besides creative genius. Some degree of mental illness was supposedly evident in famous and infamous leaders like Winston Churchill, U.S. Grant, Alexander Hamilton, Adolf Hitler, Howard Hughes, Abraham Lincoln, Martin Luther, Shaka, Florence Nightingale, and Mary Wollstonecraft, and in such prodigious performers as Sarah Bernhardt, James Dean, W. C. Fields, Clark Gable, Janis Joplin, and Vaslav Nijinsky.

Had enough of lists yet? Getting pretty tiresome? I've made my point, so I think we'll stop here. So, do all of these names provide conclusive proof of the mad-genius theory? The sheer number of positive cases might seem overwhelming evidence in favor of that conclusion. Yet we have to take into consideration a very serious counterargument. It goes like this...

Billions of people have lived on the planet since the beginning of recorded history. A certain proportion of these will suffer some mental or emotional disorder and a smaller proportion will enjoy the fruits of genius. Even if there were no association whatsoever between madness and genius, a certain number of geniuses might be expected to succumb to some psychopathology, as long as it's not totally disabling. Let's do a rough calculation on the back of a napkin. Suppose that, within the population from which geniuses originate, about 5% display some noticeable mental illness at some time during the course of their lives. Assume that genuine geniuses occur in that same population at a rate of only 1 in 10,000, making them a very elite club. Finally, let's posit, rather restrictively, that the eligible population contains exactly 1 billion adults. If genius is utterly uncorrelated with madness, then the predicted number of mad geniuses will be $.05 \times .0001 \times 1,000,000,000 = 5,000$. So, if you think the lists I gave earlier were long, just imagine how long they could have been! The full names of all 5,000 would fill an entire chapter in this book! Yet even that longer hypothetical list would prove nothing under this scenario. Fully 95,000 un-mad geniuses would carry on as counterexamples, their complete names occupying another 20 chapters. Like everybody else, the mad genius would represent just 5% of the population of geniuses—the unlucky few among the great.

To get around this problem, researchers have tried to establish a reasonable baseline expectation (e.g., Ludwig, 1995, 2002). The exact magnitude of this expectation varies from researcher to researcher and depends on each investigator's unique set of assumptions about what do and do not count as instances of psychopathology. Nonetheless, it is possible to offer five tentative generalizations.

First, relative to the general population, geniuses in many if not most domains appear to exhibit a higher rate and intensity of psychopathology (Ellis, 1904; Ludwig, 1995, 2002; Raskin,

1936). Although the disparity is contingent on the specific definition used, a rough estimate is that geniuses are about twice as likely to have lived through some mental or emotional difficulties relative to a comparable baseline (Ludwig, 1995).

Second, the more eminent the genius, the higher is the expected rate and intensity of psychopathological symptoms (Ludwig, 1995). The effect is not strong, but it holds on the average. To be blandly normal is not indicative of exalted accomplishments. At the same time, no exemplary achievements are ever produced while the genius is outright mad. Quite the opposite: When madness is in, genius is out.

Third, of the available pathologies, depression seems to be the most frequent, along with its correlates of suicide and alcoholism or drug abuse (Goertzel et al., 1978; Ludwig, 1990; F. Post, 1996). Other affective disorders and psychoses are rarer, albeit not absent altogether. The John Nash case that inspired the movie *Beautiful Mind* is practically one of a kind.

Fourth, the family lines that yield the most eminent geniuses may also tend to feature a higher rate and intensity of psychopathology (Jamison, 1993). In other words, the pedigrees that Galton identified may have both advantages and disadvantages—both madness and genius.

Fifth, the rate and intensity of symptoms varies according to the specific domain of achievement (Ludwig, 1995; F. Post, 1994). For example, psychopathology is higher among artistic geniuses than among scientific geniuses (Raskin, 1936; F. Post, 1994). Thus, according to one investigation, 87% of eminent poets experienced psychopathology, whereas only 28 percent of illustrious natural scientists did so (Ludwig, 1995). In *A Midsummer Night's Dream*, Shakespeare has a character proclaim that "The lunatic, the lover, and the poet / Are of imagination all compact" (5.1.7–8). Among leaders, the rates are much higher among social activists (49%) than among military figures (30%). Interestingly, tyrannical rulers exhibit the highest rates of all, around 91% having some psychopathology (Ludwig, 2002). Have you seen the 2006 film *The Last King of Scotland*, which won Forest

Whitaker an Oscar for his portrayal of the Ugandan tyrant Idi Amin? Anyhow, the odds of finding a mad genius hinge on the domain of achievement.

Again, I emphasize that these five conclusions are only tentative. It we had to rely on historiometric studies alone, our ability to address this question would be very limited indeed. Fortunately, these results do not have to stand alone.

Psychiatric Results: Clinical Diagnoses

Here are two questions I often ask students taking my upper-division capstone course in the history of psychology: How many of you plan to go into a mental health profession? How many of you would like to become clinical psychologists? Usually the show of hands is impressive—definitely more want to go into the helping professions than to become research psychologists like me! Many of the psychology majors I teach were once pre-med students but could not get past "o chem" (organic chemistry) or some equally horrendous obstacle. The members of one subset of these pre-med dropouts might even have aspired to become psychiatrists, yet learned from the school of hard (academic) knocks that an MD may not be in their future. In any case, these students have probably already taken the course in abnormal psychology, and perhaps also the course our department offers in clinical psychology.

If you fall into such a group, then you might have imagined something preposterous about the historiometric research just reviewed. How can one possibly diagnose a dead person? Almost every genius in the historiometric studies is very much deceased, and often lived centuries ago. If you know anything about the standard diagnostic manual in psychiatry—the *DSM–IV* (American Psychiatric Association, 1994)—you know that clinical diagnosis is not an easy task, even when the patient or client is sitting right across from you in your office!

The answer to this challenge is complex and not completely satisfactory. On the one hand, the evidence pointing to psychopathology is sometimes overwhelming. For instance, the German composer Robert Schumann had a series of manic–depressive episodes that are well documented, as is his suicide attempt and commitment to a mental institution. The Russian composer Sergei Rachmaninoff actually dedicated his Second Piano Concerto to his psychiatrist, and the American composer George Gershwin would sometimes take his therapist along when he went on vacation! On the other hand, the substantiation is sometimes weak and conjectural. For example, the Dutch painter Hieronymus Bosch is sometimes listed as a psychotic based on nothing more than the testimony of the fantastical imagery of his triptych paintings. Surely he must have been hallucinating!

So rather than lean on such retrospective assignments, why not take advantage of modern clinical diagnoses? This psychiatric attack is illustrated in a pair of investigations.

The first examined 15 writers at the Writers Workshop at the University of Iowa (Andreasen & Canter, 1974). This is a highly prestigious workshop that attracts some of the premier literary creators in the country. The writers were contrasted with control subjects who were similar except in literary creativity. The former were 5 times more likely to have been treated for an affective disorder and were 3 times more likely to be alcoholics. In a follow-up study conducted years later, it was found that 80% had some mood disorder, 30% continued to suffer from alcoholism, and 10% had committed suicide (Andreasen, 1987).

The second investigation scrutinized 47 distinguished writers and artists in Great Britain (Jamison, 1989). Over a third had sought therapy for an affective disorder. The writers were worse off than the artists, and the poets were in particularly bad shape, whereas the nonfiction writers (biographers) were in a better psychological state than other writers. This pattern closely parallels what's found in historiometric studies (Ludwig, 1995, 1998). About half of the poets needed serious medical treatment in the form of drugs or even hospitalization. Once more, depression appeared to be the most frequent symptom, with other affective disorders like mania in backup positions.

Although these psychiatric inquiries deal with contemporary geniuses who may not be in the same league as the geniuses in the historiometric investigations, the results are mutually supportive. According to both investigations, the rate and intensity of psychopathology appears to be elevated in outstanding creators. Furthermore, psychiatric inquiries also support the inference that the rate and intensity of psychopathology might (a) correlate positively with the magnitude of creative genius and (b) appear more conspicuous among artistic than among scientific creators (Juda, 1949). In addition, such studies suggest that genius and psychopathology often run in the same family lineages (Andreasen, 1987; Juda, 1949; McNeil, 1971; Myerson & Boyle, 1941).

The most telling investigation with regard to this latter point was one conducted in Iceland (Karlson, 1970). The investigator compared the data from two sources, the reference work *Who Is Who in Iceland* and the patient records from the mental hospital in the nation's capital—the sole facility in that small nation. Because Iceland provides rather extensive genealogical information as well as complete psychiatric records, it was possible to discern a revealing pattern: High-achieving Icelanders had a greater likelihood of emerging from families whose members also showed up in the psychiatric records. Those who had psychotics in their pedigree were twice as likely to attain distinction as those who didn't. And an Icelander who had a family member who was diagnosed with manic depression was 3 times more likely to become famous than one who had a family member who succumbed to psychosis. All in all, between 25% and 40% of the notable mathematicians, philosophers, novelists, poets, and painters had identifiable pathology in their family pedigree. Yet again, the Galtonian pedigrees that generate genius interweave with the lineages that produce madness.

Here we come to a disadvantage of the psychiatric method relative to the historiometric method. Where historiometric researchers can name names without any worry about violating patient confidentiality, researchers using the psychiatric approach cannot, and so the participants remain anonymous. As a consequence, I would like to close this section by giving a concrete example drawn from the historical rather than the psychiatric record, namely, the English poet Alfred Tennyson (Jamison, 1993). Probably best known for his "Charge of the Light Brigade" (even if that's not by any means his best poem), Alfred was unequivocally not someone who would receive a high score on what psychologists these days term "subjective well-being." He suffered from recurrent depressive moods, occasionally punctuated by hypomanic episodes. No doubt he inherited his gloomy demeanor from his father, an alcoholic with an apparent manic–depressive disorder. Additionally, several of Alfred's brothers and sisters were not completely well. If we omit the one sibling who died in infancy, only 3 of his 10 siblings had any semblance of normalcy, and only one might have been strictly normal. The remaining 7 were no better off than Alfred, and 2 were probably in even more dire straits, one being confined to an insane asylum for almost all of his adult life. If we take a peek at Alfred's father's family, it becomes clear that these psychopathological ailments go back for generations. The poet's pedigree was rich in depression and bipolar disorders. Yet from this pathological pedigree Tennyson's genius surfaced, even if not unscathed.

Here's a personal question for you to ponder in a private moment: Do you have any blood relatives you'd rather not mention to others? Any skeletons in the family closest? Maybe an uncle or sister a bit too strange; a manic aunt or grandfather residing in an asylum; a grandmother or brother who has committed suicide? Are you yourself peculiar, even to some extent weird? Can you also single out anybody in your extended family that has some claim to talent, if not genius? Is it you? Or is everyone in your family very, very normal? No madness and no genius?

Psychometric Results: Quantitative Assessments

Because the psychiatric studies depend on direct diagnosis, they can be considered improvements over the historiometric studies.

Even so, the psychiatric method is not without drawbacks. The sample sizes are often small, and it's not always easy to obtain appropriate control groups for comparison. What's more, diagnoses are highly qualitative and subjective by their very nature. Consequently, it might enhance our comprehension of the mad-genius controversy if we add another technique to our arsenal. That technique is psychometrics.

We're already familiar with this method. It's the method behind IQ tests. Yet psychometric investigators can assess far more than individual differences in intelligence. Researchers can also administer instruments that gauge personality traits closely related to psychopathology. Furthermore, like the average-intelligence baseline of IQ tests, these personality inventories have been standardized against large samples. This standardization allows us to detect sizable departures from the norm. The general population becomes the comparison group against which to contrast the scores of extraordinary achievers. As a final plus, personality instruments yield quantitative differentiations rather than qualitative assignments, unlike the other two methods.

Admittedly, psychometric studies have their own set of limitations relative to historiometric and psychometric methods (Simonton, 1999c). Probably the biggest constraint is that psychometric methods cannot be applied to geniuses in a wide range of achievement domains. The most clear-cut example is the domain of extraordinary leadership (J. Post, 2003). It's just not very likely that you are going to find a president, prime minister, or dictator willing to take a battery of tests to determine his or her psychological makeup. What if the results came out wrong? What if the scores indicated that the leader had serious psychological problems? In point of fact, I don't know a single psychometric investigation that has looked at genius-level political, military, or religious leaders. In contrast, exceptional creators are somewhat more willing to risk such self-exposure. They do not have to worry about their popularity in the latest polls or the probability of getting reelected to office. As a result, the findings reported in this section are uniformly limited to domains of creative achievement. Now to the results.

For the most part, creative individuals tend to score above average on several dimensions related to psychopathology (Barron, 1963; Nettle, 2006). For example, creativity is positively associated with scores on psychoticism, a dimension of the Eysenck Personality Questionnaire or EPQ (Eysenck, 1994, 1995). People who score higher than normal on psychoticism tend to be aggressive, cold, egocentric, impersonal, impulsive, antisocial, unempathetic, and tough-minded. Doesn't this profile appear like that of the typical mad scientist in a Hollywood sci-fi flick? Nevertheless, exceptional creators in the arts tend to have more elevated scores than do exceptional creators in the sciences (Feist, 1998; Nettle, 2006; Simonton, 2004c). As an exercise, just compare the personality of Pablo Picasso with that of Albert Einstein to appreciate how much higher the former rated in psychoticism!

Furthermore, it's not just the case that creative people score higher on such dimensions; it is also the case that the most highly creative people score higher than the less creative people, who in their turn score higher than the noncreative people (Eysenck, 1995; Nettle, 2006). This positive monotonic relation was demonstrated in a study of creative writers using the Minnesota Multiphasic Personality Inventory, or MMPI (Barron, 1963). This instrument contains clinical scales for depression, hypochondriasis, hysteria, hypomania, paranoia, psychotic deviation, psychasthenia, and schizophrenia. You don't need to know the meaning of each and every one of these scales to appreciate the following message: Those writers who have carved out highly successful careers score higher on every single dimension than those who are still creative but not nearly so successful, while the latter are above normal on almost every scale. A similar outcome is found for creative artists on the EPQ psychoticism scale (Götz & Götz, 1979a, 1979b). The most successful artists score higher on psychoticism than their professional colleagues, who in turn score higher on psychoticism than do nonartists (see also Nettle, 2006).

119

So far these findings fall in line with what we've learned in the previous two sections. Yet psychometric studies also provide some new empirical results that clarify the details of the connection between creativity and psychopathology. Two sets of findings stand out.

First, although highly creative individuals are prone to have prominent scores on certain clinical scales, their scores are rarely so extreme as to indicate authentic mental illness. Rather, their scores are placed somewhere between the normal and abnormal ranges (Barron, 1963; Eysenck, 1995; cf. Nettle, 2006). To give an example, although creative writers score higher than normals on almost all clinical scales of the MMPI, and highly successful creative writers earn even higher scores, the scores for both sets of creative writers stay discretely below those received by persons with full-fledged psychopathology. At these middling levels, a person will enjoy traits that can be truly considered advantageous to the exercise of creativity. For instance, elevated scores on psychoticism are correlated with independence and nonconformity, traits that help sustain originality (Eysenck, 1995). In addition, higher than average psychoticism is related to the capacity for defocused attention (i.e., reduced negative priming and latent inhibition), thus allowing ideas to enter the mind that would otherwise be filtered out during thought and perception (Eysenck, 1993; Stavridou & Furnham, 1996). This more inclusive mode of processing information is also correlated with openness to experience, an inclination that is positively associated with creativity (Harris, 2004; McCrae, 1987; Peterson & Carson, 2000; Peterson, Smith, & Carson, 2002). Defocused attention and openness also render the creator more susceptible to serendipitous events (Ansburg & Hill, 2003; see also Mach, 1896). What the average person would view as an irrelevant accident, the highly creative person sees as a significant opportunity.

Second, exceptional creators rate very high on other traits that dampen the negative effects of any incipient psychopathology. In the first place, creators enjoy a high degree of self-sufficiency and ego strength relative to the general population

(Barron, 1963; Cattell & Butcher, 1968). For that reason, they can wield more metacognitive control over any supposed symptoms. In particular, creators can take advantage of bizarre images rather than having the bizarre images take advantage of them. In so doing they can convert merely original ideas into thoroughly exemplary ideas. Additionally, the power to make use of strange ideas is most likely reinforced by an above-average general intelligence (Carson, Peterson, & Higgins, 2003). Someone who has a genius-grade intellect, or at least the intellect of a borderline genius, will be able to remain in charge of the wild proceedings.

I'm not really presenting anything very novel here. William James (1902) said over a century ago that

> the nature of genius has been illuminated by the attempts ... to class it with psychopathological phenomena. Borderland insanity, crankiness, insane temperament, loss of mental balance, psychopathic degeneration (to use a few of the many synonyms by which it has been called), has certain peculiarities and liabilities which, when combined with a superior quality of intellect in an individual, make it more probable that he will make his mark and affect his age, than if his temperament were less neurotic. (pp. 22–23)

Or, as the English playwright John Dryden (1681) asserted with more elegance: "Great Wits are sure to Madness near ally'd, / And thin Partitions do their Bounds divide" (p. 6). Genius and madness are not identical twins, but they are fraternal twins.

NOW WHAT CAN WE SAY?

It's time for a recap that combines the findings emerging from all three methods. The recap consists of six points:

First, genius does seem "near ally'd" with madness. This alliance holds in the sense that various indicators and symptoms of psychopathology appear to occur at a higher rate and intensity among geniuses than in the general population.

Second, the greater the magnitude of genius, the more likely it is that these signs will appear. Yet the level of psychopathology seen in even the greatest geniuses remains below the level characteristic of those who would be considered indisputably insane. In fact, works of genius do not appear when a genius has succumbed to complete madness. So "thin Partitions do their Bounds divide."

Third, some psychopathologies appear more frequently, with depression being the most common. Other syndromes, such as the paranoid schizophrenia of John Nash, are less common, albeit not impossible.

Fourth, family lineages that have higher than average rates of psychopathology will also feature higher than average rates of genius. Hence, even if a genius does not have a modicum of mental illness, someone in his or her family may be less fortunate. However normal Albert Einstein may or may not have been as an adult, it cannot be denied that his son Eduard succumbed to schizophrenia and had to be institutionalized.

Fifth, the rate and intensity of psychopathological symptoms varies across the diverse domains of achievement. In some domains, such as poetry, mental illness may run rampant, whereas in other domains, such as the natural sciences, mental illness will not be much more common than in the general population.

Sixth and last, any tendencies toward psychopathology are almost invariably counterbalanced by other personal traits that strengthen the individual's response to any symptoms. Especially critical are a sharp intellect and strong willpower that prevent any crazy thoughts from becoming outlandish behaviors. The symptoms of pathology thereby become resources to be exploited rather than insecurities to be feared.

Given the above six conclusions, how can they be explained? I'll focus my explanatory account on just two interconnected questions. First, why does any madness appear at all? Second, why does too much madness sometimes appear? Any areas not covered by these two will be left for Thursday's discussion section—did my teaching assistant write that down?

Why Any Madness?

It's time to go back to the Darwinian theory of creativity first introduced in chapter 3 and discussed again in chapter 4. We start by repeating the earlier observation that creative domains differ appreciably in the degree to which the ideational variations are blind. On the one hand, variations in the mathematical sciences are highly constrained by logic and data, and as a consequence the creative process in those domains is more sighted than blind. On the other hand, variations in the arts are much less restricted, and hence the variations are far more blind than sighted. Put differently, algorithmic problem solving has a much bigger part to play in the former whereas heuristic problem solving—including trial and error—has a much larger role in the latter. We have already seen that this contrast has important implications for the kinds of environments that are most supportive of creative development. Geniuses who rely more on sighted variations will have more conventional and stable familial, educational, and mentoring experiences than do those who rely more on blind variations.

Parallel cross-domain contrasts should hold for psychopathology as well. A high need for sighted variations should be associated with a lower rate and intensity of psychopathological symptoms, whereas a high need for blind variations should be associated with a higher rate and intensity of such symptoms. To explain why, look back at the correlates of psychoticism, the dimension assessed by the EPQ (Eysenck, 1995). These correlates include independence and nonconformity, two traits that provide more freedom for the generation of original variations. Moreover, psychoticism is *negatively* correlated with the capacity to filter out supposedly extraneous stimuli and information. Clearly the less rigorous such filtering, the more blind will be the resulting ideational variations (Simonton, 2004c). Indeed, the intellect will become much more open to the influx of serendipity—as occurred when Gutenberg noticed that a wine press would make a very fine printing press. Finally, psychoticism is associated with the preference for complexity and ambiguity and with the ability to generate relatively rare associations (Eysenck, 1994), two attributes long linked with the capacity for originality and creativity (Barron, 1955; Mednick, 1962). Someone who scores very low on psychoticism will have all of these aptitudes and inclinations suppressed. That is, such a person will be less independent and more conventional and conforming, less liable to engage in defocused attention, and more strongly predisposed toward the simple and unambiguous, and will have a lowered capacity for associative richness.

Each domain of creativity will have its own optimal level of psychopathological tendencies, depending on the relative proportion of sighted and blind variations required to produce original and exemplary products. This is why psychopathology is less common among scientific geniuses than among artistic geniuses and why artists who create in highly formal styles exhibit less psychopathology than those who create in highly expressive styles (Ludwig, 1998). The more blindness required in the mind, the more madness in the genius. Blind means mad.

Needless to say, even in the highly expressive arts, geniuses might go too far, their mental illness pushing them over the edge. For instance, extreme levels of psychoticism would be associated with psychopathic, schizoid, unipolar depressive, affective, schizoaffective, and schizophrenic disorders (Eysenck, 1995). When psychopathology is this intense, creativity will suffer a drastic decline and may terminate altogether if the breakdown leads to successful suicide or substance abuse. It's one thing to create when you're slightly tipsy or high, quite another to create when you're in a drunken or drug-induced stupor—even more tricky when you're cold and dead.

Yet we also have to acknowledge that one can have too little craziness for one's chosen discipline. A genius designed to become a great physicist would likely lack the wild imagination necessary to become a great poet. The variations would not be blind enough; the thought processes would be too rule bound. You'd end up with dry, academic poems instead of creative poems.

So it's a Goldilocks story: not too hot, not too cold; not too big, not too small; not too mad, not too sane—but just right. One thin partition divides genius from madness and another divider separates genius from mundaneness. The exact placement of those upper and lower bounds on psychopathological propensities depends on the degree to which the domain relies on sighted versus blind variations.

At the end of chapter 3, I merely hinted that the BVSR theory may apply to other domains of genius besides creativity. More specifically, I suggested that various forms of supreme leadership may benefit from the capacity to generate blind variations during problem-solving situations occurring in war, politics, and business. I also mentioned that the rate and intensity of psychopathological symptoms varies across distinct domains of leadership. Might these two points be connected in the same way as they are in creative domains? Does social activism require more originality than military leadership? If so, that might explain why 49% of social activists but only 30% of military leaders exhibit any mental disorder during the course of their lifetime (Ludwig, 1995). Certainly the traits associated with psychoticism would be far more beneficial to a social activist than to a military leader. Anyway, this possible interpretation is definitely worth further exploration.

Why Too Much Madness?

If each domain of achievement suggests a certain optimal level of psychopathological symptoms, then each genius must match the chosen domain to the given disposition. If you're too mad to become a physicist, then why not become a poet instead? But observe that if you're already active in a domain that harbors impressive rates and incidences of psychopathology, this option is no longer available. Poets already have an 87% lifetime rate of mental illness (Ludwig, 1995), and there's no domain that does better (or rather worse?) than that percentage (see also Kaufman, 2005; but see F. Post, 1996). Perhaps this may help explain why so many poets commit suicide, drink themselves to death, or otherwise behave in dysfunctional ways that shorten their life expectancy (Kaufman, 2003; Simonton, 1975a). Poetry attracts some really sick souls who have nowhere else to go. If you fail as a poet, what's next?

Yet we also have to recognize that some geniuses may be perfectly well suited to their chosen domain of achievement but end up being pushed over the top by unanticipated events, events so traumatic or stressful that the geniuses are pushed over the brink. Ironically, although many of these events may be of the sort that is experienced by everybody—death in the family, unrequited love, financial bankruptcy—some subset of these acute stressors may uniquely belong to the world of genius. For instance, the very act of producing a great contribution may occasion a tremendous amount of strain (Simonton, 1994). The Social Readjustment Rating Questionnaire, which assigns points according to the amount of "life change" that events produce, assigns 28 points for any "outstanding personal achievement" (Holmes & Rahe, 1967). That is about the same number of points as "litigation or [a] lawsuit," "trouble with creditors," "change in responsibilities at work," and "city or town of permanent residence changed." So how many points should a creator get for producing a work of genius? How much stress did Picasso experience when he painted *Guernica?* How did J. K. Rowling feel when completing the last Harry Potter book?

Another example of stress results from the phenomenon of fame. Fame itself can be stressful. Besides having to deal with the hurtful jabs received from critics, detractors, and competitors, it can also jar you into a mode of excessive self-consciousness. Ever been taken by surprise by a mirror in some public place and found yourself suddenly confronted by your own reflection? It's not always a pleasant experience to see yourself the way others see you, to view yourself from the outside rather than the inside. And what's a good way of ridding yourself of such psychological discomfort? Well, how about a drink, or two, or three? Or some other mind-numbing drug?

One researcher actually investigated the negative repercussions of fame on the lives of three notable creators: Kurt Cobain, lead singer and songwriter of the band Nirvana, songwriter Cole Porter, and short-story writer John Cheever (Schaller, 1997). After Cobain and Porter attained celebrity, their song lyrics betrayed an increased use of first-person singular pronouns ("I" and "me"), and a similar trend appeared in Cheever's journal entries and private correspondence. Additionally, Cheever's stories displayed a more conspicuous use of the first-person narrative voice. In Cheever's case, too, it was possible to establish a relationship between his self-consciousness and increased alcohol abuse, because the author recorded his battle with alcoholism in great detail in his journals. Taken together, the data analyses provided support for the following causal sequence: fame → self-consciousness → substance abuse. Naturally, we can probably add another item to this sequence: → decline in creativity. In Cobain's case, the decline was irreversible because he committed suicide.

The two examples given above involve processes that are applicable to a diversity of domains in which people demonstrate genius. The first applies to any great accomplishment, whereas the second applies to all accomplishments that may put a person's face on the front cover of *Time* magazine or *The New York Times*. Other trials and tribulations are unique to specific domains of achievement. Since we've spent so much time on creative genius, I should probably give an example from the realm of leadership.

Earlier in this chapter, I mentioned that a whopping percentage of 20th-century tyrants exhibited some form of psychopathology (Ludwig, 2002). Fully 91%! At that time I asked if you had seen *The Last King of Scotland*, in which just such a tyrant was vividly portrayed by Forest Whitaker. What I didn't observe back then was that tyrants display an unusual pattern of psychopathology. They tend to suffer more from paranoia than from any other mental illness. Fully 55% of tyrants are paranoid to some degree (Ludwig, 2002). The only other disorder that comes close is alcoholism, to which 41% of the tyrants succumb. The only exceptional leaders that outdo tyrants in paranoia are visionaries. Visionary leaders are very similar to tyrannical rulers in that they depend on totalitarian rule to stay in power; but where tyrants rely primarily on the military to enforce their power, visionaries depend more on their promotion of a high-profile political ideology. Furthermore, where the visionary is sincerely engaged in social engineering to create a utopia on earth, the tyrant is more cynically engaged in personal self-aggrandizement and its correlates of greed, corruption, and cruelty. While Idi Amin was a representative tyrant, Mao Zedong of Communist China was a prototypical visionary.

These differences aside, tyrants and visionaries have one thing in common: Their position at the top is insecure. They rose to the top by the sword—whether by coup d'état, rebellion, or revolution—and they could just as readily die by the sword. Easy come, easy go. This precariousness stands in stark contrast to other genres of leaders, such as hereditary monarchs and heads of state in democratic governments, whose power is sanctioned by tradition and constitution. Even authoritarian rulers, such as Spain's Francisco Franco, reached their nation's leadership by preaching the preservation of time-honored principles of law and order, and thereby obtained a legitimacy that's denied to tyrants, who simply shelve all bothersome laws, and to visionaries, who try to replace all the laws with new ones based on a radical ideology.

If you thought that you might be overthrown, even assassinated, at any time, by some wannabe tyrant or rival ideologist—by some competitor out there just following your own example—wouldn't you become paranoid? So might not this be a case where the domain of achievement induces the mental disorder rather than the mental disorder making some contribution, however elusive, to the magnitude of achievement? Can you understand why Joseph Stalin systematically destroyed all of his adversaries? He even arranged for his opponent Leon Trotsky to be brutally murdered at the victim's Mexico City home, thousands of miles away from the dictator's residence in Moscow!

A paranoid can never sleep until all antagonists, real or imagined, close or far-off, sleep forever.

IS THAT IT?

I wish the question posed by the above heading could be answered undeniably in the affirmative. Unfortunately, the reality is much more convoluted, even crazier, than has so far been revealed. Fortunately, you do have a discussion section coming up this coming Thursday. So just in case you run out of things to talk about, I'd like to pose some additional questions to stimulate conversation. There are three available discussion questions (DQs).

DQ #1: Symptoms as Blessings?

Out-and-out psychopathology appears to interfere with the operation of genius. For example, although artistic creators often suffer from depression, artists are hardly ever creative when they are deeply depressed. Yet on occasion, the symptoms of psychopathology can prove directly beneficial. An example is mania or hypomania. Mania is the state of being awfully "up"—experiencing intense emotional enthusiasm, attitudinal optimism, physical energy, and ideational extravagance. In its utmost extremity, you get the "raving maniac." Yet hypomania is a mild version of the same condition that doesn't quite leave terra firma. A number of investigators have suggested that hypomania can make a very positive contribution to achievement in a diversity of domains (e.g., Gartner, 2005).

A classic illustration can be found in the life of the German composer Robert Schumann. Subject to severe bipolar (manic–depressive) affective disorder, he was prone to mood swings of epic proportions. When Schumann was depressed, he was really depressed. But when he was at the other end of the cycle...well, he just composed and composed and composed. By far the bulk of his output appeared when he was in the manic or hypomanic phase of his bipolar oscillations (Weisberg, 1994; cf. Ramey & Weisberg, 2004). To be sure, although the quality of his work didn't necessarily increase in these states, neither did it decline. In essence, the ratio of hits to total attempts stayed about the same. That means that Schumann produced much of his best work when he was on a neurotransmitter-driven emotional high. A pathological symptom became an asset.

Or let me give an entirely different example: heavy drinking. One investigator conducted a historiometric analysis of the connection between alcohol use and creativity in the lives of 34 eminent writers, artists, and musicians (Ludwig, 1990). All had become notorious as big-time imbibers. In more than three-quarters of the cases studied, alcohol consumption had a negative impact on creative output, and this adverse effect was particularly evident in the latter phases of the subjects' lives. Drinking came to replace creating. Think Dylan Thomas and Truman Capote. Even so, according to the researcher, alcohol use "appeared to provide direct benefit for about 9% of the sample, indirect benefit for 50% and no appreciable effect for 40% at different times in their lives" (p. 953). Moreover, in almost a third of the sample, increased drinking was the consequence of creativity. After I finish writing this book, should I make another pot of coffee or break out the champagne?

So here's your task: Reflect on the various symptoms associated with the diverse disorders to which geniuses are supposedly subject. Can you imagine specific symptoms that might, if present in just the right degree, enhance rather than inhibit achievement? Can you identify a concrete case in which some modicum of madness has improved the manifestation of genius? If so, please name names and provide details.

DQ #2: Being Sane in Insane Domains?

Two persons look at a glass of water. On the one hand, the optimist—or the bipolar in a manic state—says that the glass is half full. On the other hand, the pessimist—or the bipolar in a depressive state—says that the glass is half empty. (A nerdish T-shirt adds that an engineer would say that the glass is twice as large as necessary, but we'll ignore this third possibility!) Have we been behaving like stalwart pessimists? OMG, X percent of geniuses have a mental illness of some kind during their lifetime! Shame, shame! Yet how often do we act the optimist and proclaim that Y (=100 – X) percent of geniuses have no documented evidence of mental disorder whatsoever! Take the extreme case of the poets. If 87% of eminent poets had some mental or emotional breakdown, doesn't that mean that 13% were psychopathology-free for all of their lives? Does that latter stat mean you can wholly avoid the stigma of mental illness and still offer to the world poems that are both original and exemplary?

Obviously, if we turn our attention to domains where the rate and intensity of psychopathology is lower than in poetry, the glass starts looking ever more full. According to one set of estimates, the glass is more than half full—that is, more than half of the luminaries are "normal"—in the domains of military leadership, public office, business, social activism, natural sciences, and exploration (Ludwig, 1995). So madness affects only a minority in these areas of achievement. How do we reconcile the mad-genius notion with this more optimistic spin on the statistics?

In your discussion, you may want to consider the following three possibilities.

First, it may be that the normals aren't really normal. Perhaps they have personal eccentricities that make them appear a tad off at a first meeting, but nothing that will grab the attention of a contemporary psychiatrist or future biographer. For instance, such individuals may have elevated scores on the clinical scales of the MMPI and on the psychoticism scale of the EPQ, but not so elevated that the individuals concerned betray any abnormal symptoms. Their scores would lie closer to the lower bound with respect to being average than to the upper bound with respect to being insane. When we say that 13% of eminent poets did not go through a single episode of mental illness during their lifetimes (Ludwig, 1995), does that mean that these poets would score low on psychoticism? To be more specific, does that indicate that these "healthy" poets were altruistic, socialized, empathetic, conventional, and conformist? Or was it just that their tendencies toward psychopathology stayed just below the radar? Would those who were very low on psychoticism have a higher likelihood of being poetasters rather than poets, makers of crude limericks rather than generators of grand poems?

Second, the normals may be bona fide normals, but their very normalcy affects their mark on history. For example, it's possible that such normal personalities produce work just barely original and only weakly exemplary—the kind of products generated by also-ran geniuses who just meet the minimum standards. They would be comparable to borderline geniuses according to the psychometric definition. These may be the geniuses whose posthumous reputations most quickly fade from eminence to obscurity, that is, those whose work fails to pass the test of time.

Third, perhaps we got it all wrong, and we should be looking at other factors besides psychopathological tendencies in the origins of genius. As a case in point, maybe genius just requires divergent experiences in the course of development (Simonton, 1999b). By divergent experiences I mean young talents' encounters with events and circumstances that set them apart from the norm. These conditions can come from both nature and nurture. In the case of nature, the experiences take the form of subclinical psychopathology that directs development onto a unique pathway. And in the case of nurture, these experiences assume the guise of distinctive events in childhood, adolescence, and young adulthood—such as parental loss or other trials and tribulations. An up-and-coming genius may thus be perfectly normal from the standpoint of nature but somewhat abnormal from the perspective of nurture (Simonton, 2004c).

What do you all make of these various possibilities?

DQ #3: Shrinking Genius?

Some years ago, I saw a Bizarro cartoon depicting Edgar Allan Poe at his writing desk. The poet is composing his famous "The Raven," and he is caught at the very instant when he pens the line "Quoth the Raven: 'Hey, things could be a lot worse.'" Hmm, don't recall that quote from when you took American literature in high school? The caption to the cartoon tells you why you have no such recollection. It reads "Poe and Prozac." The insinuation is obvious: If Poe had taken the medications that are readily available today, he wouldn't have created one of the most popular poems in the English language. Perhaps he wouldn't even have had to take his pills to so thoroughly kill off his creative muse. Poe might only have needed a few sessions with a psychotherapist, psychiatrist, or psychoanalyst to obliterate his poetic genius. Once Poe no longer felt all doom and gloom, full of angst and weltschmerz, he would prove incapable of conceiving a poem that depicts a forlorn lover's descent into madness.

So here's your discussion question: Is therapy the enemy of creativity? Will seeing the shrink shrink your genius? Should you go off your meds if you want to generate something decidedly original and exemplary?

Before you answer, perhaps you should consider the obverse side of the coin. Remember all of the geniuses who surrendered to suicide? Let's focus particularly on the female poets. Not only are they most disposed to endure mental illness (Kaufman, 2001), but they may also be especially prone to die by their own hands (Kaufman & Baer, 2002). Sylvia Plath suffered from depression and Anne Sexton from bipolar disorder. Plath killed herself by putting her head in a gas oven (having first sealed the kitchen), and Sexton did it by carbon monoxide poisoning (having started her car engine after first locking herself in the garage). If they had taken appropriate medication or therapy, might they all have contributed more great works to English literature? (Hint: Plath was in her early 30s at the time of her death, Sexton in her mid 40s.)

The cases of Plath and Sexton bring up another enigma: Why didn't writing have any helpful therapeutic value? After all, research on the writing cure shows that mental health can be improved by expressive writing (Kaufman & Sexton, 2006). Such deliberate activity can get repressed or suppressed thoughts and emotions out in the open, eventually inducing a catharsis. The writing cure would seem to have been especially effective in the case of two writers who created confessional poetry—works that deal directly with the poet's most intimate feelings. In Sexton's case, her therapist had initially recommended that she take up poetry as a form of self-treatment! Some have suggested that such poetry writing lacks an element that is central to therapeutic writing, namely, a proper narrative with a beginning, a middle, and an end (Kaufman & Sexton, 2006). Alternatively, the same researchers speculate that Plath and Sexton might have been so depressed that they remained very depressed even though the poetry was really having a positive therapeutic effect. Perhaps Plath and Sexton would have killed themselves years earlier if they had not become poets!

It might help your preparation for Thursday's discussion section if you read some representative poems by Sylvia Plath and Anne Sexton. Try the former's "Daddy" and the latter's "Sylvia's Death." Yes, ironic, isn't it? Sexton wrote a poem lamenting the suicide of her friend and contemporary, and then about a decade later closely imitated her example! So much for the efficacy of poetry therapy! Or not?

Is Genius Individual
or Collective?

llow me to get autobiographical again. Here's a true story from my graduate student days. I was in my first year in the social psychology program at Harvard University. At that time the social psychology graduate program was housed in the Department of Social Relations, an interdisciplinary department that also contained sociology and cultural anthropology along with the other "soft" subdisciplines of psychology. During a casual conversation with a faculty member in the nonpsychology side of the department, I mentioned my interest in the psychology of creativity. The professor's immediate response was that there was *no such thing!* Creativity is not an individual phenomenon. Instead, it is a sociocultural product. Societies and cultures create, but persons do not. The individual, even the so-called genius, is nothing more than a mouthpiece for the larger milieu or zeitgeist—the latter being the German word for the "spirit of the times." The concept of the lone genius is one of those misguided myths that psychologists alone maintain. Only sociologists and cultural anthropologists appreciate that the myth is indeed just that, a pure myth without the slightest basis in scientific fact. Creativity can be studied by sociologists and cultural anthropologists, but not by psychologists. Genius is a mere epiphenomenon; it has sociocultural causes, but no sociocultural effects. Genius is nothing more than the ephemeral froth riding the crest of a gigantic ocean wave.

In retrospect, it was no wonder that the Department of Social Relations was then in the process of disintegration. Representatives of the three component disciplines often had more disagreements than agreements about core features of human behavior. In any case, the sociologists left first, to form their own department, to be followed shortly by the cultural anthropologists, who rejoined the physical anthropologists. Eventually the psychologists in Social Relations reunited with their colleagues in the hitherto separate Department of Psychology, and the distinctive Harvard program that had lasted almost a quarter century became defunct. I had applied to a broadly interdisciplinary program but graduated from a strictly disciplinary program.

Nonetheless, the emphatic assertion of sociocultural determinism had left its mark on a young, impressionable student. For my doctoral dissertation, I decided to investigate the sociocultural factors that drive the emergence and manifestation of creative genius. These factors involve the social, political, and cultural environment. The resulting historiometric thesis, *The Social Psychology of Creativity*, was completed in 1974, and its principal results were published a year later under the title "Sociocultural Context of Individual Creativity" (Simonton, 1974, 1975b). Although I examined this question from many angles over the following years (e.g., Simonton, 1976c, 1988b, 1992a), I often felt like a traitor to my discipline. This treasonous feeling was accentuated whenever one of my fellow psychologists—most often a referee for a manuscript that I had just submitted

136

to a psychology journal—asserted that I was not a legitimate psychologist. I was called a closet sociologist or anthropologist who just happened to have a job teaching courses in a psychology department. It didn't help my reputation that my research would sometimes appear in sociology and anthropology journals (e.g., Simonton, 1976c, 1981).

Yet in time, other psychologists began to realize that creativity was not exclusively an individualistic phenomenon (e.g., Amabile, 1983; Csikszentmihályi, 1990; Harrington, 1990). So my research began to appear less and less offbeat. Now in the 21st century, other bona fide psychologists are publishing books with titles like *Group Creativity* (Paulus & Nijstad, 2003) and even *Group Genius* (Sawyer, 2007). Ironically, as the social dimension of creativity and genius became increasingly acknowledged by other psychologists, I began to shift the focus of my research toward the individual aspects of creative genius; my research remains largely in this latter area today (e.g., Simonton, 1985a, 1997a, 1999d, 2003b, 2008b). I converted from a peripheral Social Relations graduate into a (somewhat) more mainstream cognitive, personality, developmental, and social psychologist.

My transformation notwithstanding, I still believe it imperative to assign a whole chapter to the collective nature of genius. This seems only fair. The previous five chapters all centered on the genius as an isolated person, so a single chapter on the collective nature of genius doesn't come close to giving equal time to it. Surely my old Social Relations professor would insist that the book should begin and end with this single chapter! All the same, I must remind my readers that this book is part of a "Psychology 101" series rather than a "Sociology 101" or "Cultural Anthropology 101" series. I should therefore feel no guilt about having just one chapter on the collective nature of genius.

Anyhow, I'll cover just five topics: cultural stimulation, interactive relationships, collaborative groups, disciplinary zeitgeist, and sociocultural context. I'll close the chapter with a discussion of how the individual and social levels of analysis can be integrated into a unified sociopsychological conception of genius.

CULTURAL STIMULATION

As was observed in chapter 4, Galton's 1869 *Hereditary Genius* took a radical position on the nature–nurture issue. So extreme was Galton's biological determinism that he seriously argued that a genius could be born into the most deprived circumstances imaginable and still rise to prominence. This belief led Galton to found the doctrine of eugenics—literally, "good genes." Individuals with superior natural ability would be encouraged to reproduce, thereby improving the "race" in the same way that a dog breeder improves a variety through selective mating. Whatever the initial merits of this idea, positive eugenics eventually turned into negative eugenics. So-called inferior persons and groups were prevented from reproducing through sterilization and even genocide. In fact, eugenics was used to justify the Nazi ideology that led to the Holocaust during World War II.

Cultural anthropologists, such as Franz Boas and his student Alfred Kroeber, were among the strongest opponents of such views. Individuals were creatures of culture rather than slaves to their genes, and peoples were ethnic groups rather than biological races. Indeed, in 1944, as Hitler's Third Reich was being crushed by the Allies in Europe, Kroeber published a book that explicitly attacked Galton's *Hereditary Genius*. According to Kroeber, geniuses are the products of culture. In the absence of cultural stimulation, there would be no genius, whatever the person's natural ability might be. If Newton had been born in some other time or place, he might not have become Newton, nor even attained greatness in any domain of achievement. Individual geniuses are more properly seen as the outward historical manifestations of deeper changes in the sociocultural system. For this reason, Kroeber titled his book *Configurations of Culture Growth*. When a culture is undergoing a major florescence, then geniuses will emerge as signs that such a growth has taken place. But when a culture succumbs to stagnation and decay, then geniuses will completely disappear.

Kroeber offered more than theoretical speculation. He also collected lots of data to make his case. Curiously, he adopted a research strategy superficially similar to Galton's. Both compiled long lists of historic geniuses representative of diverse achievement domains. Many of the geniuses in Galton's lists are also in Kroeber's lists. Yet on closer examination, the lists are conceived in diametrically opposing ways. Galton put his geniuses in alphabetical order by surname. That's because he wanted to highlight the family relationships indicative of inherited natural ability. In contrast, Kroeber placed his geniuses in chronological order by birth year. That's because he wanted to stress how geniuses cluster over historical time into what he called cultural configurations. Geniuses would not be randomly distributed over history.

If you've had a course in the history of civilization, you should know what Kroeber was talking about. You probably learned about the Golden Age of Greece and perhaps the Silver Age of Rome. And you'll recall the so-called Dark Ages followed by the Italian Renaissance. Corresponding to these period labels are clusters or configurations of geniuses. Thus, the Golden Age of Greece featured such big names as Socrates, Plato, Aristotle, Hippocrates, Herodotus, Thucydides, Demosthenes, Sophocles, Euripedes, Aristophanes, Phidias, and Pericles. So stellar was this collection of first-rate minds within such a short period and such a small geographical area that Galton (1869) proclaimed that the ancient Greeks represented a superior race, a race even superior to that of the British, Galton's very own "race."

For Kroeber (1944), that was the crux of the problem. If the Greeks of the Golden Age had such great genes, what happened to them? Why don't the Greeks today dominate the Nobel Prizes in science and literature? Galton tried to explain the Greeks' decline in terms of reverse eugenics or dysgenics. The pure Greek "race" either failed to breed or else bred with inferior races, such as the neighboring "barbarians." This explanation is simply implausible. It would take many centuries for even the most stringent dysgenic practices to make a substantial impression on a gene pool. Maybe after a few centuries, the Greeks would only be as smart as the British! Furthermore, how did the Greeks become a superior race in the first place? Centuries prior to the Golden Age, their culture was inferior to those of Persia, Mesopotamia, and Egypt. Unless they practiced some pretty draconian eugenics—for which we have absolutely no evidence—it's hard to believe that they could acquire such good genes so quickly. Besides, if the Greeks were so brilliant, you'd think they would've figured out a method to maintain their racial supremacy!

Kroeber's alternative explanation was that each generation of geniuses depends on the previous generation of geniuses. The ideas or products of one generation stimulate the development of the next generation. This process is most patent in teacher–pupil or master–apprentice relationships. Socrates taught Plato, who in turn taught Aristotle. Each extended, modified, or contradicted the philosophy of his predecessor. Still, cultural stimulation does not have to entail direct transmission. In youth, a future genius can be exposed to ideas in a more indirect manner—by reading books, by attending concerts, or by visiting galleries or museums. Just growing up in an era replete with first-rate minds has to intensify intellectual growth. The intergenerational influence of mentors and role models is then responsible for the clustering of geniuses into cultural configurations.

Unlike Galton, Kroeber did not subject his lengthy lists to statistical analyses. So it's hard to know whether Kroeber's interpretation can account for the configurations. However, part of my 1974 doctoral dissertation was dedicated to conducting just such a quantitative examination (Simonton, 1974, 1975b). I started by expanding Kroeber's (1944) lists for Western civilization into a chronology of over 5,000 creative geniuses who made a name for themselves from the time of ancient Greece to the 19th century. I then sliced up this historical period into 127 consecutive 20-year periods or generations. Each creative genius was then assigned to that generation in which he or she reached (or would have reached) his or her 40th birthday. Using a technique known as generational time-series analysis, I then gauged whether the

140

number of geniuses in generation g was a positive function of the number of geniuses in generation g-1, that is, the previous generation.

The answer for every major domain of creativity was a resounding "yes!" The more eminent creators in generation g-1, the more would be expected in generation g. The only major qualification was that sometimes generation g-2 would have a positive effect as well. At times, genius was the upshot of the grandparental generation, not just the parental generation. Aristotle's genius could be enhanced by Socrates as well as Plato. Whatever the details, geniuses do not come out of nowhere. If generation g-1 had no geniuses whatsoever, it was extremely improbable that generation g would have any. The time-series analysis also indicated that intergenerational stimulation could fully account for the manner in which genius clustered across time. In particular, once this role-modeling/mentoring effect was removed, the distribution across time became random (Simonton, 1975b). Finally, the same results were found for other forms of genius besides creative genius, such as political, military, and religious genius, and for cultures outside the West, including the Chinese and Japanese civilizations (Simonton, 1988b, 1992a, 1997b). In all likelihood, this generation-to-generation influence characterizes geniuses throughout world history. Genius seldom emerges out of nothing.

Newton himself admitted, "If I have seen further, it is by standing on the shoulders of giants" (*Who Said What When*, 1991, p. 129). He was acknowledging that he appeared in the Golden Age of European science, at the peak of the scientific revolution. If he had been born a few generations earlier, he wouldn't have become Sir Isaac Newton.

INTERACTIVE RELATIONSHIPS

The English poet Wordsworth once wrote that Newton was "a mind for ever / Voyaging through strange seas of thought, alone" (qtd. in Jeans, 1942, p. 711). Does this mean that when Newton stood on the shoulders of giants, he was the only person standing there? That doesn't seem probable. After all, the role models and mentors to which he was exposed in the previous one or two generations would also exert some influence on his contemporaries. Maybe Newton was standing in the spot that had the best view, but surely the giants' shoulders were broad enough to hold some colleagues and competitors. What's more, it's inconceivable that Newton did not benefit from the presence of these colleagues and competitors. It's to them that he would point out the sights, and—who knows?—from time to time, one of his fellow spectators might point out something to Newton that he might otherwise have overlooked. So his creative genius might have been enhanced precisely because he was not standing alone and lonely at the top.

This inference has been confirmed empirically (Simonton, 1992c). A study examined the interpersonal interactions that 2,026 scientists had with their fellow scientists. The more eminent the scientist, the larger number of interactive links he or she had with other eminent scientists. Because Newton was one of the scientists in the sample, and because he was the most eminent of them all, his own career provides an excellent example. All told, he accumulated more than two dozen professional contacts over his lifetime. These included controversies, rivalries, and competitions with five contemporaries, more intimate relationships with seven, and contacts with a mishmash of 21 colleagues, correspondents, and associates. These interactions involved such notables as Jean Bernoulli, James Bradley, Abraham DeMoive, John Flamstead, Edmund Halley, Robert Hooke, Gottfried Wilhelm Leibnitz, John Locke, Colin McLaurin, Ole Christensen Römer, John Wallis, and Sir Christopher Wren. Beyond all these, Newton had 20 other relationships with scientists who did not attain the highest degree of eminence—those hanging on for dear life by a giant's belt buckle.

Another historiometric investigation proved that the same pattern holds for artistic genius as well (Simonton, 1984a). More specifically, the study concentrated on 772 painters and sculptors of Western civilization. Although all of these visual artists had attained some degree of fame, they still varied immensely in ultimate acclaim. The most eminent was the divine Michelangelo, whereas the least eminent was...was...just a second, it's on the tip of my tongue—yes, got it! Hendrik Bloemaert. Have you ever heard of him? You're lying if you say you have! In any event, the more eminent the artist, the greater the number of collaborators, associates, friends, rivals, and copupils (those who had studied under the same master). For an illustration, just think of the Italian Renaissance: Italy was a relatively small peninsula in southern Europe swarming with painters, sculptors, and architects great and small, with Leonardo, Michelangelo, and Raphael defining the three alpine peaks of the era. Michelangelo may have worked alone on the Sistine Chapel ceiling, but he was by no means isolated from his fellow artists.

I'd like to return to a point made in chapter 4: the highly skewed distribution of output that permits an elite few to dominate any given domain of eminence. There's a well-established principle known as the Price Law that underlines the magnitude of this elitism (Price, 1963). The law says that if k represents the total number of contributors to a domain, then $\sqrt{k}$ indicates the size of that subset that can be credited with half of the contributions. I can give an example from classical music. The compositions that define the repertoire were created by a total of about 250 composers (Moles, 1958/1968). The square root of this number is 15.8. Because we can't expect four-fifths of a composer to do much, we'll round this figure off to 16. Well, it just so happens that this is the exact number of composers who have produced half of the works heard in the repertoire. Three composers alone—Bach, Mozart, and Beethoven—account for almost 18%!

Why is the Price Law relevant to the current question? The law holds not only across historical time but also for any given generation of geniuses. Given that fact, do the math. If $k = 10$, how many geniuses produce half the work? Then if $k = 100$, and if $k = 10,000$? Notice any pattern? If not, divide the square root of k by k. Now what do you discover? You should've found the proportions .32, .10, and .01—or 32%, 10%, and 1%. Now it should be obvious to everyone. The distribution becomes more and more elitist as you increase the number of contributors to a domain. The bigger the field, the smaller the proportion of people in that field who generate half the contributions. How can that be, unless it is the presence of the lesser contributors that enhances the output of the major contributors? This enhancement may result from any of the interpersonal interactions mentioned earlier. But at the lowest possible level, the big guys and gals need the little guys and gals as an audience. The poet W. H. Auden (1948) echoes this point:

> The ideal audience the poet imagines consists of the beautiful who go to bed with him, the powerful who invite him to dinner and tell him secrets of state, and his fellow-poets. The actual audience he gets consists of myopic schoolteachers, pimply young men who eat in cafeterias, and his fellow-poets. This means that, in fact, he writes for his fellow-poets. (p. 176)

If you were a poet, do you think you'd write more poetry if you had more fellow poets to appreciate your genius? And if there were no appreciators out there, would you write less? Be honest. Amateurs may say that they do it just for their personal enjoyment, but I bet they don't spend hour upon hour doing so. And over time they would hang up their pens—or devote their keyboard to more appreciated endeavors.

COLLABORATIVE GROUPS

When delineating the various contemporary relationships that can augment genius, I included collaborative interactions. Several psychologists have stressed the importance of collaborations in outstanding creativity (e.g., Sawyer, 2007). Such collaborations are markedly conspicuous in the sciences, where many first-rate discoveries spring from large research laboratories rather than from solitary geniuses (Dunbar, 1995). In some fields, such as high-energy physics and biomedical research, the list of collaborators may take up practically the whole title page! Nevertheless, collaboration can also take place in the arts, albeit more rarely. A striking example in the history of painting occurred when the Spaniard Pablo Picasso teamed up with the Frenchman Georges Braque in the creation of analytical cubism.

Admittedly, painting is not intrinsically a collaborative art form. The Picasso–Braque collaboration lasted only a few years. And even the two artists' cubist paintings at the time were separate creations, even if each was looking over the other's shoulder. Even so, other forms of artistic expression are inherently collaborative. A most familiar case is the narrative feature film. If you're one of those moviegoers who stick around for the credits, you've got a good feel for how many different people are engaged in making a motion picture. I recently watched one of those Harry Potter films and thought the credits would never end!

Naturally, not all of these contributions are of equal merit or impact. In the 2005 *Harry Potter and the Goblet of Fire*, I'm confident that director Mike Newell contributed more to the final product than did Julie Tottman, the head animal trainer. Even among the high-profile collaborators, some contributions appear to have more force than others. For instance, those who contribute to the dramatic qualities of the film—the screenwriters, directors, actors, and film editors—have 10 times more influence than those who provide the visual qualities—the cinematographers, art directors, costume designers, and makeup artists (Simonton, 2004e, 2005a). Moreover, the members of the latter group have a bigger part to play than those who do the special effects, whether visual or sound.

Strangely, the score and song composers seem to contribute the least to the collaborative effort (Simonton, 2007a, 2007c). Regretfully, many great films lack high-quality music, and much great film music can be heard in mediocre films! In the former category is the 2004 movie *Sideways*. According to Metacritic.com, film critics gave this movie an average rating of 94 on a 100-point scale. Even so, its score received no major award, and just one major nomination (for the Golden Globe for Best Original Score). In the latter category is the 2005 *Memoirs of a Geisha,* which was rated only at 54. Yet the film's composer, John Williams, received an Oscar nomination for Best Original Score and outright won the Golden Globe for Best Original Score from the Hollywood Foreign Press Association, the Anthony Asquith Award for Film Music from the British Academy of Film and Television Arts, the Critics Choice Award from the Broadcast Film Critics Association, and the Grammy for Best Score Soundtrack Album for Motion Picture, Television, or Other Visual Media.

Some empirical research on collaborative groups has tried to tease out how a group's composition affects the group's achievement (Paulus & Nijstad, 2003). Are there certain combinations of members that are more productive or creative than other combinations? Although these studies have still a long way to go before we can say anything conclusive, it's clear that some tentative conclusions can be put forward. Probably the single most critical one is that heterogeneous membership is superior to homogeneous membership (Page, 2007; Sawyer, 2007; Simonton, 2004c). The creativity of the group is improved when the members are exposed to a diversity of perspectives (Nemeth & Kwan, 1985, 1987; Nemeth & Wachtler, 1983). In particular, group members who are exposed to behavioral or ideological dissent have a higher likelihood of discovering problem solutions that are both novel and effective (see also Nemeth, Personnaz, Personnaz, & Goncalo, 2004).

Although the conclusions at the end of the last paragraph were based on laboratory experiments, very similar conclusions emerged from a systematic study of 1,222 teams engaged in actual scientific research (Andrews, 1979). Group creativity was gauged by both subjectively rated effectiveness and objectively measured productive output. Both of these creativity criteria correlated positively with indicators of heterogeneous group membership, where the latter was assessed in terms of each member's scientific discipline, specialty area, professional role, source of funding, and research projects. A more recent inquiry into the creativity of biomedical research concluded that "members of a research group should have different but overlapping research backgrounds" (Dunbar, 1995, p. 391), a conclusion that again pinpoints the genuine advantages of group heterogeneity. Needless to say, this diversity will only prove useful if the lab encourages the free exchange of expertise among the participants. To be specific, "opportunities should be provided for the members of the research group to interact and discuss their research, by having overlapping research projects and breaking the laboratory into smaller groups working on similar problems" (Dunbar, 1995, p. 392).

Somewhat similar results have been identified in the area of political leadership. Despite the fact that political leaders are often seen as making crucial decisions in isolation—the U.S. president in the Oval Office, with furrowed brow, deciding whether or not to drop the bomb—the truth is often quite different. Before any momentous decision is taken, the head of state will usually meet with his or her closest advisors. For example, the president might meet with his cabinet or national security council. Because the leader can take advantage of diverse expertise and points of view, group decision making should be superior to any decision that might be made by any single member of the group. Surprisingly, however, this isn't always the case. Instead, the group may make a decision that's plainly ill advised. This phenomenon has been called *groupthink* (Janis, 1982). A classic instance was President Kennedy's 1961 decision to support the invasion of Cuba's Bay of Pigs by a group of U.S.-trained Cuban exiles. The invasion was doomed to failure from the get-go, and it became a humiliating fiasco—as well as a military and diplomatic triumph for Fidel Castro.

Several investigators have studied the causes of groupthink as well as the means to reduce its occurrence (e.g., Herek, Janis, & Huth, 1987, 1989; Janis, 1982; McCauley, 1989; Tetlock, 1979). Even though the causes of groupthink are numerous, most can be subsumed under a single heading: homogeneity rather than heterogeneity in the decision-making process. Rather than considering a diversity of opposing positions, and seriously considering the pros and cons of each, the group members seem more driven to reach a quick consensus—almost invariably a consensus in support of the leader's explicitly expressed opinion. Any dissent from that opinion is quickly squelched, and group discussion is confined largely to finding justifications, even if they are tenuous, for a preconceived plan of action. The end result is a decision like the one supporting the Bay of Pigs invasion, as well as U.S. nonpreparation for the 1941 Pearl Harbor attack, the 1950 UN invasion of North Korea, the White House cover-up of the 1973 Watergate break-in, and the failed attempt in 1980 to rescue U.S. hostages in Iran (Simonton, 1994). An even more recent example of groupthink, I might add, was President Bush's 2003 decision to invade Iraq.

Happily, Kennedy learned from his stupid mistake in 1961. One year later, when I was a student in junior high school, the president discovered that the Soviet Union had set up missiles in Cuba capable of reaching the United States. I remember that everyone was scared that the crisis would end in total war, so we practiced our "duck and cover" routine in class with more seriousness than ever before. Yet Kennedy had introduced special measures to avoid another instance of groupthink. Advisors were encouraged to express alternative opinions and even to play devil's advocate. Everyone took special care to consider the perspectives of the Soviet Union and Cuba, and by standing in their shoes produce a solution that would be amenable to all parties to the conflict. Because Kennedy's final decision was not contaminated by groupthink, no thermonuclear war broke out, and I lived to write this book for your reading pleasure and edification!

DISCIPLINARY ZEITGEIST

May I return to the story told at this chapter's beginning? The nonpsychologist Social Relations professor with whom I spoke cited a specific phenomenon as concrete proof that psychology was irrelevant to the understanding of genius. That phenomenon was multiple discovery or invention. This is the case in which two or more scientists or inventors arrive at the same brilliant idea in complete ignorance of the others' contributions (Lamb & Easton, 1984).

For example, it's 1858, and Charles Darwin has been working for over a dozen years on what will become his greatest masterpiece. But from thousands of miles away, a manuscript arrives unexpectedly from a younger colleague named Alfred Wallace. Darwin soon recognizes that Wallace's paper contains the gist of his very own theory of evolution by natural selection. Darwin's own stroke of genius was seemingly preempted! Fortunately, Darwin's scientific friends arranged for Wallace's essay to be read at a professional meeting along with some of Darwin's private letters and drafts—plus a promise was given that a book-length treatment would be forthcoming shortly. Darwin then worked feverishly like a student writing a term paper in the final hours before the due date. The result was the 1859 *Origin of Species*— one of the truly exemplary works in the history of science. Yet by Darwin's own admission, every essential idea in *Origin* can be found in Wallace's much briefer manuscript.

Did you take calculus in high school or college? Do you know who first invented it? Perhaps you heard that it was Newton or perhaps Leibnitz. It was actually both, working independently of each other—although Newton later accused Leibnitz of plagiarizing his ideas. When you walk into many big university lecture halls, you're likely to see a huge, colorful representation of the periodic table of the elements, an organizational scheme attributed not just to Dmitri Mendeleev but also to Alexandre-Emile Béguyer de Chancourtois, John Newlands, and Lothar Meyer (all just a few years apart). I'm sure you've learned about Gregor Mendel and the laws of genetics. You may also have been told that his work was largely ignored. But did you know that 35 years after Mendel, three different scientists, in three countries, but all in the same year, arrived at the same laws in complete independence of

149

each other—and in utter ignorance of the fact that those laws had already been discovered? These events are all the more remarkable when they are not just independent but also practically simultaneous. Alexander Graham Bell and Elisha Gray showed up at the patent office on the same day with their respective designs for the telephone. But because Bell got there first, he won the sole rights to the invention. That's why there was a Bell Telephone Company rather than a Gray Telephone Company—and how fortunate was that outcome!

Multiples of this type are not at all rare. Many years ago, sociologists and cultural anthropologists collected dozens, even hundreds, of examples (Kroeber, 1917; Merton, 1961; Ogburn & Thomas, 1922). Of course, these same researchers marshaled multiples to support their belief in sociocultural determinism. At a particular instant in the history of science or technology, a specific discovery or invention becomes absolutely inevitable. The idea is "in the air," ripe for the picking. For example, with respect to the rediscovery of Mendel's genetics, Kroeber (1917) said that "it was discovered in 1900 because it could have been discovered only then, and because it infallibly must have been discovered then" (p. 199). All scientific or technological advances are generated by the disciplinary zeitgeist at a particular moment in a discipline's history. In 1900, the discipline of biology was all set for the (re)-discovery of Mendel's laws.

Plus, it doesn't take a genius to harvest the fruit. Quite the reverse; only a mediocre intellect is required. Take the invention of the steamboat. This idea has been credited to John Fitch, Robert Fulton, the Marquis de Jouffroy, James Rumsey, Robert L. Stevens, and William Symington (yes, he's a very, very distant relation of mine). According to one cultural anthropologist, "Is great intelligence required to put one and one—a boat and an engine—together? An ape can do this" (L. White, 1949, p. 212). So these six blokes are no brighter than an ape? If it requires no intelligence, then it demands no genius to become the zeitgeist's beneficiary.

I myself, a psychologist, have compiled the largest collection of multiples ever gathered (Simonton, 1979). Fully 579 alleged cases! Even so, compilation has not converted me to sociocultural determinism. I still believe that discoveries and inventions are the work of genius rather than disciplinary zeitgeist. My reason for this belief is that I have subjected the supposed multiples to detailed scientific scrutiny (Simonton, 1978, 1979, 2004c). Such empirical analyses reveal that things are not what they seem. One problem is that many discoveries and inventions cannot be considered true multiples. In the first place, lots of times the separate claimants did not really work independently of each other. Thus, Fulton, who got the main credit for inventing the first commercially successful steamboat, was aware of the failed attempts of his predecessors. He was even present at the test runs of Symington's ship! Dozens of presumed multiples fail to meet the most basic requirement. Sorry, but no independence, no multiple. However, if genius creates ideas that others imitate—and with any luck improve upon—then the imitation can serve as a sign of the initiator's genius.

Worse yet, many of the claimed multiples do not even involve identical discoveries or inventions (Schmookler, 1966). Newton's calculus was very different from that of Leibnitz, and in fact it was the latter's version that you studied when you first took the course. Darwin and Wallace did not agree on many central aspects of evolutionary theory. For instance, unlike Darwin, Wallace did not think that evolution could explain the emergence of the human brain: Because members of the species *Homo sapiens* were far more intelligent than necessary for survival in nature, humans as brilliant as Darwin could not have evolved. Gray's telephone was not the same as Bell's, and Mendeleev's periodic table was not the same as...I should probably stop here. You'll get worn out with the examples. Suffice it to say that many suggested multiples that pass the independence test fail the identity test (and vice versa). If disciplinary zeitgeist cultivates the fruit that's just waiting for a lucky scientist or inventor, then how does one picker end up with an apple and the other with an orange?

Now for still another problem: the timing of the separate discoveries or inventions. Sometimes the alternative contributions are made simultaneously, and at other times the contributions making up a multiple are separated by many years, even decades, at times centuries (Merton, 1961). In the case of Mendel's laws, why did a whole generation elapse before the monk's findings were rediscovered? If that discovery was absolutely inevitable in 1865, why did the world have to wait until 1900 for the three independent confirmations? The sociocultural determinist cannot argue that Mendel was ahead of his time if ideas are mere products of the times! The longer the amount of time that elapses between the separate contributions, the less deterministic the zeitgeist must be. Perhaps "probabilistic" might be a more accurate term for such temporal slipping and sliding.

But what about simultaneous multiples? Surely that's impressive proof of the zeitgeist's deterministic ways! Is it? Let me ask you this: How many people do you think are currently working on the invention of the wheel? Easy question, no? It's likely that no sane person would try to invent something that has already been invented. So the answer is zero. Nevertheless, it takes time for word to get out about a given discovery or invention. Knowledge dissemination is far from instantaneous. As a consequence, simultaneous multiples should be more common than nonsimultaneous ones, not less. If Gray's work bench included a Bell telephone—or even if he saw the telephone listed among already granted patents—he wouldn't have worked on inventing the telephone himself. As a matter of fact, as knowledge communication has become ever more rapid, with the advent of printing, the telephone, and now the Internet, multiple discoveries and inventions have become ever more simultaneous (Simonton, 2004c). When scientists can post discoveries on the Web within an hour and other scientists can become aware of these discoveries through a Google search later in the day, multiples have to be simultaneous to become multiple at all!

I could give many more facts that defeat the sociocultural determinist interpretation of multiples. I've even developed mathematical models that can predict the key features of multiples without any recourse to disciplinary zeitgeist (Simonton, 2004c).

To offer one example, using what might be called an "it's all pure coincidence" model, you can predict precisely how many scientists or inventors will be involved in a given discovery or invention. But delving into all these niceties would be like beating a dead horse. Sociologists and cultural anthropologists—and my graduate school prof—have clearly inferred way too much from all too little. This is not to say that disciplinary zeitgeist is irrelevant to the emergence of genius. To the contrary, the zeitgeist provides a necessary but not sufficient basis for genius. Geniuses must work with the ideas they receive from their predecessors. So the zeitgeist is defined by the exemplary works of genius. The spirit of the times consists of the giants' shoulders on which others stand. Yet because the zeitgeist must always operate through genius, each genius will leave a distinctive imprint on the product. It is for this reason that multiples are seldom absolutely identical. Each discovery or invention will have something idiosyncratic about it that reflects the unique talents of its discoverer or inventor.

SOCIOCULTURAL CONTEXT

May I talk once more about my doctoral dissertation? Thanks! Earlier I noted that my thesis examined the history of Western civilization by applying generational time-series analysis to 127 consecutive 20-year periods to which I had assigned more than 5,000 eminent creators (Simonton, 1974, 1975b). The data indicated that the number of geniuses in generation g was a positive function of the number of geniuses in generation g-1 (and for some domains, geniuses in generation g-2 would also exert some influence). This finding was used to show how the clustering of genius into cultural configurations could be explained according to the availability of domain-specific role models and mentors in the preceding generation(s). Nonetheless, this effect cannot be the whole story. Sometimes the number of geniuses in a given generation is higher or lower than expected. Why? It turns out that the genesis of genius is the upshot of many divergent factors, not just one. On some occasions, these factors will enhance the appearance of geniuses, and at other times, these factors will hinder the appearance of geniuses.

Hence, in my doctoral thesis I also scrutinized several systemic conditions that might amplify or depress the presence of genius apart from the effects of role models and mentors (Simonton, 1974, 1975b). As one example, I looked at the consequences of political fragmentation—the circumstance in which a civilization area is divided into a large number of sovereign states. The Golden Age of Greece offers a typical illustration. At that time the Greeks were organized into numerous city states or poleis, of which Athens and Sparta were just the most famous. The Italian peninsula during the Renaissance was similarly split up into such states as Venice, Florence, Milan, Ferrara, Pisa, Siena, and Genoa. In contrast, the Roman Empire extended its imperial sway at the expense of neighboring states, eventually engulfing them all. Yet the peak of Roman military and political power was associated with a decline in creative activity. I obtained results in line with these general observations (see also Simonton, 1976b, 2004b). Not only was creative genius more abundant during times of political fragmentation, but also revolts against imperial rule had a positive impact on the emergence of genius (Simonton, 1974, 1975b). Popular revolts and rebellions even revitalized intellectual debate, encouraging the appearance of a diversity of philosophical schools (Simonton, 1976c). Tellingly, these effects tended to be seen after a one-generation delay. The political conditions and events in generation g-1 affect the geniuses in generation g. Because the adults in generation g are youths in generation g-1, the political milieu shapes the development of talent in most domains of creative achievement. Heterogeneous politics stimulates cultural creativity.

I discovered another delayed effect that was pernicious rather than benevolent: political anarchy. Whenever a civilization is plagued by political assassinations, coups d'état, military revolts, palace conspiracies, and capricious executions in generation g-1, then the number of creative geniuses will decline in generation g (Simonton, 1975b; see also Simonton, 1976b). The Roman Empire would sometimes go through periods in which one general would snatch the imperial throne, only to find himself immediately toppled by another usurper. The imperial palace in Rome would at times become a butcher's shop, the emperor's own Praetorian Guard becoming a lethal spear rather than a protective shield. On occasion, the so-called guard would sell the most powerful job in the Western world to the highest bidder. How bad could it get? In June of 68 C.E., the notorious emperor Nero was forced to commit suicide after a military coup. From that date until December of 69, Galba, Otho, Vitellius, and Vespasian succeeded each other in rapid succession, creating the "Year of the Four Emperors." The succession of rulers was determined by military revolts, usurpations, assassinations, and enforced suicides. The generation following these woeful events generated only one first-rate genius, the Stoic philosopher Epictetus, and even he had the advantage of having grown up in Asia Minor, far removed from the anarchy of the imperial capital.

Some of you may be thinking that I must have overlooked an obvious factor: War. Doesn't military conflict impede the manifestation of genius? The highpoint of the Golden Age of Greece is sometimes seen as being framed by the Persian War (546–479 B.C.E.), in which the Greeks emerged victorious, and the Peloponnesian War (431–404 B.C.E.), in which Athens was defeated by Sparta. Even so, according to the generational analysis, the net effect of war was null (Simonton, 1975b; see also C. Murray, 2003). Sometimes genius would appear during times of peace, and at other times genius would appear during wartime. There was just no consistent relationship. Even the Grecian Golden Age, which is sometimes dated between 500 and 300, partly overlapped two major wars. Still, subsequent research has found that war does have an impact, and a negative one, as long as we recognize two qualifications (Fernberger, 1946; Price, 1978; Simonton, 1980b). First, only certain kinds of war exert a noticeable influence. Balance-of-power wars within a civilization area, such as the two world wars in Europe, have a powerful effect, but imperialistic wars in which one civilization imposes its military might over another civilization, such as the European conquests in the New World, Africa, and Asia, have no effect—that is, on creative activity in the *conquering* country. Second, war's effect tends to be very short in duration. During wartime, creative output will be reduced, but it will return to normal very quickly upon the termination of the bloodshed. Because most wars do not last longer than a few years—the Hundred Years War was a series of separate wars, not one century-long continuous military conflict—the consequences are transient. That's one reason why war's repercussions on genius could not be detected using big 20-year periods.

Those of my readers who know a little history may object: Doesn't war often kindle creativity rather than deter it? What about the atomic bomb, radar, the jet, and other technological triumphs of World War II? Granted, these are bona fide counterexamples. Yet these exceptions prove the rule. During times of war, when whole nations feel that their very existence is at stake, creativity tends to become channeled into those narrow domains of achievement that are most likely to contribute to victory. The resources diverted into developing the atomic bomb could have supported a wide range of creative projects, but instead, the cash and personnel were expended on a single feat in military technology. Accordingly, the overall outcome is destructive rather than constructive.

To return to the main issue, we know have a sound basis for understanding why genius ebbs and flows during the course of a civilization's history. Genius is heavily contingent on the availability of predecessor geniuses who can serve as role models and mentors. This cross-generational influence is then amplified or dampened by other factors, such as political fragmentation, civil disturbances, and political anarchy. Certainly other positive and negative factors must participate as well: economic prosperity, population growth, prevailing ideologies, and political freedoms are only a few of the many possibilities (e.g., Kavolis, 1964, 1966;

Kuo, 1986, 1988; C. Murray, 2003; Simon & Sullivan, 1989). However, another question may have popped into your heads: If genius cannot come from nothing, then where does the first genius come from? Kroeber (1944) dealt with this issue by pointing to the fact that most civilizations are connected with previous civilizations. Consequently, when a civilization first begins, it can "borrow" its genius-grade exemplars from an older civilization. Hence, Greek civilization did not emerge out of nothing like Minerva from the head of Zeus, but instead built upon the achievements of the ancient Babylonian, Persian, Egyptian, and Minoan civilizations. Likewise, Roman civilization followed upon the heels of the Etruscan and, especially, Greek civilizations.

Furthermore, sometimes a civilization can be revitalized when it opens itself up to new influences from other civilizations. This process of intercivilization inspiration is amply demonstrated in the history of Japan. Living in an island nation, the Japanese have varied greatly in their attitudes toward cultural influences from beyond their shores. Sometimes they would open the floodgates to the external world, as they did to China during the Asuka period or to the West after the Meiji Restoration. At other times they would close their doors and discourage the importation of alien ideas, even on pain of death—as was the case during much of the Tokugawa Shogunate. Generational time-series analysis revealed that periods of openness to foreign influence in Japanese history were usually followed by a surge in high-caliber genius in most major areas of creative achievement (Simonton, 1997b). In contrast, long-term and total isolation eventually resulted in creative stagnation or decadence. Alien influences might take several forms, including famous foreign immigrants, eminent Japanese who had traveled abroad, or Japanese geniuses who had non-Japanese geniuses as role models or mentors. Significantly, it took about two generations for Japan to profit from these influences. Creative resurgence in generation g was usually a positive function of foreign influences in generation g-2. The impact had first to be assimilated by an intervening generation of Japanese before the effect could materialize.

Although such intercivilization borrowings help solve the problem of the first genius for more recent civilizations, we still must wonder about the source of the first genius in the originating civilizations. As a case in point, ancient Egyptian civilization emerged from the arid lands of the Nile valley sans predecessor. How did it start? Was the first genius of Egypt some anonymous villager with a special gift for stone carving? Or with a unique talent for storytelling? Or with an innate capacity to recruit fellow villagers to collaborate in ambitious construction projects? Is this the one clear case in which genius was born and not made? Unless someone comes up with a time machine, we'll never really know. Here's another profound question for your next discussion period!

INDIVIDUAL AND SOCIETY

So ends this whirlwind tour of how cultural stimulation, interactive relationships, collaborative groups, disciplinary zeitgeist, and sociocultural context all contribute to the appearance of genius. To offer a retrospective view of the highlights: (a) because geniuses build upon the exemplary achievements of previous geniuses, genius seldom if ever emerges out of a complete cultural vacuum; (b) geniuses can only realize their full potential if they are active in a time that's replete with high-grade geniuses in the same achievement domain; (c) for some domains at least, such as cinema and science, genius must operate within collaborative groups, groups that should have a heterogeneous membership for the group's accomplishments to be maximized; (d) although the occurrence of multiple discovery and invention has often been cited as evidence for sociocultural determinism, a thorough analysis reveals merely that disciplinary zeitgeist is a necessary but not sufficient basis for acts of genius; and (e) certain sociocultural conditions, such as specific political events and the civilization's openness to outside cultural influences, will either augment or diminish the expected number of geniuses in a given generation.

These findings are very important. They certainly deserved a whole chapter. Despite the inherent value of these findings, however, this chapter will not by any means be the longest chapter in this book. That's because, when all is said and done, genius remains a more individualistic than collectivistic phenomenon. To appreciate why, just weigh the following three considerations.

First, two individuals can be born in the same place and time but still display vastly differing degrees of genius. Einstein was not the only person born in Germany in 1879, nor was he even the only individual with any scientific talent born on March 14 of that year. Have you heard of the *birthday paradox?* According to this, if you randomly sample 23 or more people, then the chance that two have the same birthday will be 50–50 or better. If you sample 57 or more persons, the probability exceeds 99%. Hence, the chances are very large that many of Einstein's school classmates had the same birthday as he—without coming close to matching Einstein's genius. Zeitgeist might explain why Einstein was born in Germany rather than in, say, the United States, but not why of all of his German contemporaries he alone was selected as the illustration for this paragraph.

Second, contemporaries and compatriots may display equal magnitudes of genius and yet exhibit that genius in contrasting domains of achievement. Otto Hahn was born less than a week before Einstein, and in a German city only about 180 miles away from where Einstein was born. But Hahn became a physical chemist while Einstein became a theoretical physicist. In contrast, Einstein's major rivals in his specialty area of theoretical physics were born at different times and places. Thus, Niels Bohr was born in Denmark in 1885 and Henri Poincaré was born in France in 1852. Clearly, time and place of birth have very little to say about the domain in which a genius makes his or her mark.

Third, the level and type of genius is determined by numerous variables that are inherent in the individual human being.

In earlier chapters I noted (and I will note again in chapter 7) that various developmental events and dispositional traits tend to separate scientific geniuses from artistic geniuses, and that a diversity of events and traits also influences the degree of impact a genius has on his or her chosen domain. These individual-difference factors contribute to our understanding of why persons born in the same historical period and geographical region may nonetheless differ in their ultimate accomplishments. One may become a scientist, another an artist. Or both may become scientists, but one may win a Nobel Prize in physics, as Einstein did, while the other might never rise above total obscurity.

If that anonymous professor from my Harvard grad school days is now reading these words, I hope he now understands why I did not defect to sociology or cultural anthropology. If you really want to study genius-caliber creativity—or leadership or talent or whatever you like—you've got to start with psychology. Without a doubt, the psychology of genius is where it all began, and the psychology of genius is where it will all end.

Where Will Genius Science Go?

id the previous chapters tell you everything you wanted to know about genius? If you're an inquisitive person, and have an inherent fascination with the topic, your answer is probably "No! What about [fill in the blank here]?!" As a matter of fact, it's my personal experience that people have many more questions about genius than we have so far addressed. In the first place, students who take my upper-division course, Genius, Creativity, and Leadership, often raise some really weighty issues. Indeed, sometimes a student will ask a question that makes a direct contribution to my program of scientific research (a nice example of how teaching contributes to research as well as research contributing to teaching). For example, in the late 1990s, I was asked whether psychologists had studied creative genius in cinema. At the time I realized this was a subject that had attracted very little attention. So I launched my own series of investigations into cinematic creativity and aesthetics (e.g., Simonton, 2002a, 2005c; see also Zickar & Slaughter, 1999).

Provocative queries come from other sources as well. Whenever I give a talk on my research at a scientific conference, or at a research university or other organization, someone in the audience will present a challenge during the Q&A period. For instance, I began a series of studies on achievement in underrepresented groups precisely because of repeated inquiries about whether female genius was the same as male genius, or whether genius in minority subcultures was the same as genius in the majority subculture (Simonton, 1992a, 1996, 1998a, 2004a, 2008a).

Probably, however, the most challenging inquiries come from journalists and broadcasters. One consequence of becoming an acknowledged expert in the study of genius is that I find myself investigating a subject of very widespread interest in popular culture. Most people would never think of reading 1905 articles entitled "On the Motion Required by the Molecular Kinetic Theory of Heat of Small Particles Suspended in a Stationary Liquid," "On the Electrodynamics of Moving Bodies," "On a Heuristic Viewpoint Concerning the Production and Transformation of Light," or "Does the Inertia of a Body Depend Upon Its Energy Content?" But those same people become enthralled by the genius who wrote those papers, a certain Albert Einstein (the last of these four papers, by the way contains the original version of the celebrated $E = mc^2$).

It's not surprising, therefore, that I'm often interviewed for television and radio programs, from the local Sacramento CBS affiliate KOVR to the more global PBS, NPR, CNN, NBC, BBC, A&E, and ABC, for newspapers from *The Davis Enterprise* (my local paper) and *The California Aggie* (the student publication on my campus) to *USA Today, The New York Times, The Washington Post*, and *The San Francisco Chronicle*, and for magazines from the more specialized *Elle* and *Men's Health* to the more widely circulated *Newsweek, Time, US News and World Report, The New Yorker*, and *The Economist*. Many who will never leave a mark in the history books are nonetheless curious about those who do. Maybe they just want to find an explanation or an excuse for why they themselves haven't lived up to their earlier expectations. Or it's a modern form of hero worship.

At times, interviewers for the mass media have done their homework, perhaps even skimming through one of my books. Their questions are then informed and occasionally even inspired. But other times, and maybe most often, I'm expected to address matters that seem more aimed at Nielsen ratings, market share, or circulation statistics. What am I supposed to do with this question: "Do you think that all geniuses are reincarnations of earlier geniuses?" And "Were the Beatles the reincarnation of Beethoven?" Fortunately, this particular interview was not broadcast live, and so my less than amused response ended up on the cutting room floor! And, needless to say, these queries did not stir me to undertake a new line of empirical research (so here there's no parenthetical citation of "Simonton, date, date, date").

Whatever the source of the inquiry, certain core subjects are brought up over and over again. Naturally, many of the central issues raised by questioners have already been discussed in this book. Still, a few remain—questions that also deserve continued attention in future research. Rather than offer you a chaotic list of miscellaneous topics, I've decided to mention just one major topic in each of four subdisciplines of psychology: cognitive, developmental, differential, and social. I want to show that psychologists need a four-pronged attack on the phenomenon known as genius.

COGNITIVE PSYCHOLOGY: BRAIN AND MIND?

Now, Einstein's brain—I've been asked about this curious story in far too many interviews. After the death of this genius in 1955, his brain was removed, photographed from many angles, cut into more than two hundred chunks, and preserved for the benefit of scientific research. This was not the first time that a genius's central nervous system had been so abused in the name of science. A similar fate befell the brains of the eminent mathematician Carl Friedrich Gauss and the Bolshevik revolutionary Vladimir Lenin. Even so, because Einstein's brain was more recently obtained, and belonged to perhaps the most monumental mind of the 20th century, it seems to enjoy the most allure. Although Einstein's brain appears to be of average size, certain investigators claim that they can identify something distinct about its anatomy (e.g., a truncated lateral sulcus) or histology (e.g., a higher ratio of glial cells to neurons in the left inferior parietal area).

If you're aghast at the terms just tossed at you in parentheses, don't worry. I will not dignify this work with additional discussion of them. Without adequate comparison groups, these and other findings remain speculative in the extreme. Einstein's brain should not be compared with those of the average Joe or Jane on the street, but rather with those of the theoretical physicists of his day who failed to have the impact that he did. And those brains have not survived. So at present we cannot say anything whatsoever about Einstein's brain except that it looks pretty ordinary both to the naked eye and under a microscope.

Have you learned of the discipline of phrenology? This is the pseudoscience of inferring an individual's intellectual and personality traits from the bumps and indentations in the skull. The supposition is that these prominences and depressions reflect correspondingly strong and weak spots in the brain, and hence the strengths and weaknesses of the mind. Although phrenology has now been completely discredited, it has been resurrected to some extent in modern doctrines of the localization of function in the brain. As you can learn in any introductory psychology course, different regions of the cortex have identifiable intellectual responsibilities. Thus, if you have major damage to a region known as Broca's area, you may not be able to speak—except for a few emotionally charged swearwords. Nonetheless, there's no dependable reason to believe that the amount of cortical tissue in this area is related to linguistic intelligence or competence.

Great orators like Demosthenes, Cicero, Abraham Lincoln, Winston Churchill, Adolf Hitler, Charles de Gaulle, Jawaharlal Nehru, Fidel Castro, Martin Luther King, Jr., and so on and so forth, would not necessarily have more neurons in Broca's area than someone far less articulate or persuasive. It's not quantity but quality that matters.

But what exactly do we mean by "quality"? Do we mean that the cortex is organized differently in geniuses? That the neurons are more richly interconnected? That various neurotransmitters have distinct concentrations or distributions? Your guess is as good as mine! At present, we still know very little about the relationship between brain and mind in ordinary people, and even less about the relationship between brain and mind in first-rate geniuses. Of course, this proclamation of psychology's ignorance may merely represent the admission of one psychologist's ignorance, namely, mine. I am not a cognitive neuroscientist, and accordingly I'm not necessarily in the best position to judge the contributions of cognitive neuroscience to our understanding of the genius's brain. Nevertheless, I am frequently asked to review submitted articles and to write book reviews on this subject (see, e.g., Simonton, 2006a, 2006b). And, to speak plainly, so far I'm not impressed.

The typical logic in this area runs like this: (a) cognitive studies show that geniuses use mental process Y; (b) neuroscience investigations indicate that process Y has correlate X in the brain (e.g., increased activation in a specific cortical region); ergo, (c) neuroscientific correlate X explains the occurrence of genius via the process Y. This logic may seem impeccable until we subject the chain of reasoning to intense scrutiny. To give an example, if I told you that geniuses depend on the capacity to generate associations among ideas, and then described the neurological processes by which people tend to associate concepts, would you then conclude that the latter explains the former? Of course not! Lots of people out there—practically all of them—have the ability to associate ideas without being able to count themselves as geniuses.

Consider our universally favorite genius, Albert Einstein. In many ways, his mind was the same as yours and mine. He could see, hear, taste, smell, and touch. He could form memories and retrieve them. He could freely associate one thing with another. He could draw inferences and offer conjectures, just like we all do. And no doubt his brain did all these things in the same way that you and I do. Yet he, unlike everybody else with the same neurological features, came up with $E = mc^2$. In a nutshell, certain cognitive processes are necessary for genius, but they are not sufficient. Hence, the neurological underpinnings of these processes are necessary but not sufficient for the appearance of genius.

I do not want to say that the situation is hopeless. The cognitive neurosciences have made major advances using a diversity of techniques, from evoked potentials to fMRI (functional magnetic resonance imaging). Moreover, such methods have shed some light on many processes connected with genius, such as problem solving and insight (e.g., Bowden, Jung-Beeman, Fleck, & Kounios, 2005; Kounios et al., 2006). But until we get a bona fide genius to come up with an original and exemplary product while confined in an MRI scanner, all this effort is still going to entail excessive amounts of speculation and extrapolation.

Just a little over a year before I wrote the above paragraph, a well-known TV personality—I'll say no more about the person's identity—invited me to present to his audiences what we now know about the neurology of genius. This celebrity particularly wanted me to show how genius can be detected using a brain imaging machine. He would endure the test along with me, and he hoped to find a Nobel laureate or other luminary to submit to the test as well. I thought this suggestion laughable. Aside from the fact that you seldom find me at UCD's Center for Mind and Brain, where the big magnetic machine is located, he was asking the impossible. We do not comprehend well enough how the brain works to specify how it supports a first-rate mind. If we did possess this knowledge, do you think that we would still expect college applicants to take the SAT or require job applicants to endure extensive interviews and assessments? No, we'd just strap everyone into a scanner and on the basis of those results alone separate the wheat from the chaff, the winners from the losers. This magic power is just not going to come into being anytime soon. Yet I have a secret hope that someone out there will prove me wrong while I'm still around to care! All I ask is that some neuroscientist pinpoint some cortical region, neurotransmitter, or other brain feature that uniquely identifies genius. No more, no less.

DEVELOPMENTAL PSYCHOLOGY: AGE AND ACHIEVEMENT?

Born shortly after the end of World War II, I belong to that generation known as the baby boomers. Not that this membership makes me special, because by definition ("boom!") there are lots of us. And we're all entering the phase of life when there are more years behind us than ahead of us. Once you have turned 60, as I will have done by the time this book comes out, you wonder if you're over the hill. Is this particular book going to be my last contribution to the field of genius? At what time should I retire rather than embarrass myself in front of red-hot younger colleagues? Furthermore, as we enter the so-called golden years, we often wax retrospective. As I look back on my career, what would I deem my single most important contribution to the scientific study of genius? How many years ago did that work appear? And at what age did I first make a splash as a researcher in this area? When was my first hit?

Because I'm not the only baby boomer, and because many baby boomers have become journalists and broadcasters, I'm often asked about the relationship between age and exceptional achievement. At what age can one expect to first have an impact? When is one's career most likely to peak? And at what age does one begin to run out of steam? The last question is the most poignant. For even the most supreme geniuses must often recognize the day when their genius has been irretrievably lost.

Let's return to Einstein: He launched his career with a bang and ended it with a whimper. At age 26 he published the papers whose titles I listed earlier in this chapter—papers that would eventually help him win a Nobel Prize for physics. About a decade later, in his mid-30s, he made perhaps his greatest single contribution to theoretical physics, namely, the general theory of relativity. It was the dramatic confirmation of that theory in 1919 that made him the legend that he is today. Yet after Einstein received the Nobel two years later, his creative career took a remarkable turn for the worse. He began working on his unified field theory—a vain attempt to integrate all of the known forces of nature. After he generated a series of ever more implausible versions of this theory, his miserable failure became manifest to all. Because in his last two decades Einstein failed to produce exemplary work, his exalted genius seemed to have vanished into thin air. All that remained was a useless originality.

Let's look at this phenomenon in more detail, starting with the facts and then examining the meaning of these facts.

What Are the Facts?

As I noted in chapter 1, the age-achievement relationship is the oldest topic in the scientific study of genius, the first study having appeared in 1835 (Quételet, 1835/1968). Since that time, many others have researched the subject (e.g., Beard, 1874; Dennis, 1966; Lehman, 1953, 1962). It was even the subject of my own very first publication (Simonton, 1975a), and I've continued to publish on this subject ever since, producing a literature review a dozen years later (Simonton, 1988a) and a mathematical model of creative productivity almost a decade after that (Simonton, 1997a). Although most recent research has concentrated on outstanding creativity (Simonton, 1977a, 1977b, 2007a), some investigations have focused on exceptional leadership (Oleszek, 1969; Simonton, 1980a, 1984d; 1998c) and even championship sports (e.g., Schulz & Curnow, 1988) and chess (Elo, 1965; Roring & Charness, 2007).

This large body of research leads to four empirical general-izations that are valid across all major domains of achievement (Lehman, 1953, 1962; Simonton, 1988a).

First, the achievements of genius tend to be an inverted backward-J function of age. A what? An inverted backward-J! That's similar to an inverted-U function like ∩ but with the end point on the right higher than the beginning point on the left. In verbal terms, output, influence, or success first increases fairly rap-idly to a career optimum and thereafter slowly declines. It is rare that one starts with a whimper and ends with a bang. Geniuses seldom quit while they're ahead. Perhaps they're always hoping for one last artistic masterpiece, military conquest, diplomatic tri-umph, or athletic championship. Bobby Fisher, the world chess champion, left professional competition while at the top of his game—indeed, his chess-playing prowess was still growing—but that happened under less than normal circumstances.

Second, the expected shape of this overall career trajectory depends on the domain of achievement. In some domains the peak comes early, whereas in other domains the peak comes much later. In the former category are political revolutionaries, pure mathematicians, poets, and gymnasts; in the latter category are status quo politicians, applied mathematicians, novelists, and golfers. In most domains, the peak is situated somewhere between these extremes—most often in the individual's late 30s or early 40s. I'd rather not mention the peak age for psychologists, because I've already left that period well behind me. Ironically, my best single publication appeared at exactly the age predicted by my best single publication, which provided a mathematical model with which to make this prediction (Simonton, 1997a). Not even Einstein—not being either a photon or a planet—experienced such a self-confirmation of any of his theories!

Third, corresponding to the trajectory described are three career landmarks: the first great achievement, the best single achievement, and the last great achievement. Typically, the sec-ond landmark comes somewhere between the first and last, but usually somewhat closer to the first. The precise location of these landmarks again depends on the domain of achievement. In most creative domains, it's common for the first landmark to appear in the late 20s, the middle landmark in the late 30s or early 40s—about the same time as productive output maximizes—and the last landmark in the middle 50s. For most leadership domains, these three landmarks shift to about a decade later. Among the exceptions in terms of leaders are the founders of major religious faiths—such as Buddha, Jesus, and Mohammed. They are almost invariably 40 or younger when they assume their mission.

Fourth and last, for most domains of achievement, the greatest geniuses are distinguished by the longest careers. They start producing exemplary work at a young age and continue to do so until their final days. Consequently, the first career landmark may appear in the early 20s or even late teens, while the last career landmark will appear in the late 60s or even 70s. If genius is manifested by its works, then the big-name geniuses display genius for the longest portion of their lives. Hence, Pablo Picasso, whose status in the 20th-century art world is certainly comparable to Einstein's in the world of science, began his professional career as a painter in his teens, produced the first masterpieces of his Blue Period in his early 20s, probably created his last masterpiece in his late 80s, and was working into his early 90s, in the last year of his life. He was like the Eveready Energizer Bunny® in the TV commercial who just keeps on going, and going, and going.

As you would expect, there are exceptions to almost any rule. Death can sometimes put an inconvenient end to a promising career. Where would classical music be if Mozart had not died in his mid-30s? If Beethoven had died at the same age, his name might barely be known today. Even if death does not intervene, other inconveniences will get in the way. What a bummer! Napoleon loses at Waterloo and has to spend his closing years imprisoned on an island in the middle of nowhere! Sans armies crammed with cannon fodder, his career could contain no more momentous victories or defeats.

What Does This All Mean?

The empirical data on the age-achievement connection are well established. The initial findings of Quételet in 1835 have been replicated and extended over and over again. Despite various debates about methodological artifacts and other problems, it's highly doubtful that the generalizations offered in the previous section are going to change in any substantial manner. Yet what's more problematic is the interpretation of these findings. What factors underlie the career trajectories? Alas! There are too many! And very possibly it's unlikely that we'll find a single explanation that accounts for all forms of genius across the life span. In general, the factors underlying career trajectories can be grouped into the biological, the sociological, and, last but not least, the psychological, dwelling somewhere between the two extremes.

Biological Factors. Undoubtedly the relationship between age and achievement is partly rooted in basic human physiology and neurology. This connection is most obvious in the case of athletic champions: The more a sport depends on speed, strength, or endurance rather than experience or skill, the more youth tends to prevail over maturity. Age is often quite unkind to any domain of achievement that requires a quick reaction time. For this reason, performance in standard competitive chess peaks earlier than correspondence chess, in which slower intellectual reflexes are less costly. Needless to say, some infirmities of age have more palpable detrimental effects. Blindness, deafness, diabetes, arthritis, dementia, and so on. Those of us who are baby boomers—and who thus have parents in their 70s and 80s—are well aware of the range of possibilities. Unsurprisingly, these diverse disabilities cannot help but impede a person's capacity to display the full magnitude of his or her genius.

At first blush, biology's blow to the aging genius seems inexorable. Yet on closer examination, its explanatory utility with respect to the empirical findings leaves much to be desired. One core objection comes from the fact that, for many achievement domains, the trajectory of output and impact is a function of career age rather than chronological age (Simonton, 1991a, 1997a). In other words, it's not how old you are that's important but rather how long you've been active in your chosen domain. As a consequence, late bloomers can reach career peaks at ages when most of their colleagues have already entered the descending portion of the curve. One of my favorite examples is the composer Anton Bruckner. I know what you're going to say next....Anton who? Suffice it to say that (a) he was a great compositional genius of the late 19th century and (b) he illustrates the striking irrelevance of chronological age when discussing the trajectories of creative geniuses. How?

Bruckner was an obscure provincial composer of religious music until an encounter with the operas of Richard Wagner inspired him to become a symphonist working with comparable orchestral resources. His first symphony, an apprentice piece numbered "00," did not appear until he was 39 years old. That's a very, very late start. So his first career landmark—his first unqualified masterpiece—did not emerge until he was 50 years old. At ages 59 and 60, he created two more master symphonies, and he died at age 70, before he could finish the final movement of his last symphony, a work that constitutes his last career landmark. In sum, because Bruckner's career start was delayed by about 20 years, his creative prime occurred at an age when many other composers were far past their prime. This delayed trajectory makes no sense if his genius was constrained by biology. Surely Bruckner was not a better biological specimen of *Homo sapiens* in his 60s than he was in his 40s!

How can this be? By what means can genius maximize while the body imposes ever more obstacles in the path? I'm sure you've heard the expression, "Where there's a will there's a way." And genius does not lack volition. On the contrary, persistence, drive, and determination are among the hallmarks of genius (Cox, 1926; Galton, 1869; Roe, 1953; see also Duckworth, Peterson, Matthews, & Kelly, 2007). Beethoven discovers in his early

30s that he is going deaf, and he is eventually reduced to a world of total silence. He cannot hear that his piano is out of tune, with broken strings no less, but still manages to compose some of his greatest music when he can only experience it in his head, never in his ears. Can you imagine a more discouraging disability for a composer than that?

You want a more recent example? Sometimes journalists ask me: Who's the greatest living genius? What a tough one! Yet I've found an answer that works as a first approximation: Stephen Hawking. He's definitely much better known than Bruckner, and his contributions to theoretical physics, and in particular to quantum gravity and cosmology, are certainly of the highest order. And yet, have you ever seen him verbally communicate? It's an event at the same time excruciating and exhilarating. Here's a phenomenal intellect locked in a body seriously disabled by amyotrophic lateral sclerosis—what we in the United States often call Lou Gehrig's disease. How many biological disadvantages can you list that are worse than this, with the obvious exception of death itself? Genius is more than an Eveready Energizer Bunny®. Whatever the barrier that confronts its path, genius wills a way. Genius conquers all.

Sociological Factors. For the sociologist, the distinction between chronological and career age is old hat. Social customs, norms, and institutions establish certain expectations that are not always dependent on chronological age. Take your own situation as a college student. Traditionally, undergraduate education is defined according to a four-level hierarchy: the lowly freshman (or first year, to use a less sexist term), followed by the sophomore, then the junior, and, finally, the culmination in the senior year. Theoretically, each of these stages takes one year to complete (ignoring the "super-senior" who needs an extra semester or quarter to graduate). For most of you, the first stage was begun at age 18, and the last was (or will be) completed at age 22. Even so, as a college professor I know firsthand that not every undergraduate moves through college at these ages. Most frequently

I've had students who do not start their higher education until several years after high school—once they realize that a college education does yield some real returns. More rarely, particularly precocious students may start university much younger than 18, sometimes even 5 years younger. I mentioned this possibility in chapter 2. In any event, their progression through college is decoupled from the number of candles on their birthday cakes.

It's clear that certain sociological factors must condition the unfolding of a genius's career. This is most apparent in various forms of leadership in which a person must work his or her way up a hierarchy. A military genius must advance up the ranks. Napoleon did not start out as the supreme commander of the French but as a second lieutenant. Likewise for political genius: It's rare for someone to advance to the post of president or prime minister without having first occupied much less powerful and prestigious offices. Thus, just look at those running for the office of president of the United States every four years. With few exceptions, each has served in the U.S. Senate or as a state governor, with earlier and lesser positions often littering their campaign biographies.

The same hierarchical sequence often pervades creative domains as well. This is most evident in the academic world. College students often think of all professors as professors, but we professors know otherwise. In the United States, you must start out as an assistant professor, with the hope of advancement to associate professor in 7 years (or fewer, if you're really good). Then, after some years holding this intermediate title, you try to get promoted to full professor. Many universities even have additional titles after that, such as that of distinguished professor. Below the assistant professors in the U.S. academic hierarchy are the lecturers, the ones that often teach the large-enrollment introductory courses (like Psych 101). Whatever the details, professional hierarchies can be said to set the pace of career development. Moreover, this pacing is carried out in terms of career age, not chronological age. I've had doctoral students almost as old as I am, but when they launch their academic careers they have to start at the bottom just like everybody else. So you can have an assistant professor who is older than a full professor.

It goes without saying that you normally gain in power, prestige, and plain cash as you advance up most professional hierarchies. You thus acquire more opportunities for the realization of your talents. A general or admiral has more latitude than a second lieutenant, a president more than a senator, a full professor more than a lecturer. When I was a young scientist, I would have to convince editors to publish my research in their journals. Now editors invite me to contribute something to their publications! My most recent work is not necessarily better than my earliest work, but the former is certainly more easily published!

Not every sociological effect operates according to career age. Sometimes the effects may focus on chronological age. For instance, some societies may harbor prejudicial stereotypes about old age. "When the age is in the wit is out," says a character in Shakespeare's *Much Ado about Nothing* (3.5.34). Such ageist beliefs can even support various forms of discrimination. When I applied to graduate school in the late 1960s, I was surprised that one program (not Harvard's) explicitly said that its faculty would not even consider applicants over age 40! And many businesses and organizations once had compulsory retirement at a preset age. With retirement often comes the loss of the resources necessary for continued output and impact. It's hard to determine how much of the age decrement (amount of decrease) in achievement that comes with age might be attributed to ageism.

Psychological Factors. I've saved the best for last. It's conceivable that the age-achievement relationship is the result of underlying mental processes. This possibility was actually suggested back in chapter 3, when I introduced the BVSR model of creativity. I cited the derivation of a mathematical model that predicts the level of creative productivity across the course of the career (Simonton, 1984b, 1991a, 1997a, 2004c). Although the model is actually very complex, it can be expressed in simple terms as follows. Each genius is presumed to begin his or her career with an initial amount of *creative potential*. This is the total number of original and useful ideas that the person is capable of generating in an unlimited life span. This potential is then converted to actual products by a two-step cognitive process: the first step is *ideation* and the second is *elaboration*. Ideation generates the "works-in-progress" or raw materials—the kinds of stuff found in a scientist's laboratory notebook or an artist's sketchbook. Elaboration refines and reshapes these ideas into publishable form, whether as a journal article or as a finished painting. The model predicts that output will rise to a peak and thereafter slowly decline. Furthermore, this predicted trajectory is defined by career rather than chronological age. The clock starts when the process of transforming potential to actual creativity begins.

Besides accounting for the overall shape of the creative career, the model also accounts for departures from the general expectation. In the first place, the model makes allowance for the fact that the ideation and elaboration rates depend on the specific domain of creative achievement (Simonton, 1989a, 1991a, 1997a). For example, the rates of ideation and elaboration will tend to be faster for a lyric poet than for a novelist. The faster rates of the former mean that the peak will come earlier in the career and the decline will be more dramatic, just as is empirically observed. Additionally, the model explains individual differences in career trajectories. Most obviously, individuals will differ in the age at which they begin the ideation process—remember the late-blooming Bruckner—and this will push back the expected peak accordingly. But individuals will also differ in their initial amount of creative potential. The higher the potential, the greater is the annual output of ideas. Because the production of great ideas is a positive function of the total ideas produced, this individual difference has a direct consequence for the placement of the first and last career landmarks (Simonton, 1991a, 1997a). Given two creators who start their careers at the same chronological age, the one with the highest potential will make the first major contribution at a younger age and the last major contribution at an older age. Interestingly, the middle career landmark, the best work, is

176

unaffected by differences in initial creative potential. As pointed out, all of these predictions have been confirmed on thousands by studies of creative geniuses.

Although I personally believe that the above model provides the most comprehensive and precise explanation for career trajectories, I'm also very much aware of the model's limitations. I'd like to confess just two here.

One, the model only applies to creative genius. Although it might also work for those domains in which substantial creativity might be required—such as lawmaking—it's only been tested on the careers of outstanding creators.

Two, even within creative domains, the model cannot explain every single feature of the typical career. To offer one interesting case, this psychological model cannot explain the *swan-song phenomenon* (Simonton, 1989c). This occurs in the last year or so of a creator's life, when he or she realizes that the end is near. Realization of the proximity of death can inspire a genius to begin a distinctive resurgence of creativity. Hence, an artist might strive to produce a last testament or career capstone. What's especially noteworthy about this phenomenon is that the creator does not even have to be old. It's the nearness to death rather than the length of life lived that's crucial. Franz Schubert's collection of lieder known as *Schwanengesang* (*Swan Song*) was written in the last year of his life, but he was only 31 years old. Yet he was also a very ill young man, suffering from syphilis and perhaps mercury poisoning. Anyhow, my poor model cannot handle these episodes of creative resuscitation in a genius's final years.

So here's a challenge to future researchers—and to all students reading this book who plan to become scientists studying genius. Can we come up with a theory that can explain career trajectories in all domains of achievement? Can that theory account not just for the overall pattern but also for special quirks, like the swan-song phenomenon? Can the theory successfully integrate psychological factors with biological and social factors? And can the theory prove compatible with other things we know about genius? In short, can we ever get a Grand Theory of Everything?

DIFFERENTIAL PSYCHOLOGY: DISPOSITION AND REPUTATION?

Everybody wants to know what a genius is like. What makes him or her tick? Does he or she have a telltale personality? If you had one as a next-door neighbor, would you be able to tell right away from the first conversation? After all, most geniuses do have neighbors, so do those neighbors figure out at once that there's a new celebrity on the block? Can you tell from people's personalities that they are en route to fame, if they haven't already got there? Do you say, "There's something really special about so-and-so!" This issue is one of the favorites raised by electronic and print journalists. It's also one of my least favorites. The reason is that I'm always forced to give an extremely complex answer to what they see as a very simple question. I become just another pedantic academic failing to confine my response to a 5-second sound bite!

Why is my reply so convoluted? For two reasons: First, the connection between disposition and reputation is fraught with complexities. Second, we still need a great deal more research on this matter. Hence, any answer must be hedged in with qualifications. To appreciate both of these points, allow me to take up just four issues: domain contrasts, effect sizes, curvilinear functions, and situational conditions. And believe me, each of these sections will take longer than 5 seconds to read!

Domain Contrasts: One Size Fits All?

Does genius have a distinguishing personality? Ask me that, and I'll immediately react: What kind of genius are you talking about? At the very minimum, you have to decide whether you mean psychometric or historiometric genius. As noted more than once in previous chapters, a person with a genius-grade IQ is not equivalent to a person with genius-level achievement. Even when we concentrate on the latter, it's necessary to specify the type of genius. Genius in politics or war is not the same as genius in science or art, just as scientific genius is not the same as artistic genius. Even within the artists' group, we must take care to separate the highly formal and restrained artists from the more emotional and expressionistic artists. Worse still, within a highly specific endeavor, the dispositional makeup of the greatest of the greats differs from that of the also-ran geniuses. All Nobel laureates may have some claim to genius, but not all laureates are equal, nor are they all the same. Nils Gustaf Dalén received the Nobel in physics "for his invention of automatic regulators for use in conjunction with gas accumulators for illuminating lighthouses and buoys" (http://nobelprize.org/nobel_prizes/physics/laureates/1912/). How does that compare with $E = mc^2$?

None of this is new. I gave examples in chapter 5. Psychopathology exhibits an extremely intricate relationship with genius. It's much more common in some domains of achievement than in others. For example, mental illness is more common among artists than among scientists, and more common among tyrannical than among legitimate leaders. I also offered instances in chapter 4, when I discussed how certain inheritable traits differentiated artistic from scientific genius. Where the former tended to be more imaginative, impulsive, norm-doubting, nonconforming, independent, aloof, cold, anxious, and emotionally sensitive, the latter tended to be more flexible, dominant, arrogant, self-confident, and autonomous. Finally, back in chapter 3, we debated the possibility that each domain of high accomplishment may be characterized by a specific intelligence or set of intelligences. This prospect was most explicit in Gardner's (1993) linkage of particular types of genius with seven divergent types of cognitive ability.

In time, psychologists should be able to identify the unique profile of each domain of achievement. Researchers may even succeed in specifying the pattern of dispositional traits that separate genius in psychology from genius in kindred sciences (Simonton, 2002b). Ultimately we may be able just to administer a battery of tests to any given individual and on the basis of the results forecast the domain in which he or she is most likely to attain supreme success.

Effect Sizes: Big, Little, or Tiny?

Admittedly, some psychologists would interrupt with a "Why bother?" These researchers believe that individual-difference variables, and particularly variations in personality traits, are irrelevant to our understanding of genius (e.g., Sawyer, 2006; Weisberg, 1992). Geniuses do not differ from the rest of us because they are a special breed of *Homo sapiens*, but rather because they have acquired more domain-specific expertise. Einstein knew more theoretical physics than his contemporaries, just as Picasso mastered more techniques in the visual arts than any of his rivals. Otherwise neither genius departed one iota from any run-of-the-mill scientist or artist.

Why would anyone make what seems on the face of it to be such an outlandish claim? How could someone deny tons of solid empirical data published over several decades? The answer is simple: an unfortunate misunderstanding of a very crucial concept in statistical analysis, namely, *effect size* (Cohen, 1988). This is a measure of the magnitude of the relationship between two or more variables. Although there are several effect size indicators, the one that is most often used in this area of research is the correlation coefficient. You remember! I referred to this statistic in chapter 3. Well, critics argue that the correlates of outstanding creativity or exceptional leadership have small effect sizes, too small to be important. How small is small?

Let me give one example: the correlation between various personality traits and the degree of creativity displayed in scientific domains (Feist, 1998). The correlations for the best predictors are usually in the .20s, and seldom get into the .30s (Simonton, 2008b). These numbers, say the critics, aren't impressive. If the square of the correlation coefficient gives the amount of variance explained by a dispositional variable, then these stats tell us that each trait only accounts for between 5% and 10% of the variation. That means that between 90% and 95% is not accounted for by these factors. In brief, the phenomenon of genius is almost entirely free of dispositional correlates.

Not so fast, buster! These critics totally overlook two considerations.

First, these effect sizes are by no means small. Quite the reverse: They're actually pretty impressive. Too many people think that a correlation must be in the .80s or .90s to earn any respect, but this is far from the truth. Even much smaller correlations can have powerful consequences (Abelson, 1985; Rosenthal, 1990). Don't believe me? Then try out the following multiple choice test (cf. Meyer et al., 2001):

1. The correlation between regular aspirin consumption and reduced risk of death by heart attack is
   (a) .02   (b) .22   (c) .42   (d) .62   (e) .82.
2. The correlation between a professional baseball player's general batting skill and hit success at a single time at bat is
   (a) .06   (b) .16   (c) .36   (d) .56   (e) .76.
3. The correlation between parental divorce and a child's problems with adjustment and well-being is
   (a) .09   (b) .19   (c) .39   (d) .69   (e) .89.
4. The correlation between exposure to media violence and subsequent naturally occurring interpersonal aggression is
   (a) .13   (b) .33   (c) .53   (d) .73   (e) .93.
5. The correlation between employment interview evaluations and actual job success is
   (a) .20   (b) .30   (c) .40   (d) .50   (e) .60.
6. The correlation between taking sleeping pills and short-term improvement in chronic insomnia is
   (a) .30   (b) .50   (c) .70   (d) .90   (e) 1.00.

Before I give you the answers to these six questions, ask yourself these follow-up questions. If you had serious heart problems, what's the minimum size of the correlation that would motivate you to start taking daily doses of aspirin? If you were the manager of a baseball team, how large would the correlation have to be before you'd begin to consider batting average in deciding the lineup? If you were a child psychologist, how big should the correlation be before you'd pay attention to the fact that your client comes from a divorced family? If you were a parent, what would be the minimum correlation inspiring you to monitor the violence appearing in the movies and TV shows that your children watched? If you were the owner of a major firm, how large would the correlation have to be before you'd introduce face-to-face interviews for all job applicants? If you were suffering from chronic insomnia, how sizable would the correlation have to be to send you to the drug store or pharmacy?

Now for the answers: (a) in every case! So don't let me hear you say that the correlations between disposition and reputation are too small to pay any mind to them!

Second, the reported effect sizes for dispositional variables are for individual traits, not for all of the traits put together. The total predictive power of a full set of attributes will be much greater (see, e.g., Feist & Barron, 2003). To be sure, because some personal characteristics overlap to a certain degree, we can't determine the total predictability of genius by simply adding up all of the separate predictions. For example, the fact that openness to experience correlates positively with intelligence does not make these traits independent contributions to genius. So future researchers must take care to examine the total impact of all traits after first removing any redundancies. Be that as it may, because the effect size for the complete spectrum of dispositional traits cannot be smaller than the effect size for the single most predictive trait, the end result will still prove rather impressive. The genius next door is distinguishable from your nongenius neighbors.

Curvilinear Functions: Too Much of a Good Thing?

There's another reason to be optimistic about our eventual ability to predict genius from personal traits. If you took introductory statistics, you may recall that the correlation coefficient is a gauge of the *linear* relationship between two variables. If there's a positive association between A and B, then whenever A goes up, B goes up, and whenever A goes down, B goes down. So if the relationship is actually *curvilinear*, then the correlation will underestimate the effect size. Take the extreme case in which variable *B* is a perfect inverted-U function of *A*. At first, *B* increases as *A* increases, but then the relationship levels off as you approach the peak, and thereafter *B* decreases with additional increases in *A*. Even though the association is hypothesized to be perfect, the correlation coefficient between the two variables will be exactly zero—just as if there were no relationship at all! In this case, the correlation will dramatically underestimate the degree of correspondence. Instead of 1.0 (sublime, superb perfection) we get 0.00 (nothing, nada, niets, Nichts, ничто).

Obviously, the true relationship between the two variables might be described by some compromise between a linear function and a strictly inverted-U function. In fact, I brought up just such an instance in our earlier discussion of the association between age and achievement, an association best described as a curvilinear inverted backward-J function. In such hybrid cases, the correlation will not be exactly zero. But the correlation coefficient will still seriously underrate the closeness of fit between the two variables. Whatever the details, we can never appreciate fully the extent to which posthumous reputation is rooted in personal disposition until some provision is made for curvilinear relationships between the former and the latter.

Go back to our discussion of psychoticism in chapter 5. I said that psychoticism was positively related to genius, but only within reason. Outright madness will not do. Then you have psychosis rather than mere psychoticism. So that implies some kind of inverted backward-J function. Too much psychoticism and you get the downturn, the descent into psychosis. However, I also emphasized that the optimal level of psychoticism depends on the domain of genius involved. For example, the turnaround point will come sooner for scientific genius than for artistic genius. That's because the optimum level of psychoticism is lower for the former than for the latter. As a result, the science curve is closer to an inverted-U, whereas the art curve is closer to an inverted backward-J. So the correlation between psychoticism and greatness will be lower for the sciences than for the arts. And that's actually the case (Feist, 1998; Simonton, 2008b).

There are many other potential examples of this statistical intricacy. To offer another illustration, consider the relationship between psychometric and historiometric genius. We might like to think that these two alternative conceptions of genius are linked by a positive linear relationship—the more intelligence the more impact—but that may not be the case for certain domains of high-level achievement. In particular, in some leadership domains, especially in the political and military spheres, the relationship might be more similar to that seen between age and achievement: yet another inverted backward-J function (Simonton, 1985a; by now I hope you've got an inkling of what it means to take a capital J, turn it upside down, and then transform it into its mirror image, producing something like the Latin lower-case long "s" ʃ; that is so easily confused with the minuscule "f" in older documents in English like the American Declaration of Independence).

One final example of all this functional complexity: The relationship between disposition A and reputation B might assume some other nonlinear function besides those already mentioned. For example, one variable might be a U-shaped function of the other, the middle part of the curve represented by a trough rather than a peak. Or this single-trough curve might be slightly modified to produce a J curve or a backward-J curve. These examples are not hypothetical. Such dips do occur. Way back in chapter 2, I observed that the long-term impact of 342 European absolute monarchs was a curvilinear U-shaped function of their ethical or moral caliber (Simonton, 1984e). The most eminent had to be either very, very good or very, very bad—a famous versus infamous effect. Yet the linear correlation between monarchal impact and morality was almost exactly zilch.

Situational Conditions: How Do the Traits Fit?

In chapter 6, I talked about how certain sociocultural conditions can play a critical part in the development and manifestation of genius. What we need to know is the relative contribution of the individual and situational factors. Is it more a matter of being the right person or of being in the right place at the right time? So far, research has led to a tentative conclusion: For outstanding creativity, dispositional traits appear to be more crucial than general circumstances, whereas the reverse seems to be true for exceptional leadership (Simonton, 1994). In other words, the creative genius is more likely to be the right person, while the political or military genius is more likely to be in the right place at the right time. Sometimes, indeed, leadership seems totally dominated by the larger context.

An illustration from the world of the presidents of the United States is the vice-presidential succession effect (Simonton, 1985b). This occurs when vice presidents assume the presidency upon the death or resignation of their predecessors. The first example was John Tyler, who succeeded William Harrison after the latter's death, and the most recent instance was Gerald Ford, who was sworn in after the resignation of Richard Nixon. Characteristically, such unelected or "accidental" presidents do not perform well as chief executives. They tend to get into major conflicts with Congress, and often end up on the losing side of those conflicts. A psychologist might be inclined to say that vice presidents do not have what it takes to occupy the nation's highest office. Not the right person for the job, to be sure.

Yet the data do not support this explanation. First, these accidental presidents are indistinguishable from regular presidents with respect to the relevant predictors of leader performance. They have had to settle for the second spot on their party's presidential ticket for reasons that have nothing to do with their merit. Second, if these accidental presidents manage to get themselves elected to office in their own right—as did Harry S. Truman—then the decrement in the leader's performance immediately disappears without a trace. The real problem of accidental presidents is that they are put in the awkward position of having to assume the powers of an office without having been elected to that office. Lacking a mandate, they are obliged to operate in a situation that undermines

185

their effectiveness. Members of Congress can easily dismiss the president with the rhetorical question, "Who elected you?" The first accidental president was even derisively called "His Accidency."

Another possibility is even more fascinating: Disposition may interact with external factors to produce what's known as an Individual × Situational interaction effect. Put differently, sometimes it's not the right person that matters, nor is it just the matter of being in the right place at the right time; what counts is being the right person in the right place at the right time. Hence, the very personal qualities that might enhance genius in one situation might hamper genius in a totally different situation. Again, the U.S. presidency offers abundant examples. A chief executive who might do very well in certain circumstances might perform very poorly in others. To be specific, presidents may vary in how flexible or inflexible they are. Flexible presidents are disposed to bargain and negotiate, to strike compromises whenever necessary, and to try out new strategies when old ones fail. Inflexible presidents just charge full speed ahead without budging an inch from their predetermined trajectory. Which type of presidential disposition is best in the chief executive's role as the initiator and shaper of legislation?

The answer is, "It depends" (Simonton, 1987b). If a president enters office with a huge electoral mandate and with his party controlling Congress, inflexibility is superior to flexibility. But if a president just barely squeaks by on election day, and finds that Congress is controlled by the opposing party, then flexibility becomes the order of the day. Alas! Inflexible presidents are so inflexible that they are not flexible enough to become flexible rather than inflexible when flexibility is more likely to succeed than inflexibility. For instance, Woodrow Wilson was highly successful when the Democratic Party controlled Congress, but he failed completely when his party lost control.

I'm sure there are many more Individual × Situational interaction effects just waiting to be discovered. Especially with respect to exceptional leadership, genius requires a perfect match between character and circumstance.

SOCIAL PSYCHOLOGY: GENDER AND ETHNICITY?

I've saved the worst for last. Too often, journalists ask me questions that I won't touch with the proverbial 10-foot pole. It's not just that the questions involve very controversial issues. It's more the fact that I have no confidence whatsoever that my complex, abundantly nuanced, and finely informed answers will ever survive the vicious filter of mass-media oversimplifications. Rather than suffer the frustration of finding myself quoted out of context, I'd rather not be quoted at all. Silence is superior to misleading statements. If you've read the heading at the beginning of this section, you know exactly what I'm talking about. So let me get to the two debates I'd rather not touch upon outside of the ivory-tower world of academic research.

Gender and Genius

By now you already know that I got my doctoral degree from Harvard University. That's something that should be a source of pride. Yet as prestigious as Harvard may be, it can also be something of an embarrassment. For example, when I teach my course in the history of psychology, I am compelled to discuss what happened to Mary Calkins, one of the most outstanding psychologists ever to earn a PhD at Harvard. Well, to be truthful, although she completed all the degree requirements, including a stellar dissertation under the supervision of William James— whose name would later grace the psychology building where I took my graduate courses—she was denied a degree because of her gender. That was in 1895. Between then and her death in 1930, Harvard was repeatedly asked to reconsider its discriminatory decision, and it just as often refused. Between 1895 and 1930, Calkins became one of the top psychologists in the United States. In 1905 she was elected president of the American Psychological Association, and in 1918 she was elected president of the

187

American Philosophical Association (at a time when psychology and philosophy were still closely related). In 1927, just 3 years before her death, Harvard was even confronted with a petition signed by eminent Harvard graduates who felt that the sexist farce could no longer continue. Yet Harvard stuck by its guns, leaving Mary without a PhD to her last breath.

"Okay, okay," you might say—particularly if you're wearing a crimson T-shirt with "HARVARD" emblazoned across the chest—this is past history. Maybe so, but now fast forward through the annals for 110 years until you reach 2005. Early in that year the university's president, Lawrence Summers, suggested that innate differences may partially explain why women are under-represented in certain scientific disciplines. The nature–nurture debate then again raised its ugly head, only this time with a male-versus-female cast. Although the ensuing controversy eventually cost Summers his job, and he found himself replaced by Harvard's first woman president, the fact remains that the chief spokesperson for Harvard had taken a position that many (if not most) psychologists would consider unsupported by the facts.

So now it's time for me to weigh in on this question, at least insofar as it relates to genius. Yet please, I beg of you, do not pass judgment until you have read this entire section. Do not focus your attention narrowly on one sentence without taking into consideration other sentences that qualify or elaborate that sentence's apparent meaning. Agreed? If so, continue. If not, then please proceed to the concluding section of this book, skipping everything else that comes between.

Let us start with four unquestionable facts.

First, if we apply the historiometric definition of genius, the proportion of geniuses who are women is far less than 50%, the approximate baseline expectation. For instance, in Cattell's (1903) list of the 1,000 most eminent individuals of Western history, only 3% were women, and many of these were monarchs who had inherited their position, like Mary Stuart of Scotland, Elizabeth I of England, Catherine the Great of Russia, Isabella of Castile, and Christina of Sweden. Women are a little better represented among those included in Havelock Ellis's (1904) *Study of British Genius,* the percentage rising to a little over 5%. Other heterogeneous samples of famous creators, leaders, and miscellaneous celebrities reflect percentages that fall far short of the 51% of adults that women represent (see, e.g., Goertzel et al., 1978). The picture doesn't improve if we look just at creative genius. In the most recent systematic investigation, women made up 2.2% of the most significant figures in the Western, Arabic, Indian, Chinese, and Japanese civilizations and in the domains of science, philosophy, literature, art, and music (C. Murray, 2003). Their highest representation was in Japanese literature, but that was at only 8.2%. In contrast, there was not a single highly significant philosopher in any of the three main philosophical traditions (Chinese, Indian, and Western). That's a 0% hit rate!

Second, the representation of female geniuses using the psychometric definition is much more difficult to determine, if not utterly impossible. IQ tests are so constructed that men and women get the same average scores, so we cannot conclude that one gender has more g than another gender. However, it sometimes happens that men display greater variation on intelligence tests than do women (Eysenck, 1995). That means that more men get genius-level IQs than do women. To give an example, in Terman's (1925) sample of 1,528 kids, there were 857 boys and 671 girls. If the cutoff had been even higher than IQ 140, the discrepancy would have been greater. If genius is defined as an IQ of 160 or better, then men would outnumber women by 11 to 1 (Eysenck, 1995). But you men out there: Don't gloat over this supposed masculine superiority. That also means that males outnumber females at the bottom end of the distribution. That's why the 1994 movie *Dumb and Dumber* was written for two guys rather than two gals. It made things much easier for the casting director. Nevertheless, the idea that men's IQs are more variable than women's remains highly controversial. We should never forget that IQ is not a natural variable like height or weight or temperature that even physicists measure, but rather a psychological construct that is gauged only by an artificial psychometric instrument.

Third, men and women do differ biologically—as if you needed to be told this! Besides the obvious contrasts in primary and secondary sexual features, the two genders vary in hormones (e.g., testosterone) and neurological organization (e.g., hemispheric differentiation). It must also be said, nonetheless, that these physical contrasts may not be particularly pertinent to the problem at hand. Yes, gender differences might explain why men are more likely to be violent criminals or why men are more likely to be autistic savants. Yet it's a stretch to say that genius requires a disposition toward criminal autism! Besides, men and women differ very little on almost every major dispositional trait, including those traits that distinguish geniuses from nongeniuses (Hyde, 2005). Naturally, I have not mentioned the most obvious biological difference of all: a woman's ability to bear children. And there's some evidence that this essential contrast may not be irrelevant to the present issue. For most of the world's history, high-achieving women were more likely to be childless or to have few children (Hayes, 1989). Even so, this finding may say more about the sociocultural constraints imposed on the traditional "wife and mother" than about anything else. The Termites who became homemakers did not live up to their intellectual potential (Terman & Oden, 1959).

Fourth, and germane to the last point, the proportion of women who make it to the big time in any domain of achievement varies greatly across space and time (Murray, 2003; Simonton, 1992a, 2002b). Sociocultural systems that give women more opportunities to develop their talents see a larger percentage reach elite levels of attainment (e.g., Charness & Gerchak, 1996). Probably it's for this reason that the representation of women among the great geniuses of the world has tended to increase over the course of history (C. Murray, 2003; Simonton, 2002b). It is also pertinent that women have often done best in those domains where the obstacles to achievement are less severe than in other domains. For example, for a long time, and perhaps even still today, it's been much easier for women to become great novelists or poets than to become notable scientists (C. Murray, 2003).

You only need a cheap writing desk to do literature, while doing science usually requires an expensive laboratory or observatory. Anyhow, it should be evident that women have always been at the mercy of sociocultural circumstances, whether these involve norms, roles, prejudice, discrimination, or plain ordinary sexist male pigs. Keep in mind what Harvard did to Mary Calkins! Do you know what the French Academy of Sciences inflicted on Marie Curie? That august body denied her membership! Yet Marie Curie was not just the first woman to win a Nobel Prize but also the first scientist, male or female, to win Nobels in two different fields (chemistry and physics).

So what do I believe? I think that it *may* be possible that men might have an advantage over women in reaching the highest echelons of genius. That's a possibility, and it would be foolish to deny it. But please read on (particularly if you're a journalist). At present, I maintain that it's absolutely impossible for anyone to make any categorical statement to that effect. The fourth undeniable fact is put last because it's the most important. Right now, men and women do not compete on an even playing field. A woman might be born with exactly the same innate talent as a man but end up having that talent's development thwarted by the events and conditions to which she is inevitably exposed. This is one reason why Summers's assertion must cause so much distress. Just to suggest that women have an innate disability in the sciences will automatically give them an *environmental* handicap that equally gifted men don't share. The remark can then become a self-fulfilling prophecy. If Harvard's president said it, then what impact does that statement have on a talented teenager whose female gender was so disparaged?

As a consequence, before any conclusive proclamations can be made, we first need to comprehend more fully the social psychology of gender differences in the emergence of genius. Only if it becomes quite clear that these differences remain after accounting for all external inputs can we start making solid claims about innate contrasts. In the fewest words—and you can quote me on this—nature provides the residual interpretation only when the explanatory power of nurture has been exhausted. If the residual turns out to be nontrivial, then so be it. We cannot shy away from scientific truth... if it be true.

Ethnicity and Success

Now let me talk about something else that also causes me not a little discomfiture. To be truthful, it actually makes me squirm. It has to do with my hero, Francis Galton. As you already know, he was the first great scientist to study genius in any systematic fashion, and he was the first person identified as a genius by both the psychometric and historiometric definitions (Terman, 1917). Galton's 1869 *Hereditary Genius* remains one of the landmark books in the field, and even in the discipline of psychology. All this notwithstanding, I can't even read its table of contents without wincing. What, a chapter with the title "The Comparative Worth of Different Races"!? Here Galton affirmed with a straight face "that the average ability of the Athenian race is, on the lowest possible estimate, very nearly two grades higher than our own—that is, about as much as our race is above that of the African Negro" (Galton, 1892/1972, p. 397). He draws this conclusion on the basis of the high per-capita output of genius in the Golden Age of Athens relative to the British nation, and the latter's output relative to that of the African continent. He gave no thought whatsoever to whether his reference books might have been guilty of any ethnocentric biases. Nor did he take into consideration any of the sociocultural factors that might have played a part in his tabulations. Galton's neglect of all these factors contrasts strongly with Candolle's (1873) detailed inventory of the political, social, economic, geographic, educational, and religious forces that govern when and where genius will appear. And Candolle even introduced corrections for ethnocentrism!

Aside from his faulty logic, Galton's use of the word *race* rankles many psychologists today. The term is explicitly biological in nature. It reflects Galton's firm belief that nature overrides nurture. Nowadays the word has fallen out of favor as a scientific concept, with good reason. It's often too vague, too broad and inclusive, and too loaded with...well...racist connotations. This is not to say that biological contrasts don't exist between various human populations scattered across the globe. That would be an absurd claim. Certainly the natives of the Amazon region of Brazil will have distinctive genetic markers in comparison with those of the inhabitants of the Iberian Peninsula. Yet as in the case of gender differences, one has to question whether these contrasts are applicable to the issue before us. Indeed, their applicability in this case is even more questionable, given the fact that different so-called races almost always differ culturally. They constitute distinct cultures or ethnicities. And if there's anything we know for sure about human nature, it is that the culture we belong to can override all of the supposed biological dispositions in our genes. To return to a point made in chapter 6, it was culture and not race that created the Golden Age of Greece. It was culture and not race that caused the decline and fall of Greek civilization.

Let me offer two further illustrations: the Arabs and the Jews.

Prior to the advent of the Prophet Muhammad and the Islamic faith, the Arab peoples represented a cultural backwater in world civilization. Hitherto, the phenomenal achievements of the Western world had been produced by their neighbors—the Egyptians, the Sumerians, the Babylonians, the Persians, and so forth. Only in the area of poetry could the Arabs make a claim to have produced any persons of genius. But then, wham-o! They become Muslims, begin the conquest of the southern Mediterranean, Persia, and Central Asia, and within a relatively short time they are producing geniuses of the highest order in several major domains of achievement. Great rulers, great generals, great astronomers, great mathematicians, great physicians, great philosophers, great poets...lots and lots of greats. There was no quantum shift in the gene pool that rendered Arabic "blood" instantaneously capable of such incredible accomplishments. The dramatic discontinuity came from the sudden infusion of a new religion and the subsequent rapid absorption and assimilation of the high civilizations of the Arabs' neighbors. This should bring to mind what I said in chapter 6 about Japanese civilization. Indeed, what happened to Arabic culture after it turned a deaf ear to alien influences? The Arabs' later downfall was most definitely the result of their ignoring the achievements of the infidels and heretics. As a result, the Arab peoples eventually withdrew from the main stage of the history of world civilization.

The Jews offer another take on this process. Those who study genius cannot ignore the prominence of genius among those with Jewish backgrounds. In the recent history of Western civilization, their representation among outstanding creators is about 10 times higher than would be expected from their representation in the population (Arieti, 1976; Hayes, 1989; C. Murray, 2003; Veblen, 1919). Karl Marx, Sigmund Freud, and Albert Einstein are just a few of the most conspicuous examples. From this prominence we might be tempted to infer that Jews represent a superior race, perhaps rivaling Galton's Athenians. Yet there's a catch. The advantage holds true for a particular subset of the Jewish community, namely, the Occidental Jews of central Europe (the Ashkenazi), rather than for the Oriental Jews of the Near and Middle East (the Sephardi and Mizrahi). Moreover, the elevated position of the Occidental subset was a relatively modern phenomenon. In rough terms, geniuses of Ashkenazi heritage didn't emerge until after the European nations in which they resided began granting them more equality and after increasingly more Jews responded to this opportunity by integrating themselves into the majority culture. As in the case of the Arabs, this two-step combination of emancipation and assimilation happened so fast that it cannot be attributed to changes in the gene pool.

Incidentally, these two examples are connected. For a long period, the Oriental Jews had the advantage over the Occidental Jews. The illustrious philosopher Moses Maimonides wrote most of his works in Arabic, some in Hebrew, and none in Latin or any other European tongue. He was born in Muslim Córdoba and died in what is now Old Cairo, Egypt. Yet while the Occidental Jews eventually participated in the rise of European civilization to world supremacy, the Oriental Jews were too tightly bound to the decline in Arabic civilization. This reversal of fortunes once more underlines the sociocultural rather than biological basis for the fates of alleged races. The first can too quickly become last and the last can just as quickly become first.

No, I'm not going to conclude that biological differences across human populations do not matter at all. *Perhaps* they do, in some way, at some level. That possibility cannot be unequivocally dismissed by any open-minded person. I'm only saying that we cannot draw any solid *scientific* conclusions about this conjecture until we first rule out the mighty effects of the disparities that lie outside the genetic makeup of human groups. Given the complex, multicausal character of all human phenomena, including genius, it's likely that we will not be able to isolate that explanatory residual anytime soon. So in the meantime, can we please abstain from assigning hierarchies to putative races? Doctrines of racial superiority and inferiority do even more harm when they are clothed in the superficial appearance of a scientific truth. Such doctrines gave us the Holocaust and other atrocities that continue to shame the collective history of genus *Homo*.

LAST DAY OF CLASS

Let's return to the Genius, Creativity, and Leadership course that I introduced in the first paragraph of this chapter. The course is numbered 175 at UC Davis, but it would be numbered 275 if our introductory psychology course were 101 rather than just 1. When I first taught 175, I used my *Genius, Creativity, and Leadership* (Simonton, 1984c) as the textbook, but a decade later I assigned my *Greatness* for the same purpose (Simonton, 1994). Yes, we professors do assign our own book babies as required texts! And once *Genius 101* comes out, it will replace *Greatness* on the shelves at the university bookstore each quarter that I offer 175.

You might think that profs do this trick out of pure, unadulterated greed. Given all the royalties they supposedly receive on each book sold to their helpless students—a captive readership if ever there was one—you might imagine that the instructors are soon driving around in expensive sport cars, taking off on vacations to exotic places, and buying homes in the most luxurious part of town. The fact of the matter is that the used-book market quickly obliterates any fantasies we profs might have about getting rich quick. I usually only teach 175 once a year, and the enrollment is capped at 50 students. After the first couple of times that I taught the course I began to notice that almost all of my students have in their backpacks a copy of the text with the covers well worn and the yellowed pages highlighted in multiple styles—telltale signs of a recycled text. So perhaps only 100 of all the students who took my 175 actually bought the book new, and I only earn money on new copies sold. Considering that my royalties may start out at only 10% of the retail price (until so many thousands of copies are sold), you can easily figure out how much money I'll likely earn from assigning *Genius 101* as a required text for my 175 class. Just multiply the price you paid by 10 (i.e., 10 = 100×0.1). So you see, I'm not going to get stinking rich off of this book! The profits won't even pay for a new laptop!

But I need to get back to 175. On the last day of class, I always conduct a whirlwind tour of the quarter's subject matter by discussing four core themes that permeate the entire course. These themes concern four questions: How would you define genius? How would you identify genius? How would you intervene to encourage genius? And how would you most appropriately study genius? In four words: definition, identification, intervention, and investigation. These themes then become the basis for a quadruplet of potential questions for a 2-hour essay exam on finals day. The four questions are as follows:

Exam Question #1: In this course, we have been assuming that exceptional creativity and leadership define the two main manifestations of genius. To what extent does the term *genius* successfully provide a generic label for these two behavioral phenomena? Are there aspects of creativity and leadership that seem to reside beyond this broad categorization? And can you conjure up other domains of achievement or fame in which the term genius might be reasonably applied but that do not seem to fall into the subcategory of either creativity or leadership? For example, what about those personalities who found major world religions? Or rock stars? Or chefs?

Exam Question #2: Each year, the MacArthur Foundation awards handsome fellowships of $500,000 to notable contemporary achievers in virtually any domain of activity. The press refers to these as the "genius awards," and thus the recipients, besides being richer, become officially certified as geniuses. Let's say that you graduate at the end of this year and start looking for a job, only to discover in the want ads that the MacArthur Foundation is seeking someone to help select the next round of geniuses. Having done well in Psychology 175, you decide you are a shoo-in for the job, but you realize that your application must include a well-formulated position paper in which you specify the criteria that you should use to decide whether someone is deserving of the award. What things would you look for? Any developmental experiences or personality traits? Any objective behaviors or social relationships?

Exam Question #3: It is a national crisis: The president of the United States, in her State of the Union Address, has claimed that America has fallen behind the rest of the world in its per capita output of geniuses. This decline is evident in the poor showing of Americans among recent recipients of Nobel Prizes as well as in the dearth of first-rate leaders in industry and politics (herself excluded). Congress in its infinite wisdom has therefore voted to use the entire budget normally granted to the Department of Defense to launch a massive campaign to boost the U.S. percentage of world geniuses by the year 2050 A.D. Given that you did so well in Psychology 175 a decade ago, you are recruited by the president herself to assume command as the genius czar. Because money is no object, you initiate a massive program to make America rival the Golden Age of Greece. In particular, you...

Exam Question #4: During the course of this class, we have examined genius, creativity, and leadership from a great diversity of methodological techniques and theoretical perspectives. Which of these approaches seem to be the most enlightening, which the least, and why? To what extent are some methodologies tied to certain theories, while other methods seem relatively theory free? Which methods and theories are most suitable for studying creativity? Which work best for investigating leadership? How far is it possible for a psychology of genius to emerge that imposes one method and theory on all the pertinent phenomena? Are there aspects of genius that are overlooked by all current methodological and theoretical frameworks?

If you had a choice, which of these questions would you prefer to have as the subject for a blue book exam? How would you answer this question? Go on, outline what you'd need to write to get an A+.

Maybe you don't feel you know enough yet. After all, you may have only read this slim text, without attending any of my lectures, and without approaching any supplementary readings. You didn't even write a term paper!

It's no big deal. Besides, I'd like to inspire you to take my Genius 201 and 301 courses. There's still so much more to learn about this most fascinating and significant phenomenon. Lots of books, lots of articles. If you want a head start, you may want to explore my Psychology 175 Web page at http://psychology.ucdavis.edu/Simonton/p175wmain.html. I particularly recommend the links to be found on the Web page. You'll find a lot of stuff that's both entertaining and instructive.

But no guarantees! You might pass Genius 101, 201, and 301 with flying colors, but that wouldn't make you a genius. You should already realize why. (Hint: the keywords "original" and "exemplary.") But at least you now know what you need to do to become a genius. So just do it!

References

Abelson, R. P. (1985). A variance explanation paradox: When a little is a lot. *Psychological Bulletin, 97,* 129–133.

Albert, R. S. (1975). Toward a behavioral definition of genius. *American Psychologist, 30,* 140–151.

Albert, R. S. (1994). The achievement of eminence: A longitudinal study of exceptionally gifted boys and their families. In R. F. Subotnik & K. D. Arnold (Eds.), *Beyond Terman: Contemporary longitudinal studies of giftedness and talent* (pp. 282–315). Norwood, NJ: Ablex.

Amabile, T. M. (1983). *The social psychology of creativity.* New York: Springer-Verlag.

American heritage electronic dictionary (3rd ed.). (1992). Boston: Houghton Mifflin.

American Psychiatric Association. (1994). *Diagnostic and statistical manual of mental disorders* (4th ed.). Washington, DC: Author.

Andreasen, N. C. (1987). Creativity and mental illness: Prevalence rates in writers and their first-degree relatives. *American Journal of Psychiatry, 144,* 1288–1292.

Andreasen, N. C., & Canter, A. (1974). The creative writer: Psychiatric symptoms and family history. *Comprehensive Psychiatry, 15,* 123–131.

Andrews, F. M. (Ed.). (1979). *Scientific productivity: The effectiveness of research groups in six countries.* Cambridge, England: Cambridge University Press.

Ansburg, P. I., & Hill, K. (2003). Creative and analytic thinkers differ in their use of attentional resources. *Personality and Individual Differences, 34,* 1141–1152.

Arieti, S. (1976). *Creativity: The magic synthesis.* New York: Basic Books.

199

Auden, W. H. (1948). Squares and oblongs. In R. Arnheim, W. H. Auden, K. Shapiro, & D. A. Stauffer (Eds.), *Poets at work: Essays based on the modern poetry collection at the Lockwood Memorial Library, University of Buffalo* (pp. 163–181). New York: Harcourt, Brace.

Babcock, W. L. (1895). On the morbid heredity and predisposition to insanity of the man of genius. *Journal of Nervous and Mental Disease, 20,* 749–769.

Barron, F. X. (1955). The disposition toward originality. *Journal of Abnormal and Social Psychology, 51,* 478–485.

Barron, F. X. (1963). *Creativity and psychological health: Origins of personal vitality and creative freedom.* Princeton, NJ: Van Nostrand.

Beard, G. M. (1874). *Legal responsibility in old age.* New York: Russell.

Berry, C. (1981). The Nobel scientists and the origins of scientific achievement. *British Journal of Sociology, 32,* 381–391.

Binet, A., & Simon, T. (1905). Méthodes nouvelles pour le diagnostic du niveau intellectuel des anormaux. *Année Psychologique, 12,* 191–244.

Bliss, W. D. (1970). Birth order of creative writers. *Journal of Individual Psychology, 26,* 200–202.

Bloom, B. S. (Ed.). (1985). *Developing talent in young people.* New York: Ballantine Books.

Boden, M. A. (1991). *The creative mind: Myths and mechanisms.* New York: Basic Books.

Bouchard, T. J., Jr. (1994). Genes, environment, and personality. *Science, 264,* 1700–1701.

Bouchard, T. J., Jr. (2004). Genetic influence on human psychological traits: A survey. *Current Directions in Psychological Science, 13,* 148–151.

Bouchard, T. J., Jr., Lykken, D. T., McGue, M., Segal, N. L., & Tellegen, A. (1990, October 20). Sources of human psychological differences: The Minnesota study of twins reared apart. *Science, 250,* 223–228.

Bouchard, T. J., Jr., & McGue, M. (1981, May). Familial studies of intelligence: A review. *Science, 212,* 1055–1059.

Bowden, E. M., Jung-Beeman, M., Fleck, J., & Kounios, J. (2005). New approaches to demystifying insight. *Trends in Cognitive Sciences, 9,* 322–328.

Bowerman, W. G. (1947). *Studies in genius.* New York: Philosophical Library.

Bramwell, B. S. (1948). Galton's "Hereditary" and the three following generations since 1869. *Eugenics Review, 39,* 146–153.

Brimhall, D. R. (1922). Family resemblances among *American Men of Science*. *American Naturalist, 56,* 504–547.

Brimhall, D. R. (1923a). Family resemblances among *American Men of Science*. II. Degree of resemblance in comparison with the generality: Proportion of workers in each science and distribution of replies. *American Naturalist, 57,* 74–88.

Brimhall, D. R. (1923b). Family resemblances among *American Men of Science*. III. The influence of the nearness of kinship. *American Naturalist, 57,* 137–152.

Brown, F. (1968). Bereavement and lack of a parent in childhood. In E. Miller (Ed.), *Foundations of child psychiatry* (pp. 435–455). Oxford, England: Pergamon Press.

Buchanan, B. G., & Shortliffe, E. H. (Eds.). (1984). *Rule-based expert systems: The MYCIN experiments of the Stanford Heuristics Programming Project.* Reading, MA: Addison-Wesley.

Campbell, D. T. (1960). Blind variation and selective retention in creative thought as in other knowledge processes. *Psychological Review, 67,* 380–400.

Candolle, A. de. (1873). *Histoire des sciences et des savants depuis deux siècles.* Geneva, Switzerland: Georg.

Cannon, W. B. (1940). The role of chance in discovery. *Scientific Monthly, 50,* 204–209.

Carroll, J. B. (1993). *Human cognitive abilities: A survey of factor-analytical studies.* New York: Cambridge University Press.

Carson, S., Peterson, J. B., & Higgins, D. M. (2003). Decreased latent inhibition is associated with increased creative achievement in high-functioning individuals. *Journal of Personality and Social Psychology, 85,* 499–506.

Cassandro, V. J. (1998). Explaining premature mortality across fields of creative endeavor. *Journal of Personality, 66,* 805–833.

Cattell, J. M. (1890). Mental tests and measurements. *Mind, 15,* 373–381.

Cattell, J. M. (1903). A statistical study of eminent men. *Popular Science Monthly, 62,* 359–377.

Cattell, R. B., & Butcher, H. J. (1968). *The prediction of achievement and creativity.* Indianapolis: Bobbs-Berrill.

Chambers, J. A. (1964). Relating personality and biographical factors to scientific creativity. *Psychological Monographs: General and Applied, 78* (7, Whole No. 584).

Charness, N., & Gerchak, Y. (1996). Participation rates and maximal performance: A log-linear explanation for group differences, such as Russian and male dominance in chess. *Psychological Science, 7*, 46–51.

Clark, R. D., & Rice, G. A. (1982). Family constellations and eminence: The birth orders of Nobel Prize winners. *Journal of Psychology, 110*, 281–287.

Cohen, J. (1988). *Statistical power analysis for behavioral sciences* (2nd ed.). Hillsdale, NJ: Erlbaum.

Cope, D. (1996). *Experiments in musical intelligence*. Madison, WI: A-R Editions.

Cox, C. (1926). *The early mental traits of three hundred geniuses*. Stanford, CA: Stanford University Press.

Cronbach, L. J. (1960). *Essentials of psychological testing* (2nd ed.). New York: Harper & Row.

Csikszentmihályi, M. (1990). The domain of creativity. In M. A. Runco & R. S. Albert (Eds.), *Theories of creativity* (pp. 190–212). Newbury Park, CA: Sage.

Cziko, G. A. (1998). From blind to creative: In defense of Donald Campbell's selectionist theory of human creativity. *Journal of Creative Behavior, 32*, 192–208.

Davis, R. H., & Maurice, A. B. (1931). *The caliph of Bagdad: Being Arabian nights flashes of the life, letters, and work of O. Henry*. New York: Appleton.

Dennis, W. (1954a, September). Bibliographies of eminent scientists. *Scientific Monthly, 79*, 180–183.

Dennis, W. (1954b). Productivity among American psychologists. *American Psychologist, 9*, 191–194.

Dennis, W. (1955, April). Variations in productivity among creative workers. *Scientific Monthly, 80*, 277–278.

Dennis, W. (1966). Creative productivity between the ages of 20 and 80 years. *Journal of Gerontology, 21*, 1–8.

Dryden, J. (1681). *Absalom and Achitophel: A poem*. London: Davis.

Dryden, J. (1885). Epistle to Congreve. In W. Scott & G. Saintsbury (Eds.), *The works of John Dryden* (Vol. 11, pp. 57–60). Edinburgh, Scotland: Paterson. (Original work published 1693)

Duckworth, A. L., Peterson, C., Matthews, M. D., & Kelly, D. R. (2007). Grit: Perseverance and passion for long-term goals. *Journal of Personality and Social Psychology, 92*, 1087–1101.

Duda, R. O., & Shortliffe, E. H. (1983). Expert systems research. *Science, 220*, 261–268.

Dunbar, K. (1995). How scientists really reason: Scientific reasoning in real-world laboratories. In R. J. Sternberg & J. E. Davidson (Eds.), *The nature of insight* (pp. 365–396). Cambridge, MA: MIT Press.

Eisenman, R. (1964). Birth order and artistic creativity. *Journal of Individual Psychology, 20,* 183–185.

Elliott, W. E. Y., & Valenza, R. J. (2004). Oxford by the numbers: What are the odds that the Earl of Oxford could have written Shakespeare's poems and plays? *Tennessee Law Review, 72,* 323–453.

Ellis, H. (1904). *A study of British genius.* London: Hurst & Blackett.

Elo, A. E. (1965). Age changes in master chess performance. *Journal of Gerontology, 20,* 289–299.

Elo, A. E. (1986). *The rating of chessplayers, past and present* (2nd ed.). New York: Arco.

Ericsson, K. A. (1996). The acquisition of expert performance: An introduction to some of the issues. In K. A. Ericsson (Ed.), *The road to expert performance: Empirical evidence from the arts and sciences, sports, and games* (pp. 1–50). Mahwah, NJ: Erlbaum.

Ericsson, K. A., Charness, N., Feltovich, P. J., & Hoffman, R. R. (Eds.). (2006). *The Cambridge handbook of expertise and expert performance.* New York: Cambridge University Press.

Ericsson, K. A., Krampe, R. T., & Tesch-Römer, C. (1993). The role of deliberate practice in the acquisition of expert performance. *Psychological Review, 100,* 363–406.

Erikson, E. H. (1958). *Young man Luther: A study in psychoanalysis and history.* New York: Norton.

Erikson, E. H. (1969). *Gandhi's truth on the origins of militant nonviolence.* New York: Norton.

Eysenck, H. J. (1993). Creativity and personality: Suggestions for a theory. *Psychological Inquiry, 4,* 147–178.

Eysenck, H. J. (1994). Creativity and personality: Word association, origence, and psychoticism. *Creativity Research Journal, 7,* 209–216.

Eysenck, H. J. (1995). *Genius: The natural history of creativity.* Cambridge, England: Cambridge University Press.

Falconer, D. S. (1989). *Introduction to quantitative genetics* (3rd ed.). New York: Wiley.

Farnsworth, P. R. (1969). *The social psychology of music* (2nd ed.). Ames, IA: Iowa State University Press.

Feist, G. J. (1993). A structural model of scientific eminence. *Psychological Science, 4,* 366–371.

Feist, G. J. (1998). A meta-analysis of personality in scientific and artistic creativity. *Personality and Social Psychology Review, 2*, 290–309.

Feist, G. J. (2006). How development and personality influence scientific thought, interest, and achievement. *Review of General Psychology, 10*, 163–182.

Feist, G. J., & Barron, F. X. (2003). Predicting creativity from early to late adulthood: Intellect, potential, and personality. *Journal of Research in Personality, 37*, 62–88.

Feldman, D. H., with Goldsmith, L. T. (1986). *Nature's gambit: Child prodigies and the development of human potential.* New York: Basic Books.

Fernberger, S. W. (1946, August 23). Scientific publication as affected by war and politics. *Science, 104*, 175–177.

Freud, S. (1964). *Leonardo da Vinci and a memory of his childhood* (A. Tyson, Trans.). New York: Norton. (Original work published 1910)

Galton, F. (1865). Hereditary talent and character. *Macmillan's Magazine, 12*, 157–166, 318–327.

Galton, F. (1869). *Hereditary genius: An inquiry into its laws and consequences.* London: Macmillan.

Galton, F. (1874). *English men of science: Their nature and nurture.* London: Macmillan.

Galton, F. (1883). *Inquiries into human faculty and its development.* London: Macmillan.

Galton, F. (1972). *Hereditary genius: An inquiry into its laws and consequences* (2nd ed.). Gloucester, MA: Peter Smith. (Original work published 1892)

Gardner, H. (1983). *Frames of mind: A theory of multiple intelligences.* New York: Basic Books.

Gardner, H. (1993). *Creating minds: An anatomy of creativity seen through the lives of Freud, Einstein, Picasso, Stravinsky, Eliot, Graham, and Gandhi.* New York: Basic Books.

Gardner, H. (1998). Are there additional intelligences? The case for naturalist, spiritual, and existential intelligences. In J. Kane (Ed.), *Education, information, and transformation* (pp. 111–131). Upper Saddle River, NJ: Merrill.

Gartner, J. D. (2005). *The hypomanic edge: The link between (a little) craziness and (a lot of) success in America.* New York: Simon & Schuster.

Ginsburgh, V., & Weyers, S. A. (2006). Persistence and fashion in art: Italian Renaissance from Vasari to Berenson and beyond. *Poetics, 34*, 24–44.

Goertzel, M. G., Goertzel, V., & Goertzel, T. G. (1978). *300 eminent personalities: A psychosocial analysis of the famous.* San Francisco: Jossey-Bass.

Gottfredson, L. S. (1997). Why g matters: The complexity of everyday life. *Intelligence, 24,* 79–132.

Götz, K. O., & Götz, K. (1979a). Personality characteristics of professional artists. *Perceptual and Motor Skills, 49,* 327–334.

Götz, K. O., & Götz, K. (1979b). Personality characteristics of successful artists. *Perceptual and Motor Skills, 49,* 919–924.

Guilford, J. P. (1967). *The nature of human intelligence.* New York: McGraw-Hill.

Hadamard, J. (1945). *The psychology of invention in the mathematical field.* Princeton, NJ: Princeton University Press.

Harrington, D. M. (1990). The ecology of human creativity: A psychological perspective. In M. A. Runco & R. S. Albert (Eds.), *Theories of creativity* (pp. 143–169). Newbury Park, CA: Sage.

Harris, J. A. (2004). Measured intelligence, achievement, openness to experience, and creativity. *Personality and Individual Differences, 36,* 913–929.

Hart, M. H. (2000). *The 100: A ranking of the most influential persons in history* (Rev. & updated). Secaucus, NJ: Citadel Press.

Hayes, J. R. (1989). *The complete problem solver* (2nd ed.). Hillsdale, NJ: Erlbaum.

Helmholtz, H. von. (1898). An autobiographical sketch. In *Popular lectures on scientific subjects, second series* (E. Atkinson, Trans.; pp. 266–291). New York: Longmans, Green.

Helmreich, R. L., Spence, J. T., Beane, W. E., Lucker, G. W., & Matthews, K. A. (1980). Making it in academic psychology: Demographic and personality correlates of attainment. *Journal of Personality and Social Psychology, 39,* 896–908.

Helson, R., & Crutchfield, R. S. (1970). Mathematicians: The creative researcher and the average Ph.D. *Journal of Consulting and Clinical Psychology, 34,* 250–257.

Herek, G. M., Janis, I. L., & Huth, P. (1987). Decision making during international crises: Is quality of process related to outcome? *Journal of Conflict Resolution, 31,* 203–226.

Herek, G. M., Janis, I. L., & Huth, P. (1989). Quality of U.S. decision making during the Cuban missile crisis. *Journal of Conflict Resolution, 33,* 446–459.

Hollingworth, L. S. (1926). *Gifted children: Their nature and nurture.* New York: Macmillan.

Hollingworth, L. S. (1942). *Children above IQ 180: Origin and development.* Yonkers-on-Hudson, NY: World Book.

Holmes, T. S., & Rahe, R. H. (1967). The social readjustment rating scale. *Journal of Psychosomatic Research, 11,* 213–218.

Howe, M. J. A. (1999). *Genius explained.* Cambridge, England: Cambridge University Press.

Hsu, F. (2002). *Behind Deep Blue: Building the computer that defeated the world chess champion.* Princeton, NJ: Princeton University Press.

Hyde, J. S. (2005). The gender similarities hypothesis. *American Psychologist, 60,* 581–592.

Ilies, R., Gerhardt, M. W., & Le, H. (2004). Individual differences in leadership emergence: Integrating meta-analytic findings and behavioral genetics estimates. *International Journal of Selection and Assessment, 12,* 207–219.

James, W. (1880, October). Great men, great thoughts, and the environment. *Atlantic Monthly, 46,* 441–459.

James, W. (1902). *The varieties of religious experience: A study in human nature.* London: Longmans, Green.

Jamison, K. R. (1989). Mood disorders and patterns of creativity in British writers and artists. *Psychiatry, 52,* 125–134.

Jamison, K. R. (1993). *Touched with fire: Manic-depressive illness and the artistic temperament.* New York: Free Press.

Janis, I. L. (1982). *Groupthink: Psychological studies of policy decisions and fiascoes* (2nd ed.). Boston: Houghton Mifflin.

Jeans, J. (1942). Newton and the science of to-day. *Nature, 150,* 710–715.

Jensen, A. R. (1990). Speed of information processing in a calculating prodigy. *Intelligence, 14,* 259–274.

Jensen, A. R. (1999). *The g factor: The science of mental ability.* Westport, CT: Praeger.

Johnson, S. (1781). *The lives of the most eminent English poets* (Vol. 1). London: Bathurst et al.

Juda, A. (1949). The relationship between highest mental capacity and psychic abnormalities. *American Journal of Psychiatry, 106,* 296–307.

Judge, T. A., Colbert, A. E., & Ilies, R. (2004). Intelligence and leadership: A quantitative review and test of theoretical propositions. *Journal of Applied Psychology, 89,* 542–552.

Kant, I. (1952). The critique of judgement. In R. M. Hutchins (Ed.), *Great books of the Western world* (Vol. 42, pp. 459–613). Chicago: Encyclopaedia Britannica. (Original work published 1790)

Karlson, J. I. (1970). Genetic association of giftedness and creativity with schizophrenia. *Hereditas, 66,* 177–182.

Kaufman, J. C. (2000–2001). Genius, lunatics and poets: Mental illness in prize-winning authors. *Imagination, Cognition and Personality, 20,* 305–314.

Kaufman, J. C. (2001). The Sylvia Plath effect: Mental illness in eminent creative writers. *Journal of Creative Behavior, 35,* 37–50.

Kaufman, J. C. (2003). The cost of the muse: Poets die young. *Death Studies, 27,* 813–821.

Kaufman, J. C. (2005). The door that leads into madness: Eastern European poets and mental illness. *Creativity Research Journal, 17,* 99–103.

Kaufman, J. C., & Baer, J. (2002). I bask in dreams of suicide: Mental illness, poetry, and women. *Review of General Psychology, 6,* 271–286.

Kaufman, J. C., & Sexton, J. D. (2006). Why doesn't the writing cure help poets? *Review of General Psychology, 10,* 268–282.

Kavolis, V. (1964). Economic correlates of artistic creativity. *American Journal of Sociology, 70,* 332–341.

Kavolis, V. (1966). Community dynamics and artistic creativity. *American Sociological Review, 31,* 208–217.

Klahr, D. (2000). *Exploring science: The cognition and development of discovery processes.* Cambridge, MA: MIT Press.

Koestler, A. (1964). *The act of creation.* New York: Macmillan.

Kounios, J., Frymiare, J. L., Bowden, E. M., Fleck, J. I., Subramaniam, K., Parrish, T. B., & Jung-Beeman, M. (2006). The prepared mind: Neural activity prior to problem presentation predicts subsequent solution by sudden insight. *Psychological Science, 17,* 882–890.

Kroeber, A. L. (1917). The superorganic. *American Anthropologist, 19,* 163–214.

Kroeber, A. L. (1944). *Configurations of culture growth.* Berkeley: University of California Press.

Kuo, Y. (1986). The growth and decline of Chinese philosophical genius. *Chinese Journal of Psychology, 28,* 81–91.

Kuo, Y. (1988). The social psychology of Chinese philosophical creativity: A critical synthesis. *Social Epistemology, 2,* 283–295.

Lamb, D., & Easton, S. M. (1984). *Multiple discovery.* Avebury, England: Avebury.

Langley, P., Simon, H. A., Bradshaw, G. L., & Zythow, J. M. (1987). *Scientific discovery.* Cambridge, MA: MIT Press.

Lehman, H. C. (1953). *Age and achievement.* Princeton, NJ: Princeton University Press.

Lehman, H. C. (1962). More about age and achievement. *Gerontologist, 2,* 141–148.

Levy, D., & Newborn, M. (1982). *All about chess and computers.* Rockville, MD: Computer Science Press.

Ludwig, A. M. (1990). Alcohol input and creative output. *British Journal of Addiction, 85,* 953–963.

Ludwig, A. M. (1995). *The price of greatness: Resolving the creativity and madness controversy.* New York: Guilford Press.

Ludwig, A. M. (1998). Method and madness in the arts and sciences. *Creativity Research Journal, 11,* 93–101.

Ludwig, A. M. (2002). *King of the mountain: The nature of political leadership.* Lexington: University Press of Kentucky.

Lykken, D. T. (1982). Research with twins: The concept of emergenesis. *Psychophysiology, 19,* 361–373.

Lykken, D. T., McGue, M., Tellegen, A., & Bouchard, T. J., Jr. (1992). Emergenesis: Genetic traits that may not run in families. *American Psychologist, 47,* 1565–1577.

Mach, E. (1896, January). On the part played by accident in invention and discovery. *Monist, 6,* 161–175.

McCauley, C. (1989). The nature of social influence in groupthink: Compliance and internalization. *Journal of Personality and Social Psychology, 57,* 250–260.

McCrae, R. R. (1987). Creativity, divergent thinking, and openness to experience. *Journal of Personality and Social Psychology, 52,* 1258–1265.

McCurdy, H. G. (1960). The childhood pattern of genius. *Horizon, 2,* 33–38.

McFarlan, D. (Ed.). (1989). *Guinness book of world records.* New York: Bantam.

McNeil, T. F. (1971). Prebirth and postbirth influence on the relationship between creative ability and recorded mental illness. *Journal of Psychology, 39,* 391–406.

Mednick, S. A. (1962). The associative basis of the creative process. *Psychological Review, 69,* 220–232.

Merton, R. K. (1961). Singletons and multiples in scientific discovery: A chapter in the sociology of science. *Proceedings of the American Philosophical Society, 105,* 470–486.

Meyer, G. J., Finn, S. E., Eyde, L. D., Kay, G. G., Moreland, K. L., Dies, R. R., et al. (2001). Psychological testing and psychological assessment: A review of evidence and issues. *American Psychologist, 56,* 128–165.

Moles, A. (1968). *Information theory and esthetic perception* (J. E. Cohen, Trans.). Urbana: University of Illinois Press. (Original work published 1958)

Moulin, L. (1955). The Nobel Prizes for the sciences from 1901–1950: An essay in sociological analysis. *British Journal of Sociology, 6,* 246–263.

Murray, C. (2003). *Human accomplishment: The pursuit of excellence in the arts and sciences, 800 B.C. to 1950.* New York: HarperCollins.

Murray, P. (Ed.). (1989). *Genius: The history of an idea.* Oxford, England: Blackwell.

Myerson, A., & Boyle, R. D. (1941). The incidence of manic-depression psychosis in certain socially important families: Preliminary report. *American Journal of Psychiatry, 98,* 11–21.

Nemeth, C. J., & Kwan, J. (1985). Originality of word associations as a function of majority vs. minority influence. *Social Psychology Quarterly, 48,* 277–282.

Nemeth, C. J., & Kwan, J. (1987). Minority influence, divergent thinking and detection of correct solutions. *Journal of Applied Social Psychology, 17,* 788–799.

Nemeth, C. J., Personnaz, B., Personnaz, M., & Goncalo, J. A. (2004). The liberating role of conflict in group creativity: A study in two countries. *European Journal of Social Psychology, 34,* 365–374.

Nemeth, C. J., & Wachtler, J. (1983). Creative problem solving as a result of majority vs. minority influence. *European Journal of Social Psychology, 13,* 45–55.

Nettle, D. (2006). Schizotypy and mental health amongst poets, visual artists, and mathematicians. *Journal of Research in Personality, 40,* 876–890.

Newell, A., & Simon, H. A. (1972). *Human problem solving.* Englewood Cliffs, NJ: Prentice-Hall.

Nisbett, R. E. (1968). Birth order and participation in dangerous sports. *Journal of Personality and Social Psychology, 8,* 351–353.

Nobel Laureates Facts. (n.d.). Retrieved December 12, 2006, from http://nobelprize.org/nobel_prizes/nobelprize_facts.html

Ogburn, W. K., & Thomas, D. (1922). Are inventions inevitable? A note on social evolution. *Political Science Quarterly, 37,* 83–93.

Oleszek, W. (1969). Age and political careers. *Public Opinion Quarterly, 33*, 100–103.

Ones, D. S., Viswesvaran, C., & Dilchert, S. (2005). Cognitive ability in selection decisions. In O. Wilhelm & R. W. Engle (Eds.), *Handbook of understanding and measuring intelligence* (pp. 431–468). Thousand Oaks, CA: Sage.

Over, R. (1982). The durability of scientific reputation. *Journal of the History of the Behavioral Sciences, 18*, 53–61.

Page, S. E. (2007). *The difference: How the power of diversity creates better groups, firms, schools, and societies.* Princeton, NJ: Princeton University Press.

Paisley, W. J. (1964). Identifying the unknown communicator in painting, literature and music: The significance of minor encoding habits. *Journal of Communication, 14*, 219–237.

Paulhus, D. L., Wehr, P., Harms, P. D., & Strasser, D. I. (2002). Use of exemplar surveys to reveal implicit types of intelligence. *Personality and Social Psychology Bulletin, 28*, 1051–1062.

Paulus, P. B., & Nijstad, B. A. (Eds.). (2003). *Group creativity: Innovation through collaboration.* New York: Oxford University Press.

Peterson, J. B., & Carson, S. (2000). Latent inhibition and openness to experience in a high-achieving student population. *Personality and Individual Differences, 28*, 323–332.

Peterson, J. B., Smith, K. W., & Carson, S. (2002). Openness and extraversion are associated with reduced latent inhibition: Replication and commentary. *Personality and Individual Differences, 33*, 1137–1147.

Plomin, R., & Bergeman, C. S. (1991). The nature of nurture: Genetic influence on environmental measures. *Behavioral and Brain Sciences, 14*, 373–386.

Plomin, R., & Rende, R. (1990). Human behavioral genetics. *Annual Review of Psychology, 42*, 161–190.

Poincaré, H. (1921). *The foundations of science: Science and hypothesis, the value of science, science and method* (G. B. Halstead, Trans.). New York: Science Press.

Post, F. (1994). Creativity and psychopathology: A study of 291 world-famous men. *British Journal of Psychiatry, 165*, 22–34.

Post, F. (1996). Verbal creativity, depression and alcoholism: An investigation of one hundred American and British writers. *British Journal of Psychiatry, 168*, 545–555.

Post, J. M. (Ed.). (2003). *The psychological assessment of political leaders: With profiles of Saddam Hussein and Bill Clinton.* Ann Arbor: University of Michigan Press.

Prentky, R. A. (1980). *Creativity and psychopathology: A neurocognitive perspective.* New York: Praeger.

Price, D. (1963). *Little science, big science.* New York: Columbia University Press.

Price, D. (1978). Ups and downs in the pulse of science and technology. In J. Gaston (Ed.), *The sociology of science* (pp. 162–171). San Francisco: Jossey-Bass.

Quételet, A. (1968). *A treatise on man and the development of his faculties.* New York: Franklin. (Reprint of 1842 Edinburgh translation of 1835 French original)

Ramey, C. H., & Weisberg, R. W. (2004). The "poetical activity" of Emily Dickinson: A further test of the hypothesis that affective disorders foster creativity. *Creativity Research Journal, 16,* 173–185.

Raskin, E. A. (1936). Comparison of scientific and literary ability: A biographical study of eminent scientists and men of letters of the nineteenth century. *Journal of Abnormal and Social Psychology, 31,* 20–35.

Reynolds, J. (1966). *Discourses on art.* New York: Collier. (Original work published 1769–90)

Roberts, R. M. (1989). *Serendipity: Accidental discoveries in science.* New York: Wiley.

Roe, A. (1953). *The making of a scientist.* New York: Dodd, Mead.

Roring, R. W., & Charness, N. (2007). A multilevel model analysis of expertise in chess across the life span. *Psychology and Aging, 22,* 291–299.

Rosengren, K. E. (1985). Time and literary fame. *Poetics, 14,* 157–172.

Rosenthal, R. (1990). How are we doing in soft psychology? *American Psychologist, 45,* 775–777.

Rothenberg, A. (1990). *Creativity and madness: New findings and old stereotypes.* Baltimore: Johns Hopkins University Press.

Rudy, T. E. (2007). Psychometrics. In N. J. Salkind (Ed.), *Encyclopedia of measurement and statistics* (Vol. 3, p. 797). Thousand Oaks, CA: Sage.

Runyan, W. M. (1981). Why did Van Gogh cut off his ear? The problem of alternative explanations in psychobiography. *Journal of Personality and Social Psychology, 40,* 1070–1077.

Sawyer, R. K. (2006). *Explaining creativity: The science of human innovation.* New York: Oxford University Press.

Sawyer, R. K. (2007). *Group genius: The creative power of collaboration.* New York: Basic Books.

Scarr, S., & McCartney, K. (1983). How people make their own environments: A theory of genotype → environmental effects. *Child Development, 54,* 424–435.

Schachter, S. (1963). Birth order, eminence, and higher education. *American Sociological Review, 28,* 757–768.

Schaefer, C. E., & Anastasi, A. (1968). A biographical inventory for identifying creativity in adolescent boys. *Journal of Applied Psychology, 58,* 42–48.

Schaller, M. (1997). The psychological consequences of fame: Three tests of the self-consciousness hypothesis. *Journal of Personality, 65,* 291–309.

Schmookler, J. (1966). *Invention and economic growth.* Cambridge, MA: Harvard University Press.

Schubert, D. S. P., Wagner, M. E., & Schubert, H. J. P. (1977). Family constellation and creativity: Firstborn predominance among classical music composers. *Journal of Psychology, 95,* 147–149.

Schulz, R., & Curnow, C. (1988). Peak performance and age among super athletes: Track and field, swimming, baseball, tennis, and golf. *Journal of Gerontology, 43,* 113–120.

Seneca. (1932). On tranquillity of mind. In *Moral essays* (J. W. Basore, Trans.; Vol. 2, pp. 203–285). Cambridge, MA: Harvard University Press.

Shrager, J., & Langley, P. (Eds.). (1990). *Computational models of scientific discovery and theory formation.* San Mateo, CA: Kaufmann.

Simon, J. L., & Sullivan, R. J. (1989). Population size, knowledge stock, and other determinants of agricultural publication and patenting: England, 1541–1850. *Explorations in Economic History, 26,* 21–44.

Simonton, D. K. (1974). *The social psychology of creativity: An archival data analysis.* Unpublished doctoral dissertation, Harvard University.

Simonton, D. K. (1975a). Age and literary creativity: A cross-cultural and transhistorical survey. *Journal of Cross-Cultural Psychology, 6,* 259–277.

Simonton, D. K. (1975b). Sociocultural context of individual creativity: A transhistorical time-series analysis. *Journal of Personality and Social Psychology, 32,* 1119–1133.

Simonton, D. K. (1976a). Biographical determinants of achieved eminence: A multivariate approach to the Cox data. *Journal of Personality and Social Psychology, 33,* 218–226.

Simonton, D. K. (1976b). Philosophical eminence, beliefs, and zeitgeist: An individual-generational analysis. *Journal of Personality and Social Psychology, 34*, 630–640.

Simonton, D. K. (1976c). The sociopolitical context of philosophical beliefs: A transhistorical causal analysis. *Social Forces, 54*, 513–523.

Simonton, D. K. (1977a). Creative productivity, age, and stress: A biographical time-series analysis of 10 classical composers. *Journal of Personality and Social Psychology, 35*, 791–804.

Simonton, D. K. (1977b). Eminence, creativity, and geographic marginality: A recursive structural equation model. *Journal of Personality and Social Psychology, 35*, 805–816.

Simonton, D. K. (1978). Independent discovery in science and technology: A closer look at the Poisson distribution. *Social Studies of Science, 8*, 521–532.

Simonton, D. K. (1979). Multiple discovery and invention: Zeitgeist, genius, or chance? *Journal of Personality and Social Psychology, 37*, 1603–1616.

Simonton, D. K. (1980a). Land battles, generals, and armies: Individual and situational determinants of victory and casualties. *Journal of Personality and Social Psychology, 38*, 110–119.

Simonton, D. K. (1980b). Techno-scientific activity and war: A yearly time-series analysis, 1500–1903 A.D. *Scientometrics, 2*, 251–255.

Simonton, D. K. (1980c). Thematic fame and melodic originality in classical music: A multivariate computer-content analysis. *Journal of Personality, 48*, 206–219.

Simonton, D. K. (1980d). Thematic fame, melodic originality, and musical zeitgeist: A biographical and transhistorical content analysis. *Journal of Personality and Social Psychology, 38*, 972–983.

Simonton, D. K. (1981). Creativity in Western civilization: Extrinsic and intrinsic causes. *American Anthropologist, 83*, 628–630.

Simonton, D. K. (1983). Intergenerational transfer of individual differences in hereditary monarchs: Genes, role-modeling, cohort, or sociocultural effects? *Journal of Personality and Social Psychology, 44*, 354–364.

Simonton, D. K. (1984a). Artistic creativity and interpersonal relationships across and within generations. *Journal of Personality and Social Psychology, 46*, 1273–1286.

Simonton, D. K. (1984b). Creative productivity and age: A mathematical model based on a two-step cognitive process. *Developmental Review, 4*, 77–111.

Simonton, D. K. (1984c). *Genius, creativity, and leadership: Historiometric inquiries.* Cambridge, MA: Harvard University Press.

Simonton, D. K. (1984d). Leader age and national condition: A longitudinal analysis of 25 European monarchs. *Social Behavior and Personality, 12,* 111–114.

Simonton, D. K. (1984e). Leaders as eponyms: Individual and situational determinants of monarchal eminence. *Journal of Personality, 52,* 1–21.

Simonton, D. K. (1984f). Scientific eminence historical and contemporary: A measurement assessment. *Scientometrics, 6,* 169–182.

Simonton, D. K. (1985a). Intelligence and personal influence in groups: Four nonlinear models. *Psychological Review, 92,* 532–547.

Simonton, D. K. (1985b). The vice-presidential succession effect: Individual or situational basis? *Political Behavior, 7,* 79–99.

Simonton, D. K. (1986a). Biographical typicality, eminence, and achievement style. *Journal of Creative Behavior, 20,* 14–22.

Simonton, D. K. (1986b). Presidential greatness: The historical consensus and its psychological significance. *Political Psychology, 7,* 259–283.

Simonton, D. K. (1986c). Presidential personality: Biographical use of the Gough Adjective Check List. *Journal of Personality and Social Psychology, 51,* 149–160.

Simonton, D. K. (1987a). Developmental antecedents of achieved eminence. *Annals of Child Development, 5,* 131–169.

Simonton, D. K. (1987b). Presidential inflexibility and veto behavior: Two individual-situational interactions. *Journal of Personality, 55,* 1–18.

Simonton, D. K. (1988a). Age and outstanding achievement: What do we know after a century of research? *Psychological Bulletin, 104,* 251–267.

Simonton, D. K. (1988b). Galtonian genius, Kroeberian configurations, and emulation: A generational time-series analysis of Chinese civilization. *Journal of Personality and Social Psychology, 55,* 230–238.

Simonton, D. K. (1988c). *Scientific genius: A psychology of science.* Cambridge, England: Cambridge University Press.

Simonton, D. K. (1989a). Age and creative productivity: Nonlinear estimation of an information-processing model. *International Journal of Aging and Human Development, 29,* 23–37.

Simonton, D. K. (1989b). Shakespeare's sonnets: A case of and for single-case historiometry. *Journal of Personality, 57,* 695–721.

Simonton, D. K. (1989c). The swan-song phenomenon: Last-works effects for 172 classical composers. *Psychology and Aging, 4*, 42–47.

Simonton, D. K. (1990a). History, chemistry, psychology, and genius: An intellectual autobiography of historiometry. In M. Runco & R. Albert (Eds.), *Theories of creativity* (pp. 92–115). Newbury Park, CA: Sage.

Simonton, D. K. (1990b). *Psychology, science, and history: An introduction to historiometry.* New Haven, CT: Yale University Press.

Simonton, D. K. (1991a). Career landmarks in science: Individual differences and interdisciplinary contrasts. *Developmental Psychology, 27*, 119–130.

Simonton, D. K. (1991b). Emergence and realization of genius: The lives and works of 120 classical composers. *Journal of Personality and Social Psychology, 61*, 829–840.

Simonton, D. K. (1991c). Latent-variable models of posthumous reputation: A quest for Galton's G. *Journal of Personality and Social Psychology, 60*, 607–619.

Simonton, D. K. (1991d). Personality correlates of exceptional personal influence: A note on Thorndike's (1950) creators and leaders. *Creativity Research Journal, 4*, 67–78.

Simonton, D. K. (1992a). Gender and genius in Japan: Feminine eminence in masculine culture. *Sex Roles, 27*, 101–119.

Simonton, D. K. (1992b). Leaders of American psychology, 1879–1967: Career development, creative output, and professional achievement. *Journal of Personality and Social Psychology, 62*, 5–17.

Simonton, D. K. (1992c). The social context of career success and course for 2,026 scientists and inventors. *Personality and Social Psychology Bulletin, 18*, 452–463.

Simonton, D. K. (1994). *Greatness: Who makes history and why.* New York: Guilford Press.

Simonton, D. K. (1995). Personality and intellectual predictors of leadership. In D. H. Saklofske & M. Zeidner (Eds.), *International handbook of personality and intelligence* (pp. 739–757). New York: Plenum.

Simonton, D. K. (1996). Presidents' wives and first ladies: On achieving eminence within a traditional gender role. *Sex Roles, 35*, 309–336.

Simonton, D. K. (1997a). Creative productivity: A predictive and explanatory model of career trajectories and landmarks. *Psychological Review, 104*, 66–89.

Simonton, D. K. (1997b). Foreign influence and national achievement: The impact of open milieus on Japanese civilization. *Journal of Personality and Social Psychology, 72*, 86–94.

Simonton, D. K. (1998a). Achieved eminence in minority and majority cultures: Convergence versus divergence in the assessments of 294 African Americans. *Journal of Personality and Social Psychology, 74*, 804–817.

Simonton, D. K. (1998b). Fickle fashion versus immortal fame: Transhistorical assessments of creative products in the opera house. *Journal of Personality and Social Psychology, 75*, 198–210.

Simonton, D. K. (1998c). Political leadership across the life span: Chronological versus career age in the British monarchy. *Leadership Quarterly, 9*, 195–206.

Simonton, D. K. (1999a). Creativity as blind variation and selective retention: Is the creative process Darwinian? *Psychological Inquiry, 10*, 309–328.

Simonton, D. K. (1999b). *Origins of genius: Darwinian perspectives on creativity.* New York: Oxford University Press.

Simonton, D. K. (1999c). Significant samples: The psychological study of eminent individuals. *Psychological Methods, 4*, 425–451.

Simonton, D. K. (1999d). Talent and its development: An emergenic and epigenetic model. *Psychological Review, 106*, 435–457.

Simonton, D. K. (2000a). Creative development as acquired expertise: Theoretical issues and an empirical test. *Developmental Review, 20*, 283–318.

Simonton, D. K. (2000b). Creativity: Cognitive, developmental, personal, and social aspects. *American Psychologist, 55*, 151–158.

Simonton, D. K. (2000c). Methodological and theoretical orientation and the long-term disciplinary impact of 54 eminent psychologists. *Review of General Psychology, 4*, 1–13.

Simonton, D. K. (2001). Totally made, not at all born [Review of the book *The psychology of high abilities*]. *Contemporary Psychology, 46*, 176–179.

Simonton, D. K. (2002a). Collaborative aesthetics in the feature film: Cinematic components predicting the differential impact of 2,323 Oscar-nominated movies. *Empirical Studies of the Arts, 20*, 115–125.

Simonton, D. K. (2002b). *Great psychologists and their times: Scientific insights into psychology's history.* Washington, DC: APA Books.

Simonton, D. K. (2002c). It's absolutely impossible? A longitudinal study of one psychologist's response to conventional naysayers. In R. J. Sternberg (Ed.), *Psychologists defying the crowd: Stories of those who battled the establishment and won* (pp. 238–254). Washington, DC: American Psychological Association.

Simonton, D. K. (2003a). Creativity assessment. In R. Fernández-Ballesteros (Ed.), *Encyclopedia of psychological assessment* (Vol. 1, pp. 276–280). London: Sage.

Simonton, D. K. (2003b). Scientific creativity as constrained stochastic behavior: The integration of product, process, and person perspectives. *Psychological Bulletin, 129,* 475–494.

Simonton, D. K. (2004a). The "Best Actress" paradox: Outstanding feature films versus exceptional performances by women. *Sex Roles, 50,* 781–795.

Simonton, D. K. (2004b). Creative clusters, political fragmentation, and cultural heterogeneity: An investigative journey though civilizations East and West. In P. Bernholz & R. Vaubel (Eds.), *Political competition, innovation and growth in the history of Asian civilizations* (pp. 39–56). Cheltenham, England: Edward Elgar.

Simonton, D. K. (2004c). *Creativity in science: Chance, logic, genius, and zeitgeist.* Cambridge, England: Cambridge University Press.

Simonton, D. K. (2004d). Psychology's status as a scientific discipline: Its empirical placement within an implicit hierarchy of the sciences. *Review of General Psychology, 8,* 59–67.

Simonton, D. K. (2004e). Group artistic creativity: Creative clusters and cinematic success in 1,327 feature films. *Journal of Applied Social Psychology, 34,* 1494–1520.

Simonton, D. K. (2005a). Cinematic creativity and production budgets: Does money make the movie? *Journal of Creative Behavior, 39,* 1–15.

Simonton, D. K. (2005b). Darwin as straw man: Dasgupta's (2004) evaluation of creativity as a Darwinian process. *Creativity Research Journal, 17,* 299–208.

Simonton, D. K. (2005c). Film as art versus film as business: Differential correlates of screenplay characteristics. *Empirical Studies of the Arts, 23,* 93–117.

Simonton, D. K. (2005d). Giftedness and genetics: The emergenic-epigenetic model and its implications. *Journal for the Education of the Gifted, 28,* 270–286.

Simonton, D. K. (2006a). Beauty and the beast [Review of the book *Neuropsychology of art: Neurological, cognitive and evolutionary perspectives*]. *PsycCRITIQUES, 51*(10).

Simonton, D. K. (2006b). Creativity in the cortex [Review of the book *The creating brain: The neuroscience of genius*]. *PsycCRITIQUES, 51*(38).

Simonton, D. K. (2006c). Presidential IQ, Openness, Intellectual Brilliance, and leadership: Estimates and correlations for 42 US chief executives. *Political Psychology, 27,* 511–639.

Simonton, D. K. (2007a). Cinema composers: Career trajectories for creative productivity in film music. *Psychology of Aesthetics, Creativity, and the Arts, 1,* 160–169.

Simonton, D. K. (2007b). The creative imagination in Picasso's Guernica sketches: Monotonic improvements or nonmonotonic variants? *Creativity Research Journal, 19,* 329–344.

Simonton, D. K. (2007c). Film music: Are award-winning scores and songs heard in successful motion pictures? *Psychology of Aesthetics, Creativity, and the Arts, 1,* 53–60.

Simonton, D. K. (2007d). Historiometrics. In N. J. Salkind (Ed.), *Encyclopedia of measurement and statistics* (Vol. 2, p. 441). Thousand Oaks, CA: Sage.

Simonton, D. K. (2008a). Childhood giftedness and adulthood genius: A historiometric analysis of 291 eminent African Americans. *Gifted Child Quarterly, 52,* 243–255.

Simonton, D. K. (2008b). Scientific talent, training, and performance: Intellect, personality, and genetic endowment. *Review of General Psychology, 12,* 28–46.

Spearman, C. (1904). "General Intelligence," objectively determined and measured. *American Journal of Psychology, 15,* 201–293.

Spearman, C. (1927). *The abilities of man: Their nature and measurement.* New York: Macmillan.

Starkes, J. L., Deakin, J. M., Allard, F., Hodges, N. J., & Hayes, A. (1996). Deliberate practice in sports: What is it anyway? In K. A. Ericsson (Ed.), *The road to expert performance: Empirical evidence from the arts and sciences, sports, and games* (pp. 81–106). Mahwah, NJ: Erlbaum.

Stavridou, A., & Furnham, A. (1996). The relationship between psychoticism, trait-creativity and the attentional mechanism of cognitive inhibition. *Personality and Individual Differences, 21,* 143–153.

Sternberg, R. J. (1996). *Successful intelligence.* New York: Simon & Schuster.

Stewart, L. H. (1977). Birth order and political leadership. In M. G. Hermann (Ed.), *The psychological examination of political leaders* (pp. 205–236). New York: Free Press.

Stewart, L. H. (1991). The world cycle of leadership. *Journal of Analytical Psychology, 36*, 449–459.

Storfer, M. D. (1990). *Intelligence and giftedness: The contributions of heredity and early environment.* San Francisco: Jossey-Bass.

Sulloway, F. J. (1996). *Born to rebel: Birth order, family dynamics, and creative lives.* New York: Pantheon.

Teigen, K. H. (1984). A note on the origin of the term "nature and nurture": Not Shakespeare and Galton, but Mulcaster. *Journal of the History of the Behavioral Sciences, 20*, 363–364.

Terman, L. M. (1916). *The measurement of intelligence: An explanation of and a complete guide for the use of the Stanford revision and extension of the Binet-Simon intelligence scale.* Boston: Houghton Mifflin.

Terman, L. M. (1917). The intelligence quotient of Francis Galton in childhood. *American Journal of Psychology, 28*, 209–215.

Terman, L. M. (1925). *Mental and physical traits of a thousand gifted children.* Stanford, CA: Stanford University Press.

Terman, L. M. (1925–1959). *Genetic studies of genius* (5 vols.). Stanford, CA: Stanford University Press.

Terman, L. M., & Oden, M. H. (1959). *The gifted group at mid-life.* Stanford, CA: Stanford University Press.

Terry, W. S. (1989). Birth order and prominence in the history of psychology. *Psychological Record, 39*, 333–337.

Tetlock, P. E. (1979). Identifying victims of groupthink from public statements of decision makers. *Journal of Personality and Social Psychology, 37*, 1314–1324.

Thorndike, E. L. (1927). *The measurement of intelligence.* New York: Columbia University Teachers College.

Thorndike, E. L. (1936). The relation between intellect and morality in rulers. *American Journal of Sociology, 42*, 321–334.

Thorndike, E. L. (1950). Traits of personality and their intercorrelations as shown in biographies. *Journal of Educational Psychology, 41*, 193–216.

Vasari, G. (1968). *Lives of the painters, sculptors, and architects* (E. Fuller, Ed., A. B. Hinds, Trans., & W. Gaunt, Rev.). New York: Dell. (Original work published ca. 1550)

Veblen, T. (1919). The intellectual preeminence of Jews in modern Europe. *Political Science Quarterly, 34*, 33–42.

Walberg, H. J., Rasher, S. P., & Hase, K. (1978). IQ correlates with high eminence. *Gifted Child Quarterly, 22,* 196–200.

Walberg, H. J., Rasher, S. P., & Parkerson, J. (1980). Childhood and eminence. *Journal of Creative Behavior, 13,* 225–231.

Walberg, H. J., Strykowski, B. F., Rovai, E., & Hung, S. S. (1984). Exceptional performance. *Review of Educational Research, 54,* 87–112.

Waller, N. G., Bouchard, T. J., Jr., Lykken, D. T., Tellegen, A., & Blacker, D. M. (1993). Creativity, heritability, familiality: Which word does not belong? *Psychological Inquiry, 4,* 235–237.

Weisberg, R. W. (1992). *Creativity: Beyond the myth of genius.* New York: Freeman.

Weisberg, R. W. (1994). Genius and madness? A quasi-experimental test of the hypothesis that manic-depression increases creativity. *Psychological Science, 5,* 361–367.

White, L. (1949). *The science of culture.* New York: Farrar, Straus.

White, R. K. (1931). The versatility of genius. *Journal of Social Psychology, 2,* 460–489.

Who said what when: A chronological dictionary of quotations. (1991). New York: Hippocrene Books.

Woods, F. A. (1906). *Mental and moral heredity in royalty.* New York: Holt.

Woods, F. A. (1909, November 19). A new name for a new science. *Science, 30,* 703–704.

Woods, F. A. (1911, April 14). Historiometry as an exact science. *Science, 33,* 568–574.

Woods, F. A. (1913). *The influence of monarchs.* New York: Macmillan.

Zickar, M. J, & Slaughter, J. E. (1999). Examining creative performance over time using hierarchical linear modeling: An illustration using film directors. *Human Performance, 12,* 211–230.

Zuckerman, H. (1977). *Scientific elite.* New York: Free Press.

Zweigenhaft, R. L. (1975). Birth order, approval-seeking, and membership in Congress. *Journal of Individual Psychology, 31,* 205–210.

Index